Shakespeare:
The Basics

Shakespeare continues to be the most studied author in English literature courses at GCSE and Advanced Level, and also in many universities. The way in which his plays are studied has undergone considerable change in recent years, and this volume, aimed squarely at the student new to Shakespeare, provides a thorough general introduction to the plays, based on the exciting new approaches shaping the field of Shakespeare studies. The author offers a refreshingly clear guide to:

* Shakespeare's language
* the plays as performance texts
* the cultural and political contexts of the plays
* early modern theatre practice
* new understandings of the major genres.

Sean McEvoy illustrates how interpretations of Shakespeare are linked to cultural and political contexts, and offers readings of the most frequently studied plays in light of contemporary critical thinking. He explores issues of racial stereotyping, social justice, the subjugation of women and attitudes to female sexuality, as these themes are presented both in the play-texts themselves and in notable modern productions of those plays.

Demystifying Shakespeare's plays and bringing critical ideas within the beginner's grasp, *Shakespeare: The Basics* is an essential resource for all students of Shakespeare.

Sean McEvoy teaches English and Drama at Varndean College, Brighton, UK.

Other titles in the series include:

Language: The Basics
R. L. Trask

Philosophy: The Basics
Nigel Warburton

Sociology: The Basics
Martin Albrow

Politics: The Basics
Stephen D. Tansey

LONDON AND NEW YORK

Shakespeare

The Basics

■ Sean McEvoy

ROUTLEDGE

822.33
Mcev

First published 2000
by Routledge
11 New Fetter Lane,
London EC4P 4EE

Simultaneously published in
the USA and Canada
by Routledge
29 West 35th Street,
New York, NY 10001

*Routledge is an imprint of the Taylor &
Francis Group*

© 2000 Sean McEvoy

Typeset in Times by Taylor & Francis
Books Ltd
Printed and bound in Great Britain
by Clays Ltd, St Ives plc

*British Library Cataloguing in
Publication Data*
A catalogue record for this book is
available from the British Library

*Library of Congress Cataloging-in-
Publication Data*
McEvoy, Sean
Shakespeare – the basics / Sean
McEvoy.
p. cm.
Includes bibliographical references
and index.
1. Shakespeare, William,
1564–1616–Criticism and
interpretation–Outlines, syllabuses,
etc.
I. Title.
PR2976.M34   2000
822.3'–dc21   99-046914

ISBN 0–415–21288–X (hb)
ISBN 0–415–21289–8 (pb)

For Mum and Dad

Contents

Illustrations

Acknowledgements

The advice of Dr Elizabeth Clark, Professor Stuart Sim and Dr Nigel Smith was much appreciated during the early stages of the work. The detailed comments of a number of readers at a later stage were invaluable, and in particular those of Dr Jerry Brotton, Professor Rob Pope and Professor Peter Thomson.

I would also particularly like to think Alan Jenkins, Principal of Varndean College, Brighton, and the Warden and Fellows of Keble College, Oxford, without whose offer of an Education Fellowship in the summer of 1997 this book would never have been written.

Quotations from Shakespeare's plays are courtesy of *The Riverside Shakespeare*, second edition, edited by G. Blakemore Evans, copyright of Houghton Mifflin Inc., Boston.

Credits for illustrations are as follows: the emblems on pp. 31 and 32 are from Geoffrey Whitney (1586) *A Choice of Emblems*, Leyden, and Ripa (1600) *Iconologia*; Mander and Mitchenson Theatre Collection and John Haynes for p. 95; Mander and Mitchenson Theatre Collection for p. 100; Cheek by Jowl, John Haynes and the Lyric Theatre, Hammersmith for p. 103; by courtesy of The National Portrait Gallery, London, for the portrait which appears as frontispiece; and C. Walter Hodges for p. 86. In this connection I would like to thank Linda Nicol at Cambridge University Press for her help with the illustrations.

Talia Rodgers and Liz Brown at Routledge have been brilliant. I am extremely grateful for their support, advice and encouragement. Liz's creativity and tactful criticism have made an enormous difference to the finished book. Finally, if I can, I would like to thank Nicky.

Introduction

This book is written for students of English Literature in their final year of Advanced Level study at school and college, but it will also be useful to first-year undergraduates who want an accessible up-to-date introduction to Shakespeare.

In the course of the last twenty-five years there have been great changes in the way Shakespeare is studied at undergraduate level and above. These changes are only now beginning to take hold in schools and colleges, where character, plot and theme – ideas that rarely appear in contemporary Shakespeare studies – have until the very recent past been dominant. This means that when students arrive at university they feel unprepared and surprised at what they encounter in their first few lectures on Shakespeare. It means also that those students who take English only so far as A Level are not being kept abreast with the subject's development. Questions set at A Level in England and

Wales have in recent years reflected concerns beyond the traditional approach; indeed, Chief Examiners' reports and new papers set by the two biggest English examination boards have tried to encourage new critical approaches of the sort found in this book. Now the new Literature courses in England, Wales and Northern Ireland to be examined first in 2002 have brought the subject up to date. They will for the first time *require* an understanding of the political and cultural factors that influenced the writing of the plays, and guide how they are read today.

This book attempts to address the gap between the old and the new approaches by providing a thorough general introduction to Shakespeare which is based on the way his plays are often understood at the beginning of the twenty-first century.

Why Shakespeare studies changed

You might wonder why it is that the older way of studying Shakespeare in terms of his plays' themes, characters, plots and imagery has been superseded. The answer lies in the changes in philosophical and political viewpoints that have taken place, particularly in the universities, since the late 1960s.

One very influential modern idea is that everything takes place in space and time, 'in history', and that consequently there are no 'timeless' or eternal qualities which endure unchanged. The notion of a theme, like, say, 'love', assumes that love is something which is constant and abstract. A play will 'illustrate' or 'deal with' love, it is said, but love isn't located *in* the play itself. Love is assumed to be the same abstract notion for both Romeo and Juliet in sixteenth-century Verona and for two young people in twenty-first century Shepherd's Bush. But love doesn't stand outside of history. It is an emotion felt by people in actual time. What that emotion is like will depend a great deal on the kind of society they live in, and its practices and beliefs. It's the same *kind* of emotion, yes. But it is not the same idea existing independently through time outside its historical context. Shakespeare actually seems to me to recognise this in *Romeo and Juliet*. The lovers' affair is so fairy-tale and dramatic, not to say *literary* in its conduct, that it is clearly out of place in the feuding world of cynical Veronese politics, and is therefore doomed.

Character criticism is often based on a number of assumptions. 'Characters' are supposed to be accurate portraits of imaginary *real* people who can be treated as unified wholes. Typical of this approach to character are such view as that Hamlet is an intellectual who thinks so much that he cannot make up his mind; and that Othello is a 'noble' Moor who is prone to terrible jealousy. But this is not even what *real* people are like. These assumptions wilfully ignore the complex, contradictory and indefinable mass of feelings and desires that actually constitute a person. Influential modern thinkers have emphasised the subconscious, that part of us which is an unknowable but important motivating part of our psychological make-up. They have also suggested that we are created as individuals by the forms of language in which we think and express ourselves. Such ideas undermine the notion of character as something unique, unified and definable; if we are to a significant extent constituted by language, we do well to remember that language is always social and shared. Modern criticism looks first to society and social relations. Individuals are understood only in that context.

It is often suggested in traditional criticism that the action of the play flows out of the character, rather than role being seen as an expression or function of the society and culture depicted in the play. Thus character critics say that Macbeth kills King Duncan because 'he is ambitious', not because he lives in a society where status and manliness depend on committing acts of daring and violence, and where loyalty is a constantly shifting thing, depending on the balance of power between warriors (see pp.193f.). Character criticism is ultimately unenlightening, and often contains all sorts of unspoken value judgements. What is wrong, in itself, we might ask, in aspiring above your station in life, particularly in a society as rigid as Scotland's in *Macbeth*?

As for plot, just telling the story is clearly too basic for advanced study. Imagery can be understood to be pictures in the reader's mind formed by the words (see below, p. 28f.). Its study can have its uses, so long as we don't regard the images as timeless symbols of eternal qualities ('the flower'; 'the snake') as happened in the past.

Did Shakespeare really mean all this?

One other important point. If you are not used to contemporary criticism you may find yourself asking 'Yes, but is that what Shakespeare really meant?'. There are two responses I would want to make here to that question. The first is the obvious one, that the only proof of what the playwright *meant* is in the words that he wrote. We have no other evidence; we can't ask him what he was thinking at the time. But why would we want to do that anyway? Once those words have passed down to us, in the present day, all that they *can* mean is what they mean now, to us, from our own modern perspectives. Connected with this is my second response: when Shakespeare wrote he could express the ideas and beliefs of his time only in the language of his time. These ideas, beliefs and words were formed by the society and power structures of the world he lived in. Instead of the rather fruitless game of trying to work out what was in his head when he wrote, it is much more useful and interesting to examine what it is that his plays can tell us about those ideas and beliefs. We should consider also the possibility that no author might *ever* be in control of *all* the meanings in the text he or she produces, anyway.

Of course, if *he* could express himself only according to the ideas and beliefs of his time, the same constraint applies to *us*. When we read or see a Shakespeare play we can understand the texts only from where we are now, with our own ideas and beliefs. Contemporary criticism therefore finds its own political and social concerns in Shakespeare's plays, and expresses these concerns in the way it reads the plays. Feminism was a powerful force for social change in the twentieth century, and much Shakespeare criticism looks with great interest at the way women are written about in the plays. There are other contemporary issues that are important in the way we read Shakespeare today:

how power is exercised in society; the nature of social justice; how language shapes the world; questions of sexuality.

To find these ideas in 400-year-old plays should not really be surprising. Shakespeare was writing at the time when the modern world and its structures of power and authority were being formed. In English literature of the late sixteenth and early seventeenth centuries we can see the modern world under construction, for good or for ill.

How to use this book

Shakespeare: The Basics is in two parts, both of which will be useful to anyone studying any of the plays.

Part I sets out to explain why Shakespeare's plays were written in the way that they were. The intention is not only to help you to read the plays more easily, but to provide you with ideas that will help you to undertake the kind of close reading of a passage required for many examinations. It explains also why the plays are to be seen as scripts written for *performance*, whose full meanings are actually realised only on stage.

Part II takes in turn the plays' different types or *genres* and explains how modern critics read them. You may well want to read only those sections that include the plays you are studying, but I would encourage you to read the *whole* of the relevant section, not just the paragraphs which mention your play. Your understanding of one text is *always* enhanced by a grasp of other texts of the same type; I hope it will make you want to go on and read or see these other plays, too. I have taken examples from those most frequently studied at A Level and on first-year degree courses, but what is written in each section could apply to *any* of Shakespeare's plays of that genre.

There are sections throughout the book that seek to put the plays very firmly in their historical context, by giving relevant information about social and political life in England during Shakespeare's time, and by explaining the sort of theatre for which he wrote. In these sections you will find text 'boxes' in which I anchor the plays within their historical context, emphasising the value of regarding the plays themselves as historical documents. These history boxes are not *background*, and for this reason they are not lumped together at the beginning of the book. When we read or see the plays we are learning to understand the past in the way that we do when we read any document from a previous century. The plays are to be viewed within and as products of their period, not as standing out separately from it. To reflect this, I introduce the historical information at relevant points in my discussion of the plays, in tinted boxes spread throughout the book. At the same time, if you want to find only historical details, these sections, which are clearly indicated in the Table of Contents, are easily recognisable as you flick through the text. These boxes give you some information also about Shakespeare's own life, in its historical and social context. There is a Chronology that brings together all such information at the end of the book.

Throughout the discussion of these different aspects of the modern study of Shakespeare, I never lose sight of how exciting and beautiful these plays can be today, both in the theatre and in the classroom.

Whichever of the plays you are studying you will find the sections on language and performance useful. You may, however, want to read only the genre chapter dealing with the particular play you are studying. Realising that students may well dip in and out of the book in this way, I have tried to ensure that discussion of certain points is briefly repeated so that no one using the book in this way misses anything important. If you use the book for information about specific aspects relating to one or other of the plays, it would be a good idea to read the whole of the section containing that information, so that you understand how it contributes to the broader discussion.

At the end of each *genre* chapter I sum up the main points you should have grasped. I also suggest what to read next, offering comments on the suitability and difficulty of the different books and articles which I mention. In keeping with the usual scholarly practice I give references to the other books I have used. This is done by listing, in brackets, the author, the date of publication, and the page number referred to (e.g. Dollimore 1984: 48). The authors and their works are listed, in alphabetical order, in the References. Simply look for an author's surname and the year of publication, and you will find the title and other details that will help you to find the book, should you wish to consult it for yourself (a long dash instead of a name indicates that the book is by the last-*named* author).

For the sake of consistency, all quotations of Shakespeare's plays, unless otherwise stated, come from the Riverside Shakespeare (Boston, MA: Houghton Mifflin, 2nd edition, 1997). The reference I give to Act, Scene and line after each quotation will probably be very close to the format in the edition you are using. These appear as, for example, II 2 9–12, which means Act Two (II), Scene Two (2), lines nine to twelve. When I quote Shakespeare, I have glossed the difficult words and phrases. Words marked with an asterisk are explained in indented passages following the speech or speeches quoted; the number of the line in which the asterisked words occur is given in square brackets.

This book outlines only one way of studying Shakespeare

In this book I follow one type of criticism, which happens to be the one you are most likely to meet at university. It is probably the most influential, too. This approach always sets the plays firmly in the context of the time in which they were written *and* in the time in which they are read. It is also influenced by certain feminist ideas. Different versions of the approach are known as *new historicism* and *cultural materialism*. I want to stress however that this is certainly not the only way Shakespeare is read today. There is a whole range of other critical approaches based, for example, on psychoanalysis or on particular feminist standpoints, or on performance study, or on other ideas. Such critical strategies are just as interesting and just as valuable. I hope you will go on to explore these exciting ideas for yourself, once you have finished this book. No book can cover every approach to Shakespeare, and one of my main aims in this book is to give you an idea of just how many different approaches can be taken: Shakespeare studies is so much more than looking at character and themes.

This book is in large part an attempt to bring together, in a form accessible to those of you beginning advanced study of Shakespeare, important work by contemporary scholars. I hope that *they* will forgive my occasional simplification of their arguments and that the book will give *you*, the reader, the confidence to turn to these original thinkers, and so take your study *beyond the basics*.

Understanding the text

Part One

Chapter 1

Shakespeare's language (1)

Your first Shakespeare play is the hardest. People sometimes talk as if reading a 400-year-old play were a process similar to reading a modern novel. They have forgotten how different a piece of writing *Macbeth* or *Julius Caesar* is to almost anything you might have read before. This opening part of the book aims to explain those differences clearly, so that you will find it easier to understand why Shakespeare can be difficult. It gives you practical advice on how to read Shakespeare's plays on your own. Finally, it goes into detail about the ways in which Shakespeare's language is constructed, which will help you analyse his work, and so increase your appreciation of it.

Shakespeare wrote for theatre-goers, not readers

This is an obvious point to start with, but a very

Box 1: Shakespeare's audiences

In 1600, about 15–20 per cent of those living within reach of London's theatres were regular play-goers. There is considerable dispute about the make up of the audiences at the public playhouses, but it seems that the theatre was not solely an aristocratic and middle-class interest, although the gentry did attend. Many of the middle-class were in fact Puritans and opposed the theatre. Recent research indicates that a good number of play-goers would have been relatively uneducated: clerks, artisans, apprentices, women.

A skilled London worker would earn about six shillings (30p) a week. The penny entrance fee for 'the pit' was inexpensive entertainment compared to the potential costs of gambling, drinking or whoring. An afternoon at the theatre, complete with beer and hazelnuts, was affordable for many people, even if not for London's teeming poor.

It has sometimes been assumed that those who paid for standing space in the pit came along only for the spectacle, the language being beyond their comprehension. But Hamlet is clearly teasing those standing only a few feet away in III 2 9–12 in his advice to the actors. Other evidence indicates a higher level of understanding on the part of those who stood watching and listening in the pits. The most popular plays – *Hamlet, King Henry IV Parts I and II*, Marlowe's *Dr Faustus* and Kyd's *The Spanish Tragedy* – combined action and spectacle with discussion of philosophical and political ideas, which hardly indicates an ignorant, sensation-seeking audience.

There is no evidence that audiences were particularly badly behaved, or that they booed and hissed the villains. There were occasional disturbances, but it would appear that audiences on the whole listened carefully, applauding or laughing appropriately, though individuals would perhaps have been more talkative than a modern audience. Writers complain about them not appreciating their plays, not about them throwing fruit or storming the stage.

With the opening of the first indoor theatre at Blackfriars in 1608, audiences began to fragment. A new kind of 'aristocratic' repertoire developed for the more exclusive audience at Blackfriars. While the Shakespeare's company continued to present the same plays at this new indoor theatre and at the Globe, other outdoor theatres began to produce plays of a more populist style for their predominantly working-class audiences. Some argue that this was the beginning of the class-based theatrical tradition in the United Kingdom.

important one. William Shakespeare, just like all the other play-wrights of his time working in the London playhouses, did not write with *readers* in mind. He wrote lines for the actors to speak which had to be understood as soon as they were heard by the audience. He had no sense that he was writing for a future reader-ship, although of course, texts of the plays were occasionally published without his consent in a sort of 'paperback' ('Quarto') form (see Box 2, p. 25). There is also considerable evidence that Shakespeare imagined that his plays might be published together after his death and revised them with this in mind (though some scholars disagree). But that came much later. When he wrote the words to be spoken by a character, he would have had in mind an actor whom he actually knew. That man had to learn and then perform those words in a crowded, bustling, open-air theatre surrounded by bear-pits and brothels.

You might think that writing which is meant to be heard, not read, would be simpler to understand than writing intended for publication. After all, the audience cannot go back to the begin-ning of a speech if they lose track of what is happening. But this is not necessarily so. What actually happens is that the language gets more *patterned*: it tends to have distinctive rhythms and repe-titions of words, phrases and ways of saying things. This patterning helps the audience keep track of the sense of what they are hearing. If you think for a moment about a joke, a polit-ical speech, or even a school assembly you can see that this is true. A joke, for example, may often have three similar events or char-acters, each described in very similar words, moving towards the punchline the third time round. A political 'soundbite' will often use a memorable phrase, perhaps employing repetitions and contrasts and a satisfying and forceful rhythm ('Ask not what your country can do for you – ask what you can do for your country'). How Shakespeare's language works through this distinctive patterning is the main focus of this section.

Many people argue that today we are unused to long speeches, complex language and extended dialogue. Consider any contem-porary film or TV programme. The speaker in a conversation in a TV drama tends to change after no more than a couple of sentences. An interviewee on a news programme is rarely allowed much more than this without being interrupted. In Shakespeare's time people were much more used than we are to listening to long and (to us) demanding passages of speech. Because most of them could not read – it has been estimated that in 1600 72 per cent of men and 92 per cent of women were unable even to sign their own names (Williams 1995: 390) – their ability to take in spoken language had to be more developed than ours: if they did not *hear* a piece of information, there was no way they could check it by the written record. In addition, very many of those who *could* read could only read aloud. The ability to read silently, in your head, which we learn while still small children, had been developed by only a few people.

Another difference between ourselves and Shakespeare's audience is that we live in a culture crammed with visual signs. We are surrounded by TV and computer monitor screens, by advertising boards, by magazines, graphics and posters. Companies identify themselves by logos, increasingly, rather than names. Yet in 1600 people saw very few pictures or visual signs. Printing was very expensive, and woodcuts and engraving were the only means of reproducing pictures. Paintings – apart from murals on the interior walls of churches – were never seen by the overwhelming majority of people, who did not enter the houses of the great. 'Emblems' (see below, p. 29), printed pictures which expressed a moral of some sort, were probably the only kind of illustration regularly seen by most people – for whom, also, the spoken word was practically the only means of communication. They were better at listening than we are. It is no wonder we find that these plays take some getting used to in the theatre, let alone on the page.

Another problem: vocabulary changes over time

There is a second reason why Shakespeare can be hard to read: our language has changed in the last 400 years. While grammar – the internal structures of the language that determine which words and forms of words can be used together in order to make sense – changes very slowly over time, *vocabulary* – the words which make up a language – is constantly changing.

Vocabulary can change in three ways: first, individual words can disappear altogether; second, and more commonly, the meanings of words can change; and, third, new words are being created all the time and Shakespeare himself was not afraid to make up a word occasionally when no existing word served his purpose.

In 1500 English speakers would have understood that the word *eek*, meant 'also'. Few people outside of those who have studied the history of the language would understand this word today. Before a word passes out of use altogether, however, it goes through the stage of being *archaic*: we still understand what it means, but we immediately recognise its use as self-consciously old-fashioned. If I tell you that I have just *bade* farewell to my *damsel*, boarded an *omnibus* to the *hostelry*, then *quaffed* a tankard of foaming ale, you would understand that I had just said goodbye to my girlfriend, got on a bus to the pub and had a pint. You would, however, realise that I was using these old-fashioned words for effect. Shakespeare is, not surprisingly, full of words which are on the way out of the language. In fact, many archaic words have been kept in use solely because we have learnt them in school when studying Shakespeare!

Linguistic conservatives are constantly trying to prevent words changing their meaning, but change is a normal and constant feature of all language, particularly where social relations are concerned. In the 1920s, it was considered ill-mannered, but not illegal as it is now, for a man to *make love to* a woman in public; but what has changed is the meaning of the expression (in those days it meant to chat someone up), not the law on public decency. My 95-year-old grandmother might think that my brightly-coloured tie makes me look *gay*, but she is using the word, I imagine, in its 1940s sense of 'jolly', not in its current sense. New readers of Shakespeare are often flummoxed by such changes in word meaning, particularly those subtle changes where the new meaning is related to the old one. For example, Hecate, the leader of the witches in *Macbeth*, says that they are going to deceive the tyrant king Macbeth into thinking he is invincible, so that when fate finally turns against him and destroys him the blow will be all the harder. She reminds the other witches:

Hecate You all know security
       Is mortals' chiefest enemy

(III 5 32–3)

She is using 'security' not in its modern sense of 'being safe' – clearly that would not make sense – but in its 1604 sense of 'complacency', a groundless feeling that nothing can touch you, so confident do you feel. There is a subtle but important difference. Less confusingly, although we still use the word 'chief' to mean 'most significant', 'chiefest' is an archaic form – we can see immediately what it means, but we wouldn't say it today.

As for new words, Shakespeare's period was a time of great innovation. Some call the sixteenth and seventeenth centuries the 'early modern' period, which I think is useful because it suggests that Shakespeare's time stands at the beginning of the modern era in which we still live, and was different from the medieval period which preceded it (see the discussion of feudalism, pp. 153–4). Others call the period the Renaissance, meaning 'rebirth'. This is taken to imply that the art and culture of that period were in some way vastly superior to those of the 'Middle Ages', a questionable value judgement but again an indication of a marked change. Whatever we call the period, it was a time when education, scientific knowledge and contact with other countries and cultures were all rapidly increasing. Words from Greek, Latin, Italian, Spanish, Dutch and other tongues were finding their way into the language to enable people to describe and understand the new horizons – geographical, social, political, philosophical and scientific – which were opening up before them. The vocabulary of English grew at a faster rate than at any time before or since. The language grew and developed so quickly that by the early 1600s it was as different from the English spoken in 1500 as it is from the English spoken in Britain today (White 1998: 3).

Some words in Shakespeare that have gone from our language

aroint	*go away*
beshrew	*a curse upon*
cautelous	*crafty*
decoct	*heat up*
hest	*a command*
kibe	*chilblain*
murrain	*plague*
neb	*mouth or nose*
reck	*pay attention to*
strossers	*trousers*

Some words with the same primary meaning, but which in Shakespeare have an alternative meaning which has now passed away

clown	*peasant*
colour	*disguise*
round	*frank*
use	*interest gained from lending money*
union	*a pearl*

Some words in Shakespeare with different meanings now

anchor	*hermit*
boot	*something extra*
clip	*embrace*
diffidence	*mistrust*
doom	*opinion, judgement*
fond	*stupid, silly*
gentle	*of high birth*
habit	*clothes, costume*
incontinent	*at once*
nice	*shy, fastidious*
physical	*good for the health*
quick	*alive*
reprove	*disprove*
success	*outcome, whether positive or negative*
tomboy	*prostitute*

As well as reflecting the changing language of his period, Shakespeare's works have a considerable influence on contemporary English. Because the plays have long had a major role in British education and culture, many of the words and idioms (distinctive ways of saying things) that were new when Shakespeare was writing have found their way into the standard vocabulary of the British English in use today.

Above are some examples of the kinds of difference in vocabulary you may find in reading the plays.

You have to rely on a good modern edition with clear explanatory notes on these changes, clearly – preferably on the same page. The Oxford School Shakespeare does this well. More scholarly editions for A Level and degree study are the Oxford Shakespeare, the New Cambridge Shakespeare and the *new* (i.e. 1995 onwards) Arden Shakespeare.

Isn't it *all* hard going? Registers of language

Sometimes new readers of Shakespeare think that they are having trouble understanding the text simply because it is Shakespeare. In fact, the problem often arises because Shakespeare is deliberately making the language difficult in order to express what the character in the play is trying to do. Consider these two brief passages. In the first example, King Lear, a very old man, is waking up from a long sleep. Before he fell asleep he was raving mad, lost on a heath in a storm and deserted by almost all those who owed him respect. He has not seen his youngest and best-loved daughter Cordelia since he banished her in a fit of rage.

King Lear Pray do not mock me:
   I am a very foolish fond old man,
   Fourscore and upward, not an hour more nor less;   60
   And to deal plainly,
   I fear I am not in my perfect mind.
   Methinks I should know you and know this man,
   Yet I am doubtful: for I am mainly ignorant
   What place this is, and all the skill I have   65
   Remembers not these garments; nor I know not
   Where I did lodge last night. Do not laugh at me,
   For, as I am a man, I think this lady
   To be my child Cordelia.

                                    (IV 7 58–69)

It may be worth checking two words against the notes at the bottom of the page in the edition you are using: *fond* (59) means silly, not affectionate; *fourscore* (60) means eighty. Otherwise the language is clear, simple and powerful. But that is because the play requires King Lear to come across as having a clear mind at last. The simple language is dramatically effective and moving in its plainness. This is a play where language has been used, up to this point, for flattering and lying, or for riddles, or to express the confused meanderings of madmen's minds. Clear, simple speech comes as a striking relief. But it shows also that Shakespeare can be very simple when that's what the dramatic situation requires.

Consider in contrast this speech from *Troilus and Cressida*. For the first time, the audience sees Agamemnon, King of Mycenae and leader of the mighty Greek forces which have been unsuccessfully besieging the city of Troy for seven long years. What then will bring them ultimate victory? He addresses his generals:

Agamemnon Princes:
    What grief hath set these jaundies o'er your cheeks?
    The ample proposition that hope makes
    In all designs begun on earth below
    Fails in the promis'd largeness. Checks and disasters   5
    Grow in the veins of actions highest rear'd,
    As knots, by the conflux of meeting sap,
    Infects the sound pine and diverts his grain,
    Tortive and errant, from his course of growth.

                                                    (I 3 1–9)

Agamemnon is saying, in essence: 'It's no surprise we haven't taken Troy yet. The things we do never turn out as we expect them to.' In the first place, this less than inspiring message to the Greek high command is conveyed in a convoluted word order: the words don't come in the order which would make the overall meaning as clear as possible. Then the main ideas are conveyed in unusual ways: for example, '*ample* proposition' (3) means 'good prospects'; 'actions *highest reared*' (6) means 'important actions'. The comparison with the grain of a pine tree is not an obvious one, to say the least, and the vocabulary uses a Latin word instead of an English one whenever possible. *Conflux* (7), meaning 'flowing together', and *tortive* (9), 'twisted', were pretentious new English words adapted from the Latin by Shakespeare – this is the first time they are seen in English. He even describes the commanders' glum expressions by a medical term – 'jaundies' (2) means 'jaundice'.

He goes on to repeat this message in the next six lines, and then says that the gods send us difficulties so that we can see who the superior men really are (i.e. himself). Yet he is proposing to *do* precisely nothing. The complexity and difficulty of Agamemnon's language masks the stupidity of what he is actually saying. Either he is deliberately putting up a smokescreen for fear that the other leaders will see that he has run out of ideas, or he is so pompous and vacuously self-important that he fails to realise what high-sounding nonsense is coming from his mouth. Whichever is true, the language reveals him to be an inadequate leader, to say the least.

Whenever Shakespeare's language gets difficult, and the explanatory notes at the bottom of the page multiply accordingly, there is usually some reason connected with what the drama is trying to do. The difficulty is not just that *this* is Shakespeare: it is because Shakespeare is attempting to produce a particular effect on his audience. Sometimes it will be because he is reproducing the street-language of the poor; at others, because he is sending up self-important schoolteachers or blindly passionate lovers, or stupid, brutal soldiers. These different styles or modes of language are sometimes called *registers*.

Sometimes, of course, the language is complex, as you'd expect, because Shakespeare is trying to reproduce complex states of mind or feelings. If a character is trying to come to terms with, for example, the fact that his lover had betrayed him – a lover on whom he depended for his whole sense of personal identity – the complexity of the language will reflect the complexity of the thoughts and feelings it describes. Look, for example, at Troilus' speech from *Troilus and Cressida* on p.221 below.

How to read Shakespeare

First, if at all possible, read it aloud – for all the reasons outlined above. Second, don't stop when you reach a word you don't understand. If you are reading verse, ignore the line endings (at least for the moment). Consider who is speaking to whom, what they want and where they are at this point in the play. Use the punctuation. Pause briefly when there is a comma, and for a longer time when there is a full stop. Follow these rules and you should always get the sense.

What comes next is some advice about the structure and patterns of Shakespeare's thought which you might find useful.

Very often the key to getting a clear understanding of a speech depends on recognising which words or phrases are being spoken in direct connection with certain other words and phrases in the sentence. Usually the two connected words are contrasted in some way: maybe they're opposites in meaning; maybe one indicates a state of time later than the other; maybe they refer to different people or situations. The full sense of both words depends upon the balancing effect of each upon the other. If you stress the contrasted or balancing words as you read it aloud, the sense is usually made plain. This balancing of words and ideas is very common. When it involves a contrast of terms with conflicting meaning it is known as *antithesis*.

Here is an example from *Romeo and Juliet*. I have chosen it because it expresses a common Christian way of thinking in the early modern period: there are two sides to everything. A single thing (including an individual human being) has an equal capacity for good or ill. The Christian world was strictly divided between God and the Devil, the saved and the damned, the good and the evil. No wonder antithetical thinking was so common.

Friar Lawrence is a monk with a good knowledge of the natural powers of herbs and plants. At his first appearance he lets the audience in on some of his lore (the superscript numbers indicate which words are paired together by contrast, e.g. mother[1]/tomb[1] and grave[3]/womb[3]):

Friar The earth that's nature's **mother**[1] is her **tomb**[1];
  What[2] is her burying **grave**[3], **that**[2] is her **womb**[3];   10
  As from her womb children of divers kind*
  We sucking on her natural bosom find:
  Many[4] for many virtues excellent,
  None[5] but for **some**[4], and yet **all**[5] different.
  O, mickle* is the powerful grace that lies   15
  In plants, herbs, stones and their true qualities;
  For **naught**[6]* so vile but **on**[7] the earth doth live
  That **to**[7] the earth some special good doth give;
  Nor **aught**[6]* so good but, strained* from that **fair use**[8],
  Revolts[9] from **true**[9] birth, stumbling on **abuse**.[8]   20
  Virtue[10] itself turns **vice**[10] being misapplied,
  And **vice**[11] sometime by **action**[11] dignified.

                                                    (II 3 10–22)

  * [11] *divers kind* different or many kinds [15] *mickle* great [17]
  naught nothing [19] *aught* anything *strained* led astray

If you read this rather difficult speech aloud, stressing the words
in bold type, it will make more sense; and if, at the same time, you
always make it sound as if the first of each numbered pair needs
the second of that pair to complete the sense, the passage will be
even more intelligible. (Think about how the football results are
read out on Saturday afternoons: for example, 'Manchester
United 1' is always read as being only half the information – and
you can always tell from the tone whether or not the result is a
surprise or predictable: 'Queens Park Rangers 3'.) Find the
balancing words, read them with the right emphasis, and the
pattern of logic and thought will become clear.

  Two other points to notice about this speech. First, the fact
that it is in rhyme has an important effect on its meaning. In
English folk-culture, well-known sayings which encapsulate some
wisdom are often expressed in rhyme: *Red sky at night, shepherd's
delight* is a banal example. In early modern plays, rhyming
couplets that express opinions often carry with them this appearance of wisdom, which has rubbed off from this oral tradition.

These rhyming statements are referred to by the Latin word *sententiae*.

Second, the pattern of balancing words is actually quite varied. For example, you will often find a second balancing pair completed before the first term has been matched: *a* is followed by *b*, then *b* is repeated before we reach *a* again (look at lines 19–20 in the passage above, for example). After all, if the pattern of the balancing pairs was the same all the way through, the verse would be monotonous and tedious – boring – in sound and rhythm. The skill of the writer here consists in using the habits (conventions) of early modern verse drama in a varied way according to the effects he wishes to produce.

To conclude this section, I want to examine how a particular speech looked in print just a few years after Shakespeare's death. This demonstrates once again the importance of the conditions of spoken performance to the writing of Shakespeare's plays. The speech in question is the first that King Claudius is given in *Hamlet*, the world's most produced play. Claudius has just become King of Denmark in succession to his brother, Old Hamlet. He has also married Old Hamlet's widow, Gertrude, within a month of his brother's death. This might well cause tongues to wag; the original audience would have been aware also that the bible forbids a man to marry his brother's widow. Claudius is addressing the assembled court. He has to make his mark and appear forward-looking and dynamic – particularly since Denmark is currently under threat of invasion by Norway. However, he must not make it seem as if he's already forgotten about his brother. The new king must make it clear that he has married Gertrude to provide political stability rather than for reasons of recently adulterous lust or ambition. He knows too – though no one else, including the audience, does yet – that he actually murdered Old Hamlet.

First is the 1987 Oxford text, edited by G.R. Hibbard. I have put in bold type, as previously but without the numbering, the balancing words which the reader needs to stress to bring out the sense. The second is the speech as it appeared in the 1623 First

Box 2: Playtexts in Shakespeare's time

A popular play might be printed in *Quarto* format (an A5-sized paper pamphlet), but theatre companies opposed this practice, as it made the texts available to other performers. After Shakespeare's death, however, his friends John Hemmings and Henry Condell in 1623 published the so-called First Folio of his plays (a folio is a large leather-bound book). Some of the plays of Shakespeare exist only in this volume; others exist in both the Folio and the Quarto form, and there are considerable variations between the versions: whole lines are missing or differ, and speeches in one are not in the other.

Throughout the nineteenth and much of the twentieth century scholars assumed that there was one perfect (but lost) original text on which both Quarto and Folio are based: what Shakespeare *really* wrote. Where several versions of a play like *Hamlet* existed, an amalgamated version, considered to represent what Shakespeare must have written, would have been produced.

A modern view is that it is a mistake to regard a play as existing in a single perfect form. Shakespeare was a working playwright well-used to the fact that performances vary from one staging to the next. A popular play like *Hamlet* or *King Lear* would be adapted each time it was performed. Government censorship also required alteration of texts. Since 1559 a licence has been required to perform a play, available then from an official called the Master of the Revels. In 1606 the same official was granted the right also to license the printing of plays. The Master of the Revels could and did insist on certain cuts before a performance could take place. For example, the scene where Richard abdicates in *King Richard II* was thought too subversive at the time, when Elizabeth was increasingly infirm, but found its way into the Folio version after her death. When a play toured with a small cast cuts would be made. In *King Lear*, the differences between the Quarto and the Folio text are so significant that the Oxford Shakespeare offers two plays, *The History of King Lear* and *The Tragedy of King Lear*. The point is that there is no 'pure' text. A playscript is a blueprint for live performances, all different, and none the 'true' version.

Folio, a collection of Shakespeare's plays published after his death. It is very likely that it was typeset from the scripts used by the actors in performance, which were hand-written, perhaps by Shakespeare himself.

Oxford text

Claudius Though **yet** of Hamlet our dear brother's death
The memory be green, **and** that it us befitted*
To bear our hearts in **grief**, and our **whole** kingdom
To be contracted* in **one** brow of **woe**,
Yet so far hath **discretion** fought with **nature**   5
That we with **wisest sorrow** think on **him**
Together with remembrance of **ourselves**.
Therefore our sometimes **sister**, now our **queen**,
Th'imperial jointress* of this warlike state,
Have we, as 'twere with a **defeated joy**,   10
With one **auspicious*** and one **dropping** eye,
With **mirth** in **funeral** and **dirge** in **marriage**,
In equal scale weighing **delight** and **dole**,*
Taken to wife.

* [2] *that it us befitted* though it is right for us [4] *contracted* furrowed like the brow of a worried or upset man – but also in the legal sense of 'dutifully united' [9] *jointress* another 'coinage' (i.e. a word made up by Shakespeare for the occasion) which seems signify a woman who is joint-sharer, or perhaps a woman who joins things together [11] *auspicious* optimistic [13] *dole* grief

First Folio text

King Though yet of *Hamlet* our deere Brothers death
The memory be greene: and that it vs befitted
To beare our hearts in greefe, and our whole Kingdome
To be contracted in one brow of woe:

Yet so farre hath Discretion fought with Nature,   5
That we with wisest sorrow thinke on him,
Together with remembrance of ourselues.
Therefore our sometimes Sister, now our Queen,
Th'Imperiall Ioyntresse of this warlike State,
Have we, as 'twere, with a defeated ioy,   10
With one Auspicious, and one Dropping eye,
With mirth in Funerall, and with Dirge in Marriage,
In equal Scale weighing Delight and Dole
Taken to Wife;

                (I 2 1–13)

In 1623 there were no standardised rules for spelling. You could spell words more or less how you wanted – and, shocking to relate, the world didn't fall apart. Indeed, Shakespeare spells his own surname differently in the different signatures we have. I am more interested here in the way that the punctuation is used. Modern punctuation tends to be used to express the logical connection between phrases. For example, we use a full stop to show where the sense of one particular proposition is complete – at the end of a sentence. A colon (:) usually indicates that a list or a phrase follows which exemplifies what has just been stated. A capital letter indicates a proper name or the beginning of the sentence. This is not how these conventions were used in the 1623 First Folio of Shakespeare's plays. A full-stop was used for the strongest sort of pause, even in the middle of an unfinished sentence. A colon was used as an emphatic pause, no matter what the logical or semantic connection is between what goes either side of it ('semantic' means 'concerned with meaning'). Capitals are used both for proper names *and* for words which are particularly important in the context of the speech. It is worth noticing that italics are not used for emphasis but for proper names and quotations. If you read the speech using the punctuation marks as a guide for pause and emphasis, you will find that they, too, are very useful in helping you get the sense. You will get a different yet corroborative reading from that suggested by paying attention to the balancing words. Claudius comes across as even smoother and more slippery than the politically persuasive speaker who emerges from a focus on the balancing words.

My point here is that meaning is produced by performance: sound, rhythm, pause and emphasis are actually more important than is a knowledge of what the words mean: you can spend a long time looking them all up and still be unsure sometimes about the meaning of the passage.

Comparisons, images and analogies

The language of early modern drama is not generally that of plain description. A great deal of the written English of the time was in verse form, and the use of *figurative* language, which is particularly characteristic of poetry, was common. By *figurative* I mean language that describes one thing by comparing it, either directly or indirectly, to something else. As a simple example, to say that a freezing cold day has an *icy grip* on you is to speak figuratively: the air is likened to a cold hand firmly grabbing hold of you. A significant part of the dramatic and the poetic effect in Shakespeare's plays is the result of carefully developed comparisons which, when they work to create a particular picture in the audience's mind, are known as *imagery*. It has been a feature of poetic writing since the time of the ancient Greeks, but in Shakespeare it gains a sophistication and a precision which call for comment.

Here is another passage from Shakespeare's Trojan War play *Troilus and Cressida*. Troilus, one of the many sons of Priam, King of Troy, is in love with Cressida. He has not spoken to her yet – he has only admired her from afar. He is employing her uncle, Pandarus, as a go-between to sing his praises to Cressida in the hope that she will agree to a meeting with him. The first time he is on stage alone with the audience he describes his situation to them in a particularly striking image:

Troilus Her bed is India, there she lies, a pearl:　　　　　　100
　　　Between our Ilium* and where she resides,
　　　Let it be called the wild and wand'ring flood;*

Ourself the merchant, and this sailing Pandar
Our doubtful hope, our convoy and our bark.*

(I 1 100–4)

* [101] *Ilium* another name for Troy [102] *flood* the sea [104]
bark a ship

The image of Cressida as a pearl lying in a bed conveys a great
deal about Troilus' idea of her: her whiteness (in 1600, the fairer
the skin the greater the beauty; white skin connoted goodness,
and black skin wickedness in the racial thinking of the time, too.).
The image also suggests her feminine roundness and her exotic
strangeness as a woman ('India'). A pearl is hard and unyielding,
too, of course, as well as perfect in the way that no human being
ever is. From the start he idealises her impossibly. An erotic
charge is clearly an ingredient – he is already imagining her in
bed.

A pearl is also a thing of great value, difficult and perhaps
dangerous to obtain. But he does not cast himself in the role of
the adventurer who crosses the sea to win the prize. Instead he is
the speculator who remains at home and waits for the employee
in whom he has invested his money to do the work for him. Thus
Troilus, despite the extravagant lover's language of the first part
of the image, sees Cressida as an object or possession to be
purchased at only material – financial – risk. Subtly, a great deal
of information about his attitude to her (which will foreshadow
the course of their affair) is contained in this image.

As I pointed out above, (see p. 14), early modern audiences
were familiar with a limited range of visual representations. An
emblem was a picture which symbolised, usually allegorically, a
piece of wisdom or a belief about life. The illustrations in Figure
1.1 contain some examples. 'Chapbooks', cheaply produced and
roughly printed unbound editions, were often composed solely
of woodcut emblems. In a society of widespread illiteracy,
cheap emblem sheets were as close as you got to genuine popular
literature. We know that the pages of such books were often fixed
to the walls of even humble cottages. There was a whole set of

well-known emblems on which 'theatrical' pictures – both on the
stage itself and in the language – would draw to enhance their
meaning. Queen Elizabeth was portrayed holding a sieve, not to
boast her prowess in the kitchen, but because it was associated
with the chaste Roman virgin Tuccia who proved her chastity by
her ability to run with a sieve full of water without losing a drop,
and also with an emblem which symbolised true judgement –
being able to sieve the good out from the bad (White 1998: 9).
The people of the time must have been used to doing this sort of
analysis on mental pictures, too.

Shakespeare uses allegorical images as emblems to make a
moral or political point. (By *allegorical* I mean telling one story
in terms of another in order to pass comment on the first story.
Thus George Orwell told the story of the Russian Revolution in
Animal Farm (1944) by recounting a story about animals who
take over a farm from the human owners, but themselves end up
as the slaves of pigs, who rule under the slogan: 'All animals are
equal, but some are more equal than others.') To return to King
Lear: when the old King is out on the heath, deserted by his
family and his court, homeless and despised, he sinks into
madness. Yet in his mad ravings there is a kind of wisdom. He
has seen that a king is just a man; he has experienced the sufferings of the poorest. He comes to see the nature of the power held
by the rich over the poor.

King Lear Through tattered clothes small vices do appear:
    Robes and furred gowns hide all. Plate* sin with gold,   165
    And the strong lance of justice hurtless breaks;
    Arm it in rags, a pygmy's straw does pierce it.
    None does offend, none, I say none. I'll able 'em.*

                   (IV 6 164–8)

    * [165] *plate* i.e. put in plate, sheet metal, armour [168] *I'll*
    able 'em I can vouch for this from my own experience

There are two images or emblems here. In the first we see two
men, a poor man in rags and a rich man in expensive clothes.

(a)

(b)

(c)

FIGURE 1.1 Three emblems from contemporary collections

Note Each suggests a moral message of some sort:
(a)   Even the most wealthy, proud and youthful will die one day.
(b)   The serpent and the flower: beware the superficially attractive; danger may well lurk beneath it (see *Macbeth*, I 5 65–6).
(c)   *Occasio* or *Fortuna*, an emblem of the goddess of luck. Good fortune is a beautiful woman (because she is desirable, but also proverbially fickle in her affections). She has only one lock of hair because you have only one chance to grab her as she goes by. She stands upon a wheel because fortune moves in a circular fashion: when you are at the height of your good luck there is one way only to go, down – and vice versa (see *Hamlet*, II 2 228–36, and 492–7).

Both do wrong to others, but we cannot see the offence of the rich man because his wealth conceals it. The image is of the sores and rashes – external markers of internal moral disease – visible through the rags of the poor man but hidden by the robes of the rich. The poor and desperate who turn to crime, on the other hand, are caught and condemned. In the second emblem, wickedness is depicted as encased in a suit of golden armour: money. Even the strong lance of the state's justice cannot pierce it. Clothe wrongdoing in rags, and even the straw of a puny man can punish it. The image is saying that if you are rich you are far more likely to get away with illegal, even wicked, behaviour than if you are poor.

Lear has, in the past, abused his power as a monarch. Now that he is poor and outcast he can see how right and wrong in society tend to be defined by those with wealth and power. Blaming our ills on the crimes of the poor as if only they did wrong will get us nowhere. We need a better way of organising our society: this idea often emerges in the play. Notice how a political argument is expressed in a verbally realised visual image. This is characteristic of how early modern English drama works.

This sort of analysis could be replicated thousands of times for the complex images which throng the plays. It is important to remember that Shakespeare and his contemporaries were working in a climate of ideas and beliefs very different from our own. Medieval thinking had been dominated by the idea that God had organised the world into a series of linked hierarchies, so that human beings were ranked as (just) inferior to the angels but superior to animals, which in turn were superior to plants, and so on. Within these hierarchies, or 'domains', lay further hierarchies: a king was at the top of the human pyramid, a lion above all beasts and an eagle above all birds. While ideas were changing in Shakespeare's time, this type of thinking was still influential, and this means that we, from our modern perspectives, might find some of his analogies or comparisons surprising. For example, in medieval thought an eagle had far more in common with a king or a lion – as the chief creatures in their own domains – than it did with other birds. Such correspondences were simply the way God had organised the world. The extensive use of comparison and analogy in the plays of the time reveals the way in which people might seek to acknowledge the links in what was known as the 'Great Chain of Being' and to exploit these for effect. The images become increasingly complex because, of course, Shakespeare was living in post-medieval times (and even in medieval times there were those who did not agree or act in accordance with the Great Chain). Old ways of thinking were becoming mixed with new views of the way the world worked. As the example from *King Lear* shows, politics was no longer a

Box 3: The Great Chain of Being and radical politics

The Great Chain of Being organised the world into a *fixed order*, with God at the top, descending successively through angels, men, women(!), animals, birds, fishes, insects, trees and plants to stones. There were seven orders of angels, with archangels at the top. Men were organised in a fixed order from king down to serf.

Such domains within the greater hierarchy meant that the structure of each class of being reflected the structure of creation as a whole. Even parts of the human body corresponded to other elements in society: the head was the king, the arms warriors, the hands workers, and so on. As you went up the chain, each 'link' had power over the link below. To disobey those in authority was to defy the divine plan: superiors had to be obeyed even when they seemed to do wrong (see Ulysses' speech in *Troilus and Cressida*, pp. 231f.).

In Shakespeare's time, those who were in positions of power wanted everyone else, including Elizabeth's government, to know their rightful place, and so argued that this medieval hierarchy was divinely ordained. But in London, where a merchant class was making its own way to wealth and power, not everyone was convinced. The rise of individuals through business undermined the theory that a person is born into a particular class and must remain there. At the same time, science was developing, and men like Copernicus, Galileo and Francis Bacon showed that observation and experiment could explain the world in new ways. Copernicus' proof that the earth went around the sun, and not vice versa, was known in London at this time: man was no longer at the centre of the universe. There was also a small but influential group of 'sceptical intellectuals' who made it their work to doubt everything, discarding worn-out beliefs. The writings of one such thinker, the Frenchman Michel de Montaigne (1533–92), were read by many, including Shakespeare himself. Hamlet's soliloquy (III 1 55–87), doubting the Christian idea of the afterlife, can be seen as an example of how a radically minded student may have thought at this time.

Puritanism had a significant impact. Puritans argued that a poor man's reading of the Bible was as valid as a rich man's, building upon a radical popular tradition which for hundreds of years had argued that all people should be equal. The Puritans' commitment was to God first, and to civil authority only thereafter, so that for them the king was no longer necessarily God's mouthpiece. Much of the age's political conflict can be ascribed to this moment when obeying God and obeying the monarch became two different things. By 1642, a king who did not behave in a godly way was no longer a king to be obeyed, and Civil War followed.

simple question of obeying the king and accepting your place in a God-given hierarchy.

Comparative–analogical thinking of this kind came much more naturally to Shakespeare's audiences than it does to the modern reader or audience member. The creation of verbal images also was very powerful, achieving subtle, sometimes political, effects. Today we are sophisticated readers of the visual image. The challenge in reading early modern drama is to hear and feel the mental pictures created by the language with the same sort of sophistication.

Chapter 2

Shakespeare's language (2)

Verse and prose

When you flick through a Shakespeare play, you immediately notice the different ways in which the language is set out on the page. The majority of all but a few plays is written in verse, but a significant amount of each is written in prose. Prose, broadly speaking, is any sort of writing which is not poetry; I am writing prose now. When you are writing prose and you come to the edge of the page, you start a new line – unless, of course, you begin a new paragraph. In verse, you start a new line whenever the effect you're trying to produce calls for it. Often this is because you are keeping your lines to a regular length. In Shakespeare this is usually a standard five-beat line – more on which below (see p. 40).

Verse is the principal means of expression in Shakespeare, though prose is used in particular circumstances. Here I want to point out certain of the effects that are achieved by shifting between verse and prose. Generally, prose is of lower social status than verse: poetry is 'elevated', noble; prose is 'prosaic', ordinary. Working-class and comic characters usually speak prose; their 'betters', the serious characters, verse, by and large. Domestic scenes between women tend to be in prose, too. And, finally, when one character has to work hard to persuade another on stage, prose tends to be used.

But that does not mean there is something unrefined and second-rate about prose speech. Here is an important moment from one of the funniest and most exciting of all the plays, *King Henry IV Part I*. At the end of the play, King Henry finally engages his rebel enemies in battle. His wayward son Prince Hal (Henry or Harry) has spent most of the play in a London tavern, drinking and jesting with a boastful, cowardly but very funny fat old knight called Sir John Falstaff. In this final battle the prince, now reconciled with his father, comes face to face with the rebels' greatest warrior – Harry Hotspur, son of the Duke of Northumberland. During their fight to the death, on which the fate of the crown depends, Sir John Falstaff waddles on stage to cheer from the sidelines. To his horror, he himself is attacked by Douglas, Hotspur's Scottish ally. No warrior, Falstaff falls down 'dead'. Douglas leaves him lying there, and leaves the stage. Hal eventually kills Hotspur and speaks nobly, in verse, over his enemy's body. Then he notices the 'corpse' of his fat old friend.

Prince Harry What, old acquaintance! Could not all this flesh
    Keep in a little life? Poor Jack, farewell!
    I could have better spar'd a better man.
    O, I should have a heavy miss of thee,   105
    If I were much in love with vanity!*
    Death hath not struck so fat a deer to-day,
    Though many dearer, in this bloody fray.*
    Embowell'd* will I see thee by and by.
    Till then in blood by noble Percy lie. *(Exit)*   110
    (Falstaff riseth up)
Falstaff Embowell'd? If thou embowel me today, I'll
    give you leave to powder* me and eat me too,

tomorrow. 'Sblood,* 'twas time to counterfeit, or that hot
termagant* Scot had paid me, scot and lot, too.
Counterfeit? I lie, I am no counterfeit. To die is to be a   115
counterfeit, for he is but the counterfeit of a man who
hath not the life of the man; but to counterfeit dying,
when a man thereby liveth, is to be no counterfeit, but
the true and perfect image of life indeed. The better part   120
of valour is discretion, in the which better part
I have saved my life.

(V 4 102–21)

* [106] *Vanity* spending your time on pleasure [108] *fray* fight,
battle [109] *Embowelled* Hal means buried, put in the 'bowels'
of the earth, though Falstaff takes it to mean 'disembowel',
to gut, as you would an animal before eating it: of course, the
portly Sir John certainly is 'embowelled' – possessed with
ample guts [112] *powder* season with salt and pepper [113]
'Sblood a swearword, 'by God's blood' [114] *termagant* a
boastful, blustering, hot-tempered character from the old
Mystery Plays

Sir John's attitude in this speech to the audience comes across as
more like common-sense than the sentiment of a coward. The
honour and nobility of the duel between the rival young Harrys
has left one of them dead on the ground. Prince Hal, speaking
over the body of Falstaff, cannot resist making jokes about his
size. There's an almost offensive lack of respect in the way that
Hal mocks his friend, even in death. The prince uses heroic
language, but there's an aristocratically arrogant harshness about
it, despite its poetic qualities – final rhyming couplet and all. In
some productions of the play the audience is turned further
against Hal by having Falstaff's face, unseen by Hal, towards the
audience so that the actor can respond to what he's hearing in his
silent changes of expression. Or sometimes the 'fight' between
Douglas and Falstaff is played in a way to make the audience
think that Sir John really is dead. Hal exits at line 109. There is

then a pause before Falstaff, still supine, roars the word 'Em-bow-ell—ed!' before sitting bolt upright. Audiences sometimes cheer at this point! Verse can be uplifting and beautiful, and also witty and full of energy; but it can also lose the common touch, the audience contact, that prose can give.

The point again is that we should be aware of the conventional uses of language in order to see how the writer exploits these uses for dramatic effect. When the duke enters to quell the street-fight between the Montagues and the Capulets at the beginning of *Romeo and Juliet*, he speaks the first sustained verse in the play (I 1 78–100). The earlier insults and squabbling (between the servants – see I 1 1–62) were conducted first in prose and then in two-line snatches of verse as the nobility become involved (I 1 63–77). Here, with the duke's entrance, extended verse conveys order, dignity and authority. This is the normal use. As readers, we have to identify these conventions in order to see when the dramatic situation needs to turn them on their heads.

Indeed, prose is often used purely for its dramatic impact without reference to the social status of the speaker. Sometimes it is used to break the pattern of a scene which has been running in verse, so marking the end of a particular event or atmosphere; or to signal the beginning of a new dramatic moment. Falstaff's shift into prose (in line 111 above), given the situation, would be just as effective whatever the social status of the speaker.

Verse

The majority of the time, however, Shakespeare writes in *blank verse*. This term refers to lines of unrhymed poetry, each of which has five stressed syllables. The stress conventionally falls on the second, fourth, sixth, eighth and tenth syllables. The classical name for this verse form is *iambic pentameter*, each line of verse consisting of five iambic 'feet' (a 'foot' being a two-syllable unit comprising an unstressed syllable followed by a stressed syllable). This requires explanation.

A syllable is a unit of sound. *Shakespeare* has two: Shakespeare. The first unit is stressed. English pronunciation requires us to put emphasis on certain syllables rather than others. We pronounce the writer's name *Shakes*speare, not Shake*speare*. 'Manchester' has three, with the first one stressed: *Man*-ches-ter. Poets like to organise the stressed syllables in regular patterns to create rhythm and musicality. The characteristic rhythm of the (five-stress) iambic pentameter is de-**dum**-de-**dum**-de-**dum**-de-**dum**-de-**dum**. This pattern of line is found in Chaucer, then in the poets and playwrights of Shakespeare's time, then Milton, Pope, Keats, Tennyson ... all the way up to contemporary poets like Simon Armitage and Carol Ann Duffy. In other words, it is the standard line in English poetry. Chaucer made his pentameters rhyme. The first writer to use unrhymed pentameters was the Earl of Surrey, in his 1557 translation of the Latin Epic Poem *The Aeneid*. By the time Shakespeare started writing, Kyd and Marlowe had made it the standard verse form for drama – and it remained so until the writing of verse drama went out of fashion in the eighteenth century.

Here is a line of Shakespeare with the stresses just where you would expect to find them. It is Hamlet's advice to his mother soon after he has seen his father's ghost for the second time: she should be sorry for marrying Claudius and so avoid the vengeance that is coming:

Hamlet Re**pent** what's **past**, a**void** what **is** to **come**.

(III 4 150)

As you can see when you read it, the second, fourth, sixth, eighth and tenth syllables are stressed. Some are long sounds (*past*) and some are short sounds (*is*). Of course, if every single line had this regular pattern of stress over the course of a three-hour play it would get rather monotonous. What happens is that the writer uses this as a framework, and then varies from it in all sorts of subtle ways. This not only gives the sound of the language interest and variety but produces particular effects which add to the meaning of what the character is saying. So, on many occasions, the pattern of the stress is irregular: this is known as

41

modulation. Sometimes the actual length of the line varies, too. It all depends on the overall impact the speech is supposed to have within the context of the play.

Look now at a speech from *Hamlet.* Old Hamlet, the King of Denmark, has been murdered by his brother Claudius so that he could seize both the crown and the hand of Queen Gertrude. The murdered monarch's ghost appears to Prince Hamlet, his son, in the middle of the night. The prince has been told that a ghost looking like his father was seen walking the castle battlements, but until now he has not seen it for himself and remains unsure whose ghost it is. If it is his father's, it may well mean that there is some act of revenge required of him by the unsettled spirit before it can rest. The ghost identifies itself, and tells him of its sufferings in purgatory (according to Roman Catholicism, the place where the souls of the dead go if they had committed sins not grievous enough for hell; they suffer there until the penalty for their misdeeds is paid, and then they can go to heaven).

I have marked the text to show the actual way in which an actor or reader would stress these lines in contrast to where you would expect the regular stress to fall. The italicised syllables show where the stresses regularly fall in blank verse. The bold syllables show where I think the stresses of the line, when actually spoken, don't coincide with the normal stress pattern of the five-beat line. You might see a slightly different pattern – there's no absolutely right answer here – but my suggestions are in line with normal British English speech patterns, both in 'received (dictionary) pronunciation' and in most regional accents. In other words, as you read it you naturally stress the underlined syllables – but you will stress the bold syllables as well. This modulation – deliberate variation from the normal de-dum-de-dum-de-dum-de-dum-de-dum pattern – gives more than variety and musicality to the line. The ear is expecting a certain regular pattern of stresses, so that when this expectation is unrealised the words which you didn't expect to hear stressed call attention to themselves and stand out. Usually (but not actually in every case) these words have significance in the dramatic impact of the speech overall. Look at the stressed words marked in bold, which fall outside the normal stress pattern.

Ghost **I** *am* thy *fath*er's *spi*rit,
Doom'd *for* a *cer*tain *term* to *walk* the *night*

10

And *for* the *day* con*fin'd* to *fast** in *fires*,
Till *the* foul *crimes* **done** *in* my *days* of *nat*ure
Are *burnt* and *purged** a*way*. **But*** *that* I *am* forbid
To *tell* the *sec*rets *of* my *pri*son-*house*,
I *could* a *tale* un*fold* whose *light*est *word*

15

Would *harr*ow *up** thy *soul*, **freeze** thy young *blood*,
Make *thy* two *eyes* like *stars* **start** *from* their *spheres*,*
Thy *knot*ty *and* com*bined locks* to *part*,
And *each* par*tic*ular *hair* to *stand* on *end*,
Like *quills* up*on* the *fret*ful* *porcu*pine.

20

(I 5 9–20)

* [11] *Fast* go hungry [13] *purged* cleansed; *But* except [16] *harrow up* torment [17] *spheres* sockets [20] *fretful* bad-tempered

The first word in line 9 ('I') is unconventionally stressed – the first syllable in a blank verse line isn't, in theory. But of course, for Hamlet, this is a terribly important syllable. With it the ghost identifies itself and satisfies the question both Hamlet and the audience have been asking. The first word of the next line ('Doomed') is not only unconventionally stressed but very long in sound. When a stress – particularly an irregular one – falls on a word with a long vowel sound, as here, the word has even more force and impact in the sentence. The fact that the ghost is inescapably condemned to years of horrific torture and fretful unrest is powerfully conveyed in that word – because of its place in the stress patterning of the line. To me it sounds as if the ghost is feeling particularly sorry for itself, but it could also be said in a way which scares. The fact that the ghost is eagerly looking forward to the point at which its sufferings will stop, and regrets the sins it committed on earth which have condemned it to this fate are conveyed in the next words which stand out: 'Till' and 'done' in line 12. The next irregularly stressed word, 'But' in line 13, is an example of how modulation sometimes doesn't bring out the meanings of words so much as stress the overall logical development of a speech. Here the main effect is strongly to signal the beginning of a new sentence; but I suppose it also indicates the force of the divine prohibition on telling the truth about Purgatory. The final two irregularly stressed words have the effect of making the physical impact of hearing the ghost's account of the horrors of the afterlife even more striking. The sudden icing-up of Hamlet's young blood is brought out in the emphasis on 'freeze'; the word 'start' jumps out at you – and that's what 'start' means, here (as in 'you gave me a start'). Hamlet's eyes would jump from their sockets in shock if he saw the torments his father must face in Purgatory.

I am not, of course, suggesting that a full appreciation of Shakespeare's verse requires this sort of detailed awareness of variations in the stress patterning all the time. The variations work almost subconsciously, just as, no doubt, the writer put them in without consciously striving for technical effect. But when you are looking closely at a passage from a play this is certainly something you need to be aware of in order fully to grasp how the language achieves the meanings it does.

Here is another, most dramatic, example. At the end of *King Lear*, the heartbroken old king holds in his arms the dead body of his daughter Cordelia, killed before news of her reprieve from execution could reach her. The speech includes these lines:

Lear **Why** *should* a *dog*, a *horse*, a *rat* have *life*,
   And *thou* no *breath* at *all*? Thou'lt *come* no *more*,
   Ne*ver*, **ne***ver*, **ne***ver*, **ne***ver*, ne*ver*.

(V 3 307– 9)

In a moment of terminal grief, Lear speaks a line the stress pattern of which is wholly inverted. This comes after two very nearly regular lines, apart from the powerful question posed by the irregularly stressed 'Why' in line 307. In this way it is forcefully brought home to the audience that Lear's world really has been turned upside down; chaos is here.

Modulation of stress patterning is an important way in which the writer manipulates the rules of blank verse to produce particular effects. Altering the line length is another way of doing this. As Shakespeare developed as a dramatist this is something he did more and more. Take for, example, the first line of the ghost's speech: 'I *am* thy *fath*er's *spi*rit'. This is two stresses short of the standard five. There are, in fact, three syllables (dum-de-dum) missing from the full blank verse line. What this does, of course, is make the actor pause to preserve the rhythm pattern. This silence is dramatically required for the ghost's announcement to sink in. The actor playing Hamlet no doubt reacts physically, and this two-beat pause gives the audience a space to become aware of the prince's reaction.

Line 13, on the other hand, has an extra stress. It is a six-beat line, technically called an *alexandrine*. Clearly, its irregularity emphasises its meaning: to tell more is forbidden, and that is underlined by the way 'forbid' stands out. But its disturbed line, with a heavy full-stop followed by the irregularly stressed 'but', does not flow at all smoothly. Consequently it conveys the ghost's turmoil as it contemplates the horrors and the loneliness of its predicament: being unable to share with Prince Hamlet the nature of its suffering. In order to lessen the damage to the overall rhythm, the actor may well pause for a couple of seconds at the full-stop here. In the 1623 Folio there is a question-mark instead of a full-stop – at the time a question-mark was used as we today would use an exclamation-mark, as well as to indicate a question. Clearly, excitement and mental disturbance are to be conveyed here.

One of the commonest modulations involves stressing the first syllable (or even missing out the first unstressed syllable, the so-called 'headless' line) in order to give more impact to the opening of the line. Another is to add an extra unstressed syllable to the end of the line to give it a softer – falling – ending. Such line-ends were called 'feminine' (and, yes, the hard-stressed ending of a line was indeed called 'masculine').

Another verse technique used by Shakespeare concerns the interplay between sentences and lines. In the early years of the Elizabethan theatre an idea expressed in verse sometimes would have its sense clumsily completed at the end of the line: so-called 'end-stopping'. In *Hamlet* a play is put on for the court in which the characters are made to speak in old-fashioned, rhyming, end-stopped lines. Here is the Player King in the *Murder of Gonzago*, as performed before the Danish court, telling his wife that he does not wish to hold her to her promise that she would never remarry after his death:

> *Player King* I do believe you think what now you speak,
> But what we do determine* oft we break.
> Purpose* is but the slave to memory,
> Of violent birth, but poor validity.

(III 2 186–9)

* [187] *determine* decide [188] *Purpose* intention

End-stopping can be lumbering in its effects; but even this old-fashioned (for 1600) use can have weight and dignity, as is appropriate for the *sententia*-like wisdom (see above, p. 24) which the Player King is passing on. Had Hamlet listened to his advice, events would certainly have turned out differently. End-stopping can be powerfully dramatic when combined with rhetorical figures (see below, pp.51–3). Look at the famous abdication speech from *King Richard II*. King Richard, an indecisive and rash monarch open to the influence of favourites, alienates important noblemen on whom he depends for support. One of them, Henry Bolingbroke, rightful Duke of Lancaster, first exiled by Richard, then deprived of both lands and titles, returns home to reclaim them. Richard panics and hands over power to Bolingbroke without the latter even asking for it – though neither does he refuse it. This is the moment when Richard gives in:

> *King Richard* Now mark me how I will undo myself:
> I give this heavy weight from off my head,
> And this unwieldy sceptre from my hand,   205

The pride of kingly sway* from out my heart;
With mine own tears I wash away my balm*
With mine own tears I give away my crown,
With mine own tongue deny my sacred state,
With mine own breath release all duteous oaths;   210
All pomp and majesty I do forswear;*
My acts, decrees and statutes* I deny.

(IV 1 203–12)

* [206] *sway* rule [207] *balm* the sacred ointment applied to
kings during the coronation ritual [211] *forswear* deny, cast
off [212] *statutes* laws made in parliament

The powerful finality of each of Richard's actions is reinforced in
the way the meaning is linked with the conclusive ending of each
line. Contrast the way Richard's language runs on between the
lines in this speech, a few scenes earlier. The king has fallen into a
depressive state, fearing that he is about to lose his throne:

King Richard For God's sake, let us sit upon the ground   155
     And tell sad stories of the death of kings:
     How some have been depos'd, some slain in war,
     Some haunted by the ghosts they have deposed,
     Some poisoned by their wives, some sleeping kill'd,
     All murdered. For within the hollow crown   160
     That rounds* the mortal temples of a king
     Keeps Death his court; and there the antic* sits,
     Scoffing his state and grinning at his pomp,
     Allowing him a breath, a little scene,
     To monarchise, be fear'd, and kill with looks,   165
     Infusing* him with self and vain conceit,
     As if this flesh which walls about our life
     Were brass impregnable; and humoured thus,
     Comes at the last, and with a little pin
     Bores through his castle wall, and farewell, king!   70

(III 3 155–70)

Box 4: Kings and queens

Thirty years before Shakespeare was born, Henry VIII had nationalised the possessions of the Roman Catholic Church and created the – Protestant – Church of England, of which he was Supreme Head. His daughter, Elizabeth I (1558–1603), was queen for most of Shakespeare's lifetime. The early part of her reign was a time of relative peace and stability. She largely completed the process begun by her father and grandfather (Henry VII) of centralising power and of breaking the independent fiefdoms of lords and nobles. She brought about a truce between the different wings of the Church and beat off a Spanish invasion fleet in 1588. In the years following, however, bad harvests, increasing poverty and social unrest made England a much less peaceful place. I say *England* because Britain, in its modern sense, did not then exist. Elizabeth I was Queen of England – and of Wales, which had been brought under the English crown by the Acts of Union of 1536 and 1543. Irish resistance to English power continued throughout Shakespeare's life. Scotland was an independent country and another hostile neighbour. Elizabeth was succeeded in 1603 by the King of Scotland, who became James I (1603–25). James had a more autocratic style than Elizabeth and faced opposition from Catholic rebels (the Gunpowder Plot of 1605, for instance) and from the Puritans in parliament. He and his son Charles I (1625–49) adopted a new political belief, most powerfully expressed in Catholic monarchies: *absolutism*. A feudal monarch respected the honour and rights of other lords, but the absolute monarchs saw themselves as God's sole representative on earth. Their will was absolute and they owed respect to no one. Public and court display under James I moved its emphasis increasingly away from the idea of the country as a single body, with each part carrying out its proper function, towards that of a divine king separate from the kingdom below him. The Civil War (1642) put an end to this idea.

Many Renaissance writers ended up in prison for slandering monarchs or foreign dignitaries. Shakespeare, however, seemed to have a great deal of political acumen. In February 1601 the Earl of Essex asked for a special performance of *Richard II* to signal his impending rebellion against the queen. Shakespeare's company complied, but clearly did not lose royal favour in consequence as it performed before Elizabeth on the eve of the earl's execution. This has caused much speculation about the company's political sympathies, but it seems likely to me that as shrewd businessmen they took the money and reported the affair to the authorities.

* [161] *rounds* surrounds [162] *antic* joker, teaser [166] *Infusing* filling up

The first sentence, listing the ways monarchs have lost their lives, runs over four lines. Then it ends suddenly and heavily in the middle of line 160: 'All murdered'. A line of blank verse has a natural pause, a *caesura*, which tends to come after the second beat – but obviously can be placed anywhere for effect. The full-stop falling on the caesura makes the realisation strike even harder: that, rather than living happily ever after, kings are usually done to death. This feature of verse, when the sense runs on from one line into the next, is called *enjambment*. When it happens, emphasis tends to get thrown on to the word which ends the line of which the sense overruns, or on to the first word of the next line. This can be seen at the ends of lines 167 – 'as if this life/Were brass impregnable' – and 169 – 'with a little pin/Bores through his castle wall'. In the first case, the emphasis on the word 'life', left exposed and hanging on the end of the line before the hard and rumbling sound of 'brass impregnable', makes it seem all the more vulnerable. In the second, the word 'pin' seems similarly to be left hanging: it appears all the tinier – so that its effect, in killing a king through his castle wall, is to make the king appear more fragile still. Again, a political idea is expressed through a visual image, created verbally.

Blank verse isn't blank when it rhymes. As his career progressed Shakespeare used rhyme less and less, but there are two distinc-tive uses of rhyme in the plays. Most notable is the use of a pair of rhyming lines, a 'rhyming couplet', to signal the end of a scene or the whole play. The rhyming couplet seems to give a sense of completeness. *King Lear* ends with four consecutive couplets (V 3 320–7).When a play ends without a rhyming couplet, as does *The Winter's Tale* (V 3 154–5), a sense of incompleteness is bestowed on the ending. And, indeed, since the ending of that play presents a 'statue' coming to life as a woman who was supposed to have died sixteen years earlier, the lack of concluding couplet is part of the general air of strangeness and provisionality surrounding the end of that play.

The other use of rhyme is to mark out a passage as distinctive from the rest of the blank verse and prose around it. It can be used to give to a saying or maxim the appearance of folk-wisdom, as in the Player King's speech quoted above (p. 46). Alternatively, it can be used in dialogue to give to rapid dialogue an energy and a backwards and forwards movement. In an early play, *The Comedy of Errors*, two sisters, Adriana and Luciana, are arguing about men. They are waiting for Adriana's husband Antipholus to come home for dinner. He is late, and Adriana feels aggrieved at the way men feel they can make women wait at their leisure; the younger and unmarried Luciana takes the man's point of view:

Adriana	Why should their liberty than ours be more?	10
Luciana	Because their business still lies out a'door.*	
Adriana	Look when I serve him so*, he takes it ill.	
Luciana	O, know he is the bridle of your will.	
Adriana	There's none but asses will be bridled so.	
Luciana	Why, headstrong liberty* is lashed with woe:	15

    There's nothing situate under heaven's eye
    But hath his* bound in earth, in sea, in sky.
    The beasts, the fishes and the winged fowls
    Are their males' subjects and at their controls:
    Man, more divine, the master of all these,   20
    Lord of the wide world and wild wat'ry seas,
    Indued with intellectual sense* and souls,
    Of more pre-eminence than fish and fowls,
    Are masters to their females and their lords:
    Then let your will attend on their accords.*   25

                     (I 3 10–25)

* [11] *still lies out a'door* is always away from home [12] *serve him so* treat him in the same way [15] *headstrong liberty* wilful self-assertion [17] *his* its [22] *intellectual sense* reason [25] *accords* wishes

The rhyme in lines 10–13 gives the dialogue something of the quality of a ball-game, with language being lobbed from one player to the other. But do the rhyming couplets of Luciana's speech (15–25) give its sentiments an air of wisdom? Or is it that putting in rhyme these very conventional Renaissance ideas about male natural superiority makes them seem glib and naive, particularly in the mouth of the inexperienced Luciana?

Rhetoric

Look at these two items of twentieth-century language. I expect you will find them familiar:

(a) Beanz Meanz Heinz

(b) We shall not flag or fail. We shall go on to the end. We shall fight in France, we shall fight on the seas and oceans, we shall fight with growing confidence and strength in the air, we shall defend our island whatever the cost may be. We shall fight on the beaches, we shall fight on the landing grounds, we shall fight in the field and in the streets, we shall fight in the hills; we shall never surrender.

The advertising copywriter of (a) would not have kept the job if what had been written was: 'Heinz beans are very nice. If you want beans they are the best ones to get.' The slogan combines humour, a memorable jingle, and three words building to a climax. Similarly with (b): Winston Churchill would not have inspired much resistance to the threat of German invasion in 1940 without the speech's carefully structured repetitions building towards a conclusion. It is the form of this part of the speech, as much as the sentiment it contained, which makes it memorable after all these years.

It was believed, both in ancient times and in sixteenth century Europe, that certain linguistic effects can naturally produce emotional reactions, in both speakers and hearers. The study of these effects was – and still is – known as *rhetoric*. From the fifth century BC the different means by which speakers decorated their

Box 5: Social mobility

The period during which Shakespeare was writing saw great hardship for many people, but it was also a time of new social mobility. In the countryside class divisions were still pronounced. Men and women alike worked on the land, either as servants or day-labourers. Those able to rent land were known as *husbandmen*; and if they could also afford to employ servants and labourers, *yeomen*. Above yeomen were the gentry and the aristocracy, whose incomes were mostly from the land they owned. Unemployment and hunger were generally seen as the results of laziness or greed, although parishes made some effort to help the poor. Leaving your parish to look for work was risky. Under the 1597 Poor Law, 'masterless men' could be classed as vagabonds and sentenced to be whipped until bloody, and then returned to their home parish. Poor Tom in *King Lear* would have been a recognisable figure to audiences. Despite the risk, around 6,000 people a year entered London looking for work. There and in the towns, obedience to your social superior was still very important, but at this time people were making their way in the world by their own efforts. Merchants didn't always have a 'gentle' background, but commerce made them the most powerful social group in London: they made up the council of alderman which administered the city.

Those whose livelihood was the theatre also demonstrated a certain social mobility. Shakespeare was not born into a prosperous, well-educated, land-owning family. His father John Shakespeare dealt and traded in whatever was profitably passing through Stratford-upon-Avon, including animal skins, coal, corn and malt for beer. He was probably a butcher, too. At one time chief alderman of Stratford, he was eventually arrested for debt. William Shakespeare turned out to be a far more successful businessman. He became a shareholder in the theatrical companies for which he wrote and performed, and began to acquire some wealth. In October 1596 he secured a coat of arms for his father and with it the rank of *gentleman*. When the Lord Chamberlain's Company became The King's Men, in May 1603, royal patronage confirmed Shakespeare's social status. Around 1613 he was able to retire to Stratford a reasonably wealthy man. He had bought the largest private house in the town, a rambling old building called New Place, and was clearly regarded as a local worthy.

Many did still feel that you should remain within your social class, where God had placed you. In fact, the social mobility of those in the theatre was often used against them by their critics, along with the accusation that actors should not go on stage disguised as their social superiors.

language to make it persuasive, memorable or moving were listed, taught, and learned in schools and universities. In the sixteenth century it was a major part of the curriculum. Skill in rhetoric was the essential quality of a public man.

Outside of academic philosophy, the word today has acquired a generally bad press: we us the phrase 'just rhetoric' to mean bluster empty of reason and logic. But, in fact, we use rhetoric all the time in our speech and writing – and nowhere more so than in advertising. In Shakespeare's time there was no pretence that rhetoric was anything other than an essential part of all literary writing. Without it, wrote George Puttenham in his *Rate of English Poesy* (1589), language is 'but as our ordinary talk'. The skilful writer picks the effects that naturally inspire certain feelings and reactions, and refines them to be both elegant and appropriate to the subject matter. 'Nature herself suggesteth the figure in this or that form: but Art aideth the judgement of his use and application', wrote Puttenham.

A *figure* is one of the two main types of rhetorical effect: it is concerned mostly with the placing and positioning of words in the sentence to produce particular patterns, usually by use of repetition and its effects. Scholars catalogued very many different types of repetition, giving them Greek names such as *anaphora, parison, ploce* and *anadiplosis*. It is the overall effect of these figures, rather than their particular differences, that I want to examine. 'Figures' also include devices where the speaker exclaims and emphatically addresses his hearers (*apostrophe*), or asks of them the so-called 'rhetorical question', the answer to which is obviously implied (*interrogatio*).

The other type of rhetorical effect, the *trope*, is concerned with effects created by changing the meaning of a word. These effects are distinguished by the terms according to which we analyse poetry in school and college today: metaphor (a comparison that works without using the words 'like' or 'as'); simile (a comparison using the words 'like' or 'as'); irony; understatement; exaggeration; allegory (see above, p. 30); and by such less-familiar terms as synecdoche (where the part stands for the whole – 'hand' for a worker) and metonymy (where the greater is substituted for the lesser – calling a king 'England', for example).

In the plays, rhetorical figures are used by characters who are overtly seeking to persuade, but they are also a common feature of the language of verse drama.

Look at another speech from *King Richard II*. Richard has recently stepped down, and Bolingbroke is about to ascend the throne and become King Henry IV – Prince Hal's father, in fact. The Bishop of Carlisle, who is attending proceedings, objects strongly. Richard, who was God's chosen representative on earth, is still alive, but absent. No man, the bishop argues, has the right to depose God's anointed ruler. Bolingbroke (who is called 'Herford' here – 'Duke of Hereford' was one of his titles) is no more than a thief. God will punish England for this sacrilege and condemn the country to generations of civil war. The other speaker involved, Northumberland, is one of Bolingbroke's temporary allies.

Bishop of Carlisle I speak to subjects, and a subject speaks,
    Stirred up by God thus boldly for his king.
    My lord of Herford here, whom you call king,
    Is a foul traitor to Herford's king,   135
    And, if you crown him, let me prophesy,
    The blood of English shall manure* the ground,
    And future ages groan for this foul act.
    Peace shall go sleep with Turks and infidels,*
    And in this seat of peace tumultuous wars   140
    Shall kin* with kin and kind* with kind confound.*
    Disorder, fear, horror and mutiny
    Shall here inhabit, and this land be call'd
    The field of Golgotha* and dead man's skulls.
    O, if you rear* this house against this house,   145
    It will the woefullest division prove
    That ever fell upon this cursed earth.
    Prevent, resist it; let it not be so,
    Lest child, child's children cry against you 'woe!'
Northumberland Well have you argued, sir, and for
    your pains   150
    Of capital* treason we arrest you here.

                                   (IV 1 132–51)

* [137] *manure* fertilise [139] *infidels* non-Christians [141 *kin* family; *kind* race; *confound* mix together in opposition [144] *Golgotha* the 'place of the skull', where Jesus was crucified [145] *rear* rear up, like a horse [151] *capital* punishable by death

It was indeed believed by some sixteenth-century historians that the furious civil wars of the fifteenth century had been a divine punishment for the usurpation (wrongful seizure of power) of Richard by Henry Bolingbroke. Two things are clear about the way the bishop's speech is written. First, we can see how Carlisle's rhetoric seeks to persuade by making it clear that the unnaturalness of the act will lead to a horrific future. Second, we can see how the bishop's faltering control over the techniques of persuasive language will give the audience an impression of how desperate and forlorn his attempt to stop Bolingbroke is. There are many subtle uses of repetition for effect here. I shall focus on just a few.

Each of lines 133–5 uses the word 'king'. The first is genuinely meant, and refers to Richard, Carlisle's true king. The second refers, sarcastically, to Bolingbroke. The third refers back to Richard, but in a clinching way. In rhetoric the third term in a repetition tends to act as a climax. This is *tricolon*, 'the rule of three'. Richard is *really* 'proud Herford's king'. This is asserted by the movement of the language towards this third use – so how can Hereford–Bolingbroke be king?

The repetition of 'foul' – used first in line 135 to describe Bolingbroke – in line 138 to describe his act of taking the throne, not only connects the abstraction *sacred kingship* with this ambitious personality but, coming as it does after the strange description of blood as 'manure', gives a strong impression of an England where blood and kingship have literally been turned to shit. Bolingbroke is an execrable man, and fouling will be the result of his sitting on *this* throne!

The harsh reality of civil war is well conveyed in line 141. 'Shall kin with kin and kind with kind confound' alternates a hard-*k* sound with a hard-*n* sound five times in ten syllables. Words which refer to welcoming and gentle relationships are rubbed up against each other in harsh-sounding syllables. Family relationships are turned into bruising conflicts: this much the repetition of sound and word suggests.

But after this Carlisle begins to lose his way. Just as students were taught the effective and appropriate use of rhetoric, so they were taught also to see where it is badly used. On stage, Carlisle is facing massed ranks of hard-faced and ruthless Bolingbroke supporters. As the speech unfolds, their jaws drop and their stares harden at the bishop's politically innocent effrontery. The bishop begins to realise that he is out of his depth. His language becomes more extreme, uncontrolled and less effective. The reference to Golgotha (line 135) in fact picks up the idea, expressed in certain images earlier in the play, of Richard as Christ, but the repetition of 'and field of skulls' would in this case be seen as unnecessary – *Golgotha* means 'place of the skull', as both the onstage and offstage audiences would have been aware. 'Woefullest division' is both clumsy and inadequate to describe the apocalyptic civil war predicted. The repetition in the final line, 'Lest child, child's children, cry against you woe', sounds ugly, and is weak and hard to understand. In this one speech we see rhetoric working to move us; then the dramatic situation changes and the crafted balance of word and sound breaks down, as the bishop's confidence collapses.

Rhetorical effects are not all about the language of political persuasion. Sometimes they are effective in communicating the most profound emotions, too. In Act I of *Antony and Cleopatra*, Mark Antony, the great Roman general, has fallen deeply in love with the sensual Queen of Egypt, Cleopatra. They are both mature and experienced people, in their forties, but there is in their feelings for each other an intensity more commonly encountered in the expressions of those less used to such passions, which is totally absorbing. Antony has, in fact, been neglecting his responsibilities as one of the three joint-rulers of the Roman Empire and has to leave Cleopatra in Egypt to recover his political position in Rome. At this moment in the play, though they don't know it, they are happy and trustful of one another as they will never be again. Cleopatra teases and irritates him. Then she relents and strives to put her feelings into words:

Antony   I'll leave you, lady.

Cleopatra Courteous lord, one word:
   Sir, you and I must part, but that's not it.
   Sir, you and I have loved, but there's not it;
   That you know well. Something it is I would –   90
   O, my oblivion* is a very Antony,
   And I am all forgotten.

                                       (I 3 86–92)

   * [90] *oblivion* forgetting

The structure of Cleopatra's speech is fully as rhetorical as the Bishop of Carlisle's. Yet it has an intimate personal quality that is quite different. She is trying to find the words to express her feelings for Antony in the face of his departure. She knows she is losing something precious but cannot say clearly what it is. It might perhaps be a sense of foreboding that she is about to be abandoned and forgotten by Antony. The repetitions of line 88 seek to modify her first attempt to express herself: It is not their parting; it is not the love they have experienced together – it is something she feels, but cannot say. It is the rhythms and sounds of the repetition that communicate this, not just the words themselves: it is as full a use of rhetoric as any more obviously persuasive speech.

Summary

- I have outlined the features of Shakespeare's language which you need to understand to read it with appreciation and understanding.
- I hope I have made clear that it is the *sound* of the language, in specific crafted ways, that is crucial to its meaning. This is quite unlike the characteristic modern experience of reading prose silently in your head.
- You need to be aware also of how the structure of verse and prose, and the use of rhetorical features and imagery, contribute essentially to the meaning conveyed by spoken language.

Further reading

Brook (1976) is a very good place to read more about Shakespeare's language; Blake (1983) is very comprehensive, but more advanced. There is a facsimile of the 1623 First Folio available, edited by Moston (1998). A version is also available on the world wide web at: http://etext.virginia.edu/shakespeare/folio

Chapter 3

Types of stage action

The forms of drama we live with day to day are what we see on TV, film and video. By comparison, what can actually happen in a Shakespeare play acted on stage is quite limited. The physical resources of the theatre – the number of actors involved, the size of the stage and so on – constrain the sort of action which can be shown to audiences; and, in Shakespeare's time, the types of stage activity which were deployed by playwrights were limited in number.

Broadly speaking, what happens on stage in a Shakespeare play will consist of such elements as the following:

- dialogue involving two or more characters who ignore the audience's presence;
- dialogue involving two or more characters who occasionally speak to the audience in 'asides';

- soliloquy – one character alone on stage talking to the audience;
- a spectacle of some sort – a sword fight, a masque, a dumbshow, a tavern scene, a song, a dance or similar; sometimes the spectacle is watched by other characters who form an on-stage audience;
- a direct address to the audience by a chorus figure.

The first of these is a dramatic form with which we are very familiar. Our constant exposure to popular TV programmes, film and naturalistic theatre has attuned us to think that naturalism is 'proper' drama. Indeed, a significant proportion of Shakespeare's plays consists of action of this sort, the actors making no acknowledgement that an audience is observing them. But, as you can see from the list above, a great deal of the on-stage action tends to involve a direct recognition of the audience's presence – and as a consequence apparently loses its claim to be a representation of reality. As the actors perform, they constantly signal to us that they know they are actors in role. If you are used to film-style naturalism, where we praise most highly acting that conveys 'realism', this acknowledgement of role awareness will seem unusual, to say the least.

It seems, in fact, that the actors constantly varied their styles of performance. Sometimes they could be depicting the thoughts and feelings of characters so vividly that the audience is swept along with, and emotionally affected by, the 'reality' of what is being portrayed. Richard Burbage – the son of theatre-owner James Burbage – who played many of the leads in Shakespeare's plays, was described by a near contemporary as capable of 'wholly transforming himself into his part and putting himself off with his clothes' (quoted in White 1998: 59). The theatre's Puritan enemies (see Boxes 6 and 11, pp. 63 and 155) regarded this ability to enchant and ensnare through the truthfulness of its representation of human behaviour as one of the stage's most dangerous qualities. They felt that wicked deeds were presented in so convincing and attractive a way that some of the audience would want to copy them. Yet the illusion would frequently be broken by an actor stopping to address the audience or breaking into soliloquy once other characters were out of the way.

A range of acting styles was deployed. Sometimes it was naturalistic; sometimes actors delivered a speech formally, as an orator would at court; at others the actors used an 'epic' style which acknowledged both the presence of the audience and the fictionality of what was happening on stage. Often these styles would follow one after another in the space of a few minutes. Just as the shocking and the tragic lived side by side with the silly, the absurd and the smutty in the same scene, so the style of acting would have to shift and change in an instant. Consistency, whether of character, style or mood, was not a salient characteristic of the English stage at this time. Narrative drive, engaging the audience, and dramatic impact were always more important than 'consistency'; in fact, many plays glory in their inappropriately juxtaposed, but nonetheless connected, moments. Look at the way the action of *The Winter's Tale* shifts from pathos and sentimentality to horror, absurdity and smuttiness, then to mockery of that horror, all in the space of the fifty lines around the stage direction '*Exit pursued by a bear*' (III 3 51–107; see p. 262). Look at the way Hamlet explicitly reminds us that the voice under the ground isn't his tormented father's soul in Purgatory, whose suffering we have just heard horrifically described (I 5 13–19), but a boy actor moving around the stage 'cellarage' below their feet (I 5 150–1, 162). This is how the theatre worked.

I want to consider, first, the notion that quite frequently the on-stage action acknowledges its fictional status. One of the effects of this dramatic technique is that, at those moments, the play asks the audience to reflect on the connections and contrasts between the on-stage and off-stage worlds. In particular, I want to introduce two important ideas characteristic of early modern drama: *estrangement* and *reflexivity.*

Estrangement

The notion of *estrangement* will be familiar to you if you have come across the idea of an 'alienation effect' in drama or theatre studies. In the late nineteenth and early twentieth centuries most theatre strove to persuade the audience that it was watching a piece of reality unfold – as if the fourth wall of a room had been removed so that everything within was revealed. In the theatre this is known as *naturalism*, though in film and TV, which have in the main adopted the same style, it tends to be known as *realism*. In the twentieth century writers like Bertolt Brecht and Edward Bond have had to strive to produce the opposite effect, that of an 'epic' theatre which doesn't want to evoke mere unthinking emotional escapism in its audience: it doesn't want its audience so lost in identification with the characters and their feelings as to be unable to reflect upon the morality and politics of what is being enacted. Instead these dramatists wanted audiences to maintain a distance, and be constantly aware of the fictionality of what was portrayed. They had to struggle, so wedded were audiences to naturalism – though those same audiences were happy to accept these effects in popular forms like pantomime and music hall. Brecht and Bond wanted to make audiences reflect on the meaning of the events on stage in relation to their own lives – to consider why things are happening on stage as they are – rather than be emotionally and uncritically caught up in the story in the manner, for example, of a Hollywood film audience. In order to do this they developed ways of estranging the audience, of breaking the illusion of reality. In one of Brecht's plays, for instance, a character will suddenly come out of role, come down to the front of the stage and sing a song to the audience about the on-stage situation. In one of Bond's plays a piece of violence might occur which is so gruesome and nasty that audiences are shocked into wondering why the play is putting them through this experience.

In plays of Shakespeare's time, the actors were constantly talking to audiences, reminding them that what they were watching were only plays. This may be surprising if you are not used to it, but the response expected from audiences was quite

Box 6: Early modern views on theatre

The Council of London Aldermen would not allow playhouses to be established in areas under their direct control. Many of the reasons they gave were practical. Those who attended the afternoon performances should have been working, so the theatre damaged the city's economy. The crowds that gathered caused disturbance; they attracted criminals and prostitutes; and they spread infectious diseases.

All this was true. But the mostly Puritan aldermen had more profound objections. Acting was not a 'respectable' but an artisan profession. Actors were associated with travelling jesters and jugglers. Any actor had to be licensed, or he would be classed as a vagabond and subject to the harsh laws applied to vagrants. (I say 'he' because women did not take the stage: performing *for* men would be an admission of whoredom.) Successful actors seeking social advancement were mocked, even by others in the theatre. It was said that because they made their living pretending to be what they were not, actors were inherently untrustworthy people. On stage, boys pretended to be women, and common men kings. Players were thus usurping God's role in deciding how people should appear on earth. The clothes worn were often those of real lords and bishops, left to a servant who had sold them on to a company. In a society where strict 'sumptuary laws' (until 1604) restricted according to social class and income the types of fabric and the colours people could wear, a further complaint against actors was that they overturned social distinctions by adopting clothes they were not qualified to wear. The theatre was seen to show social rank to be merely conventional and, therefore, to teach a subversive message. What is more, it encouraged crime and disobedience through the 'copy-cat' effect it would have on its audience.

Writers, actors and audiences knew, however, that what they were sharing was actually happening and yet was also a pretence: it was both fantasy and the truth about their lives; it reinforced those values which it also subverted. The theatre did both good and ill, as you would expect from serious art. Despite Puritan objections, theatre companies received the patronage of the court and the aristocracy. By supporting the theatre, monarchs shared in and took credit for its fame and glamour, thus protecting the institution until the Civil War broke out in 1642, at which time all the London theatres were closed and then pulled down (The Globe in 1644).

different from what is standard now. Our TV and film culture is built around star lead actors, and we are asked to identify with them and their 'personal' problems. Shakespeare's plays don't set out to examine the character traits and the problems of individuals as such and without reference to the wider issues. On the public stage, in front of a mixed audience, plays aimed to show a whole society at work together with the problems of people within that society. That is why in a single play there are kings and servants, warriors and jesters, noblewomen and whores – and all their lives are shown to be interconnected. It is the *why* and *how* of the events on stage that evoke the emotions and the laughter. There is no single vantage point, no one dominant character, from whose perspective we are asked to view the action of the whole play. We are given many different voices and many different perspectives between which we are asked to judge.

The theatre of Shakespeare's day was a product of a society in a state of transition. The feudal medieval world of loyalty to your lord in an unchanging society dominated by religion was giving way to a modern and increasingly 'secular' society (in which religion was no longer central to people's lives). This society was characterised both by acquisitive individuality (where people seek to make themselves rich, and put their own welfare before that of those around them) and by constant technological and political change. All these competing forces are evident in the plays put on stage. In this society in flux, no one way of looking at the world has become so powerful that it is accepted as natural, so no one viewpoint on stage is fixed, natural, 'real'. The characters seem to keep suggesting questions to the audience: 'Do you approve of what I am doing? Can you see why I'm behaving like this? Could things be otherwise?'

Reflexivity

The way in which the on-stage action keeps referring back to itself is known as its *reflexivity*. Self-reference is obvious from the language itself, with its puns and word-plays drawing attention to how a particular word or phrase is being used (as when Hamlet tells Claudius that he is 'too much in the sun ["son"]' (I 2 67; see p. 80. It is also evident in the constant playing with the conventions of verse forms and rhetoric (see p. 51 above). The delivery of the lines in live performance will bring out this self-consciousness even more clearly than when the text is merely read. But more obviously it is also there in the plays' habit of setting up *other* performances on stage and turning some characters into a second audience which the paying audience observes watching. Look, for example, at the hidden Othello observing what he *thinks* is his lieutenant Cassio boasting about taking Othello's wife Desdemona as his mistress (IV 1 74–170). Shakespeare's theatre was fascinated with what we call *representation*. How is it that we can represent fictional men and women on stage in such a way as to make that fiction a recognisable simulation of 'reality'? What happens when we do that? What is revealed about our views and ideas by our choice to represent a black man, a whore, a bishop, a legendary hero or a famous historical character on stage? The plays seem self-consciously to do this, and are constantly watching themselves at work both critically and ironically – yet all this is done with a great sense of playfulness.

Here are three of the principal techniques by which the audience is made to think in these ways. They are not unique to early modern English theatre, but they are among its important constituents.

Soliloquies and asides

A soliloquy is addressed by a character, alone on stage, directly to the audience. An aside is a remark or speech directed at the audience *unheard* by the other characters on stage at the time, and is usually quite short. Teachers sometimes say that a soliloquy or aside is a character voicing his or her inner thoughts. When Macbeth voices his doubts about going ahead with King Duncan's murder (I 7 1–28) the audience is *actually hearing* what Macbeth is saying or thinking to himself. Indeed, many film versions of Shakespeare deal with the soliloquy by using the 'voice over' convention of cinema, which we take to represent what is going through a character's mind. But this is to assume that the character is real and has 'inner thoughts'. Such teachers and critics are being led astray by the false presumption that the plays are naturalistic and that the character doesn't know that the audience is there. We sometimes think because a soliloquy is addressed to us rather than to another character, that it must have some special authority. But why should it? *All* speeches reveal 'states of mind', and in fact a character is just as capable of seducing and misleading an audience as he or she is of another character.

Because asides and soliloquies involve a character talking to the audience, some sort of relationship is established between that character and the audience. Sometimes the whole audience will share one view of that character; more often individual audience members will react in different ways. In any case, we are being asked again to make a judgement about whether we accept what is being said to us, or of the credibility of the character as a reporter. Audiences will often laugh at pompous or foolish characters who confide in them. The actors sometimes respond in character to this laughter. Audiences can find themselves siding with the 'darker' forces in a play through these means, too.

Soliloquies and asides also make us complicit in what the speakers are doing. We share their viewpoints for a moment – or longer – even if we cannot agree with what they say. It is another means of making us aware that no single viewpoint predominates in a play. Here is a soliloquy from *Othello* spoken by Iago. Othello is a very successful Moorish general working for the state of Venice. He has just promoted an officer, Cassio, to be his lieutenant. This has dashed the hopes of another of his junior officers, Iago, a man in whom Othello has complete trust. We know from the first moments of the play that Iago hates his general, not least because he is black. Othello has just eloped with and married Desdemona, the daughter of a rich Venetian, against her father's wishes. Iago has secretly done his best to wreck the marriage, but the Moor's credit with the Venetian government is such that the state ignores her father's disapproval and the marriage is blessed in spite of the difference in their age and race. At the end of the third scene Iago comes, alone, to the front of the stage to share his plans for a more thorough revenge.

Iago I hate the Moor,
   And it is thought abroad that 'twixt my sheets
   He has done my office.* I know not if it be true,
   But I, for mere suspicion in that kind,
   Will do as if for surety.* He holds* me well,   390
   The better will my purpose work on him.
   Cassio's a proper man. Let me see now:
   To get his place, and to plume up my will
   In double knavery – How, how? Let's see –
   After some time to abuse* Othello's ear   395
   That he* is too familiar with his wife.
   He hath a person and a smooth dispose
   To be suspected* – framed to make women false.
   The Moor is of a free* and open nature,
   That thinks men honest that but seem to be so,   400
   And will as tenderly be led by th' nose
   As asses are.
   I have't.* It is ingendered.* Hell and night
   Must bring this monstrous birth to the world's light. *(Exit)*.

                       (I 3 386–404)

* [388] *done my office* had sex with my wife [390] *Will do as if for surety* Will act as if I were sure it is true; *holds* regards [395] *abuse* deceive [396] *he* Cassio [397–8] *He hath a person and a smooth dispose/To be suspected* His attractive appearance and smooth manners make it easy to suspect him of being a womaniser [399] *free* generous [403] *have't* have it; *ingendered* conceived

Iago's outrageous suggestion that he will act as if Othello has slept with his wife even though he's not sure it's true (388–9) might be done with a cynical leer; it might also be done with a deranged expression. Either way, the audience becomes complicit in Iago's intention and, like it or not, is soon involved in his vengeful plotting. He actually asks them what he should do ('How, how? Let's see' [394]) Many actors who have played the part have been capable of getting members of the audience to share Iago's delight in his own powers of evil invention. We may well laugh at his accurate description of Cassio, perhaps accompanied by a comic impression (392; 397–8). Iago has an energy, an affability, a dash of that common humanity which the distant, heroic, wordy Othello lacks. We will be forced to think about the connection between male 'mateyness' – for Iago is certainly 'one of the lads' – and decent behaviour in general. What is there in his language which makes his racism, his contempt for women and his lying have an energy that proves attractive, both now and then? This is how the soliloquy works at a more significant level than that just of revealing 'character': it is about the relationship between representation and audience. In other words, when we recognise and connect with what is happening on stage, to what extent do we have to share the moral and political views which are written into the representation of the world in that on-stage action?

On-stage plays

We have already noted that Shakespeare depicts a group of actors putting on a play for the Danish court right at the centre of *Hamlet*. The prince has persuaded the group to insert some action into the play which mimics the murder of his father as described by the ghost. Hamlet is watching his uncle Claudius closely to see how he reacts to this dramatic re-enactment. If he shows fear or embarrassment, it will prove the ghost's words to be true, and he can then confidently take his violent revenge. Yet the words the actors speak in the on-stage play are advising the prince *not* to act on resolutions made in passion (III 2 187–97), and warning us that our actions often have unseen consequences (III 2 210–13). Hamlet himself gets so excited during the performance that he keeps interrupting it and has to spell out the

Box 7: Women and sex

In Shakespeare's time, upper-class women had to be virgins at marriage. Property mostly was passed on to a man's first-born legitimate son, and virginity was proof, in theory, that the first born was the husband's offspring. Women of other classes, too, were supposed to marry as virgins, but sex before marriage, using primitive though sometimes effective forms of contraception, was the norm. People generally married when they were in their mid-twenties, allowing couples the time to have built up some sort of reserve of property or capital. If a woman became pregnant, marriage followed irrespective of age, and this seems to have been the sequence for a large number of early modern brides. Anne Hathaway was two months' pregnant when Shakespeare married her in November 1582. He was 18, young to marry, while his bride was 26.

The high mortality rate meant that many of both sexes were widowed at a relatively young age. Remarriage was common. A widow bequeathed her husband's property was in an unusual position, as this was the only situation in which a woman might legally own and dispose of goods and estate. Otherwise women lacked the legal rights of men. In fact, according to the law a son need no longer obey his mother once he had ceased to be a minor at the age of 8.

Many writers of the time asserted women's inferiority to men. Some drew on the medieval tradition that blamed mankind's fall on Eve; and the same tradition saw a woman as a temptress, sexually insatiable once she had lost her virginity. Others thought of a woman as an incomplete man, lacking the faculty of reason and the ability to control her emotions. She was controlled, like the tides, by the fickle moon, as her menstrual cycle showed. Fluidity and excess were qualities often attributed to women in literature (see pp. 247f.). Women's inability to control her tongue elevated silence to the position of highest female virtue. Yet all this stands against the many intelligent, witty and determined women we find in the plays of the period. And for most of Shakespeare's life the monarch was a woman.

Adultery by the wife was considered wrongful, but it was a particular disgrace on the man to be thus 'cuckolded' by his wife. On the other hand, male infidelity was, it seems, almost excused. In London brothels were plentiful and were frequented by men of all classes. While no particular shame was associated with this, there was also no cure for the venereal diseases caught there.

Reading the works of Shakespeare and his contemporaries, it seems that, outside of Puritan households, men and women were much more sexually frank than they are today. This was a society in which, after all, very little privacy was to be had: bedrooms, even beds, were very commonly shared by family members other than the husband and wife.

plot of the play to Claudius to make sure he gets the reference (III 2 261–4).

It is unclear from the text how Claudius reacts – it is a matter for the actor and director to decide what reaction the king actually shows. But it is clear that Hamlet thinks that drama can make us regret our actions. It can, indeed, have a *political* impact on us; but, that said, what is the effect of *Hamlet* on its audiences? Is it suggesting that it is acceptable to murder a wicked king? Is revenge always justified? But, if drama can teach moral and political lessons, why is it that Hamlet pays no attention to what the Player King is telling him? And why does the play need Hamlet as a 'chorus' (III 2 245) to interpret its meaning for the audience? Here again the very nature of stage representation is put up for our scrutiny.

Similar reflections are prompted by the performance of *Pyramus and Thisbe* by Bottom's company at the end of *A Midsummer Night's Dream* (V 1 32–355). On this occasion it is questions about dreams and art that are raised. We are asked to think about the connection between love itself and the stories we tell about love, and the contrast between the life an audience leads and the sort of world represented on the stage. When you read these lines, you also might think it hard to regard the Athenian men with much sympathy after their reactions to the workmen's play. There are also fully staged performances of different sorts in *The Tempest* (IV 1 60–142), *Henry VI Part II* (I 4 1–40) and *Pericles* (II 2); and there is an hilarious improvised play in *Henry IV Part I* (II 4 376–480). To these plays one could add the numerous disguises and roles played by characters pretending to be other people in Shakespeare's other plays, from Viola pretending to be the eunuch Cesario in *Twelfth Night* to the

Duke's disguise as Friar Lodowick in *Measure for Measure*. Actors in Shakespeare must expect not only to play someone else but to play someone playing someone else again: they need to learn how to portray acting. This may well mean having to think about what it actually means to *act*.

Sub-plot and juxtaposition

Eighteenth-century neo-classical writers criticised Shakespeare because he disobeyed the *Dramatic Unities*. These ideas originated with the Greek philosopher Aristotle, but it was the commentaries of the Italian Ludovico Castelvetro (1505–71) that came to influence authoritively how plays *should* be written. According to Aristotle and Castelvetro, the action of a play should occur in one setting (the unity of place) over the course of a single day (the unity of time); and there should be only one plot (unity of action). Shakespeare must have known of these rules – other playwrights like Ben Jonson made a point of not breaking them; see, for example the Prologue (lines 31–2) to *Volpone* (1606). But Shakespeare had no intention of keeping to them; nor had many of his contemporaries. His plays set out to depict a society at work, not the small group of kings, gods and heroes who are the subject of Greek tragedy.

Sometimes new students of Shakespeare wonder about the purpose of the minor plots in the plays. It is usual in a play for there to be a main line of action involving the noble characters, and one or more subsidiary plot-lines which at first glance might be seen to be of no immediate relevance to the main narrative. They are, however, crucial to the play's overall impact. In Chapter 2 I explained how in *King Richard II* Henry Bolingbroke, Duke of Lancaster and Hereford, had taken the throne that rightfully belonged to his cousin Richard II (see pp. 46 and 54). In *King Henry IV Part I*, a group of Bolingbroke's former allies led by the Duke of Northumberland and his son Harry Hotspur are attempting, in their turn, to depose King Henry and put *their* claimant on the throne. The sub-plot of the play concerns Sir John Falstaff and his relationship with King Henry's son Prince Hal.

Falstaff is on one level Hal's alternative father, one who represents a life devoted to pleasure, irresponsibility and self-centredness. He might be seen as the sort of over-indulgent parent who has not grown up himself. He is a real contrast to the king's own stern seriousness and sense of vast responsibility. Both men show Hal affection in their different ways. Yet Falstaff is also, in a positive way, the opposite of Hotspur, England's greatest warrior, for whom honour is the most important thing in life. Indeed, with his dying breath he tells Hal that the dishonour of his defeat in single combat matters more to him than the loss of his life (V 4 78–80). Yet Hotspur's defeat and death at Shrewsbury are the product of his own naive worship of that ideal honour. Hotspur's father Northumberland and his forces fail to arrive at Shrewsbury in time to fight. The rebels consider not facing the royal army in battle because they are outnumbered. Hotspur insists they should fight against these overwhelming odds because it will increase the glory and honour won by their combat (IV 1 77–8). Yet his colleagues have no such sense of honour. Vernon and Worcester, his allies, keep from him King Henry's final offer to satisfy all the rebel grievances because they think he might accept them. They also know that the king is likely to forgive Hotspur, but never themselves (V 2 1–25).

Falstaff puts all this in context in a soliloquy spoken on the morning of the battle, immediately before Worcester and Vernon plan to deceive the valour-obsessed Hotspur:

Falstaff I would 'twere bed-time, Hal, and all well.   125
Prince Why, thou owest God a death.* *[Exit]*
Falstaff 'Tis not due yet, I would be loath* to pay him
    before his day. What need I be so forward with him
    that calls not on me? Well, 'tis no matter, honour pricks*
    me on. Yea, but how if honour prick me off* when   130
    I come on? How then? Can honour set to a leg? No.
    Or an arm? No. Or take away the grief of a wound?
    No. Honour hath no skill in surgery then? No. What
    is honour? A word. What is in that word honour?
    What is that honour? Air. A trim reckoning!*   135

Who hath it? He that died a'Wednesday. Doth he
feel it? No. Doth he hear it? No. 'Tis insensible*
then? Yea, to the dead. But will't not live with the
living? No. Why? Detraction* will not suffer it.
Therefore I'll none of it, honour is a mere scutcheon.*   140
And so ends my catechism.*

(V 1 125–138)

* [126] *death* probably pronounced nearly the same as 'debt',
which would explain Falstaff's next remark [127] *loath*
unwilling [129] *pricks* spurs [130] *prick me off* 'marks me off
on a list', presumably of casualties – but there may also be on
obscene play on words here [135] *A trim reckoning* 'A neat
little amount that adds up to!' [135] *insensible* not detectable
by the senses [139] *Detraction* people gossiping and criticising
behind your back [140] *scutcheon* the shield on a nobleman's
tomb [141] *catechism* questions and answers learnt by children when preparing for confirmation into the Roman
Catholic Church

Falstaff's palpable common sense serves to point out a more
sensible and human way of living, which takes into account the
empty boastfulness and violence of the feudal code of honour. In
1600 Hotspur's ideals were shared still by many of the aristocracy
– the lords, earls and dukes of the realm. But as values they had
no real place in a world of professional soldiers armed with
muskets, and in a world where political leadership had long since
ceased to be associated with skill in battle.

But it is not just the characters in sub-plots who offer an alternative view of the values central to the main narrative: *events* in
the sub-plots also comment upon the main plot in an important
way. In Act I of *King Henry IV Part I* Falstaff hatches a plot to
rob a party of pilgrims at Gadshill on the way to Canterbury that
night (see pp. 170–1). Hal and his friend Poins join the mugging
party, but disappear just before the attack takes place. Once
Falstaff and his cronies have robbed the pilgrims, Hal and Poins
appear in disguise and rob Falstaff in turn! (II 2) The idea behind

Poins' joke is to hear the 'incomprehensible lies that this same fat rogue will tell us when we meet at supper, how thirty at least he fought with ...' (I 1 187–8) – which they can then expose as lies. But of course these events echo the events of the main plot. The 'martyred' Richard (Canterbury was the shrine of the martyr Thomas à Becket) was robbed of the crown by Henry Bolingbroke (Falstaff, Hal's alternative father); now there is another group of robbers (Hal and Poins, mirroring Hotspur, Northumberland and Worcester) out to rob the robber – and, as in the main plot, these robbers are apparently the friends of their intended victims.

What is being said by this parallel narrative? An equivalence is being established between highway robbers and warring medieval barons. In a political world where military force actually decides the right to rule, and might is right, what difference is there between its exercise on a lawless highway and on a battlefield where the crown is the prize? In another echo, in the final battle at Shrewsbury in Act V the king dresses up several of his knights to look like him, perhaps so that he might appear to be everywhere in the battle. Disguise may not be honourable, but it is effective, whether at Shrewsbury or at Gadshill. The difference is that highway robbers and footpads are punished with death by the state. Robbers of the crown are in a position where no one can punish them, so long as they maintain the might which brought them to power in the first place. They can tell the story of their coming to power in a way that justifies it, as Falstaff does in the attempt to explain his defeat.

The parallel actions of non-noble characters in Shakespeare have the effect of undermining the acts of the nobles by exposing high politics to an unflattering comparison. The actions of characters like Falstaff reveal that the difference between their deeds and those of their social superiors is one of scale, only. There is nothing special about the problems of the rich and powerful; it is just that sometimes they have the capacity to turn their wrong-doings into myths which glorify them. Sometimes the sub-plot is comic; then it serves as a mockery, a parody, of the play's main concerns. But when we laugh at serious matters we often reveal the real truth about them.

This placing together of contrasting scenes and events in order to bring into focus key points of comparison can be called *juxtaposition.* It is similar to the notion of *montage* in film studies, and in a Shakespeare play forms an important element in the way the many voices and characters from the different social groups combine to produce that drama's overall effect. Sometimes the sub-groups have a major part to play, as in *King Henry IV Part I*; at other times the role is less significant, as in *Othello*. Sometimes main-plot characters change their way of talking and behaving, and become in effect the commentating sub-plot. This is what happens in *King Lear* (see pp. 30–3): when he is mad on the heath, the king joins the ranks of the homeless and destitute, and thereby points out for the audience the direct connection which exists in the same society between the conduct of the rich and powerful and the fate of the poor (III 4 28–36; IV 6 150–66).

The ways in which the various plays use juxtaposition is a topic dealt with in subsequent chapters (see e.g. pp. 167–70 and 252 for discussions of *King Henry V* and *The Tempest*), in which juxtaposition is considered in terms of the plays' different types, or genres.

Summary

In this chapter I have argued that Shakespeare's plays, rather than attempting to present a 'realistic' picture of life, are very often aware of themselves as fiction. The means employed to remind us of their fictional status include:

- remarks indicating that the actors are speaking lines from a play; actors speaking directly to the audience;
- staging a smaller play within the main play;
- juxtaposing contrasting scenes and plot-lines to encourage us to stand back from the main action in judging what is happening, rather than allow ourselves to be carried away by an emotional identification with the imaginary world of the play.

Further reading

Detailed discussions of the issues covered here can be found in White (1998: Chapters 3 and 6). More advanced is Kiernan (1996); see especially Chapter 5. See also Heinemann (1985).

Chapter 4

What the plays mean in performance

The first three chapters have looked at the language and structure of Shakespeare's plays, with one eye fixed on their meaning for theatre audiences. The plays were written for performance. To that extent it is obvious that we are missing something very crucial if we read them as if they were poems written in dialogue form or an unusual kind of novel. In fact, the study of the play-scripts *solely* as literary texts seems to miss the entire point of how and why they were written – as blueprints for a live performance, not as texts for reading and study. Yet that is how they were primarily regarded for a very long time, and very often still are, to judge from the way they are taught and examined at school, college and even, sometimes, at university. Some nineteenth-century critics like Charles Lamb, and even the occasional twentieth-century critic like Harold Bloom, have felt that *any* staging sullies the ideal 'performance' – which it is argued exists only in the reader's mind. But this view seems wilfully perverse. In a media studies course, we wouldn't be expected to study the *scripts* of films except in so far as they are adjuncts to our understanding of the finished film. The text alone is an incomplete realisation that leaves us with a two-dimensional account of the whole experience. What we should be studying, many modern critics say, is the *performance text*: that is, the play in actual performance as experienced by an audience.

As an indication of how much there is to be added to the depth and complexity of the play-script in front of us once we imagine an actual production of the text, we can look at a crucial moment in *Hamlet*. This will demonstrate the inadequacy and thinness of a purely text-based reading of the play. It will also throw up some of the difficulties and challenges of this way of reading a Shakespeare play.

Just after his long opening speech in Act I Scene 2, which we looked at in Chapter 1, Claudius turns his attention to Prince Hamlet. The stage direction (see p. 201) indicates that Hamlet does not come on stage in his due place according to social rank, but enters last. Or does he? The stage direction I quote is from the Riverside Shakespeare, based on the Second Quarto of the play published in 1604. The Oxford Shakespeare takes its stage direction from the 1623 First Folio, and that has Hamlet in his proper place, entering third in order behind the king and queen (Hibbard 1987: 154). This is not just a matter for dry textual scholarship. If, in such a status- and ritual-conscious society, Hamlet is out of his normal place in the procession as it enters the court, what is signalled is an imbalance in the court hierarchy prompted by his desire to rebel against convention. In fact the Quarto text may preserve playhouse practice; the Folio, published after Shakespeare's death, could well have been 'tidied up' by someone else. In any case, Hamlet has to be positioned somewhere when he gets on stage. But whatever his location – sitting on a chair to his uncle's left and with Gertrude on his right; or close to one side of the stage, particularly if positioned downstage (i.e. nearest to the audience) and with his back to the king, where his expressions will be clearly visible during all that precedes his first line – the audience will find it significant and interpret it accordingly.

It is important to notice, too, that there is no single 'true' text to guide us here. We have three different versions of the play published between 1601 and 1623. Even if, like the Arden, modern editions 'conflate' the three into a single version, to understand *Hamlet* means appreciating that there is no precisely fixed authoritative text. And this should be understood of all the plays first produced in this period (see Box 2).

If he is wearing black – as the text indicates he should be (I 2 68, 77) – he will stand out against the wedding clothes of the king, queen and courtiers. This is something easily missed in a reading of the play. But what does Hamlet look like? On what basis should a casting decision be made? Is he a large mature man, as Burbage must have appeared? Or does he appear a youthful and laid-back student, dressed to appeal to the youth of his time, like David Warner in Peter Hall's 1965 production, complete with Dr Who scarf? Is he good looking? When he speaks does he sound royal or does he have a regional accent? Or, again, is his pronunci-ation 'non-received', as was Nicol Williamson's in the 1969 Round House production (Williamson's was allegedly the first recorded use on the *London stage* of a non-RP accent for the role of Hamlet)? These are not mere trivialities of character, and while they may not occur to us when we read the play, they *do* affect our response when we see it performed. It is also worth pointing out that the reactions of individual audience members to the portrayal of Prince Hamlet will vary according to their age, gender, sexual orientation and background.

King Claudius has been talking to Laertes, the son of his chief minister, and has just granted Laertes permission to return to France. Then he turns to Hamlet:

King But now, my cousin Hamlet, and my son—
Hamlet (Aside) A little more than kin, and less than kind.* 65
King How is it that the clouds still hang on you?
Hamlet Not so, my lord, I am too much in the sun.*
Queen Good Hamlet, cast thy nighted colour off,

And let thine eye look like a friend upon Denmark.*

(I 2 64–9)

* [65] *A little more than kin and less than kind* There are two meanings here, one rude and one polite. Hamlet's idea seems to be that Claudius won't be able to publicly acknowledge any hidden insult – even if he hears it. The polite meaning is: 'I am more than just a relative [kin], but not actually your son [kind].' The rude meaning is: 'I am a close relative of yours [kin], but you don't exactly treat me with affection [less than kind]' [67] *too much in the sun* Again, there two meanings: the first is: 'You are generous in lavishing your royal presence on me' (conventionally, the king was compared to the sun); the second is: 'You are treating me like your son when I'm not and don't want to be '(a play on sound: *sun, son*) [69] *Denmark*: the king

The stage direction '*(Aside)*' (line 65), which indicates that Hamlet speaks to the audience, is again from The Riverside Shakespeare version. In fact it is not an aside in any of the three known early seventeenth-century versions (First and Second Quartos and Folio) of the play. The direction was added by an editor, Theobald, in 1726, though it may have come down as a stage tradition from Shakespeare's time. It certainly works well when delivered as an aside: it immediately establishes a conspiratorial intimacy between Hamlet and the audience – as Iago does in *Othello* (see p. 67). If, on the other hand, it is spoken publicly, so that the whole court can hear it, we have a bold, provocative and cheeky rather than a joky and conspiratorial Hamlet. Does Hamlet rise and bow to deliver his next line, or is he already standing? Is Claudius so annoyed by his riddling that the Queen has to intervene uninvited (line 68) to prevent her new husband losing his temper in public? Is there any reaction on the part of the court? Is there bitterness in Hamlet's words, or is he looking for a snigger with his sarcastic tone? Are his arms folded defensively, or do they make theatrical gestures as he speaks? These are decisions the director will make with the actor, and each such detail helps define the significance of the moment. The responses from the audience will depend also on how well members know the play and how they've seen this scene done before.

I have spent some time on this moment and these questions to illustrate that once we start thinking about the text in performance – how the play would look and be received in the theatre – as distinct from reading it as an object of study, we quickly see that its full meaning depends on a series of interpretative decisions and these will differ from production to production, and even, perhaps, from performance to performance of the same production. Equally, the full meaning will tend to differ for each audience member! Despite the textual variation that often exists, the play in print, on the other hand, tends to be a very much more stable entity. When we strip away the performance possibilities, the play is much more manageable as a literary artefact; but to treat it as such is a distortion of what it really is. The solution lies, I think, in the recognition that when we study a play-script we are studying something provisional. A play-script is not the finished artistic product. Literary interpretations have to be made in order to understand and present the play, they must go hand in hand with a constant awareness of how the play will operate in the theatre – and with all the possibilities of meaning that the play has to realise for different people. There *is*, after all, a fairly stable heart to the text: the play can't mean whatever you want it to mean. In studying the plays we're looking at the possibilities for meanings in the theatre that the scripts open up; we're not looking for *the* truth about any particular text.

Since the conditions of both performance (see the next section) and audience reception were obviously very different in Shakespeare's time, it is likely that the plays meant something to the audiences then which differs, to a greater or lesser extent, from what they mean to audiences today. In looking at the conventions of the original staging, as far as we can recover them, we can in fact discover a great deal about *why* the plays were written the way they were, and this allows us to deal with some of the matters that puzzle the modern reader used to the conventions of naturalism.

These conventions are considered next; discussion then focuses on how, in a similarly conventional way, the plays' meanings in modern times have been produced by the active work of both performers and audience at particular historical moments.

Performance *then*

We have already looked at the construction of the plays and the types of language and action employed, but there are many other features that are unlike the conventions of modern drama. If you are not familiar with these plays, the way in which, for instance, change in the location of the action or the passing of time is conveyed might seem to you very unrealistic. If there was no scenery or lighting in the modern sense, wasn't the presentation rather unconvincing? Didn't it get confusing, with actors doubling-up on roles (as they must have done) to play the large number of parts required in many of the plays? And how could anyone take seriously a youth playing the female-lead role – Lady Macbeth or Cleopatra?

But why do we think that *our* art forms are just like 'real life', and therefore superior? The American performance scholar Alan Dessen (1986: 87–8) has written very well about the strange cinematic conventions we have no difficulty in accepting:

> Although to a modern sensibility cinema may embody the epitome of realism, what is 'real' about sitting in a darkened auditorium, watching figures larger than life (especially in close-ups) projected on to a flat screen and seen through camera angles that often do not correspond to our normal viewing range, while listening to voices, not from the lips of speakers, that boom around us in stereophonic sound accompanied by music from a full orchestra (and how many of us have thought through the implications for 'realism' of background music in cinema or television)?

Audiences, from Elizabethan times to the present, have had their own expectations of what makes a representation credible. What mattered in Shakespeare's time was that the story was told and the action kept moving. Costumes, hand-held props or extra characters would identify a place if location were necessary. If a jailer came on leading a prisoner in chains it was clear where the action was situated. An actor with a napkin and a knife has clearly just been eating, and his entrance will establish the locale as outside a hall or private chamber. If necessary, the script just *says* where they are: 'This is Illyria, lady', says the sea captain (whose costume indicates that the action takes place at a port or on a beach) to Viola when she asks where she is (*Twelfth Night* I 2 1–2). No more was necessary; the audience didn't expect to see 'real life' as if the fourth wall of a room had been removed and they could see the action going on within, as in modern TV or conventional drama (see pp. 68 and 93).

The theatre was a representation, a self-conscious fiction; but, in being so, it was also much *truer* than an art which pretends that it can copy nature exactly. Pauline Kiernan (1996) has argued that Shakespeare explicitly rejected such early modern views about art as those propounded by Sir Philip Sidney. Sidney considered art that produced an exact replica of nature to have surpassed nature itself because, unlike nature's offering, this artefact would be eternal and unchanging. Shakespeare realised, says Kiernan, that this is to produce something false. Art can never reproduce nature exactly because it is *not* nature. The truth of life and nature is mutability and change. By choosing to be a playwright Shakespeare chose an art which puts the human body, not an invisible realm of ideas, at the centre. By constantly acknowledging that its representations were both physical and fictional manifestations in real time, Shakespeare's theatre emphasised the truth that only the physical present is real; that time moves on and the past is irrecoverable; that no representation can be 'true'. The more we strive to recreate the past exactly, the more the skill of the recreation becomes what you notice (Kiernan 1996: 10–12); either that or we are fooled into believing that we are seeing what 'really' happened. Both these reactions, but particularly the first, are found in response to Hollywood historical blockbusters. In that sense Shakespeare's drama is far more real than any naturalistic, 'mimetic' art form.

But why should action require a specific location anyway?

Later editors always put a place identification at the beginning of each scene because they were assuming the use of realistic painted backdrops, the fashion in theatres from the eighteenth century onwards. But as shown in Figure 4.1, Shakespeare's public stages were open, perhaps based on the idea of a galleried inn yard with a central stage.

Spectators stood in the yard area or 'pit', while permanent galleried seating ran almost all the way round the stage. The theatrical experience was quite different in these conditions: on the open stage it is the drive of the story and the action which hold you, so that specific location becomes incidental. If it matters to the action, place will be indicated; otherwise it will not. For example, the balcony above the stage, when not used for musicians or spectators, could become a separate acting area, indicating the walls of a besieged town or the balcony of a house (this is, however, the least visible part of the acting space). It seems that flying effects were possible from the canopy over the stage, which was painted with the sun, moon and signs of the zodiac. Ghosts could appear from or disappear into a space below the stage via a trapdoor – or devils appear, as if from hell. It was also possible that there was a 'discovery space' in the tiring house. This would be an alcove covered by a curtain which could be pulled back to reveal a particular scene, giving the sense of a hidden, perhaps interior, space being revealed.

If we accept the replica Globe on London's Bankside as a true approximation of an early modern theatre, the depth of the stage (30 feet at the Globe) meant that actors entering from the tiring house would be visible to the audience for as much as the duration of two lines of speech before reaching the front of the stage where the action is taking place. This offered great comic and dramatic potential. The spaces in front of and to the sides of the two pillars were shut off from the main acting area, and long asides unheard by other characters would seem plausible. This was used as unlocalised space from which the comic characters would interact with the audience – they may even have done this from the pit, in the midst of the audience (White 1998: 95). As well as unlocalised, this area was undefined – being both part of the play's space and in some sense part of the audience's *real* world, too. It was the focal point for the entire playhouse. In this position, so close to the 'standers' that they could touch his feet, an actor delivering a soliloquy could command the attention of the entire audience, those farthest removed from the stage being no more than 40 feet away. This area seems to have been a privileged space wherein marginal characters could offer criticism of the central characters of the drama, frame dispassionate evaluations of the conduct of the principal action, and where behaviour and language which break the rules are allowed because the world of the play is at least partially left behind. It is the space in which Iago, Thersites and Falstaff are active for much of their time. The German critic Robert Weimann has called this area the *platea* (Latin: 'an open street', and therefore 'an unspecified place'), as distinct from the *locus* ('a specific place'), the realm of the fully localised and historical action further upstage (see Dubrow 1997: 43–4).

Scenes which take place in the dark might seem to be a problem in an outdoor theatre where all performances took place in daylight. But the convention of torches being carried, or that of characters appearing in night-gowns, for example, worked perfectly well. Very often the characters just said it was dark and acted accordingly. In fact, Alan Dessen argues, it had certain dramatic advantages compared to modern practices. In the moonlit scenes between the lovers in Acts II and III of *A Midsummer Night's Dream*, for example, the confusion produced by the blindness of love and its analogue, magic – not darkness – is underlined by the daylight setting (Dessen 1986: 96). At the indoor Blackfriars theatre there was candlelight, but the torch convention seems to have applied there, too – though with perhaps some lowering of the light level (White 1998: 150).

If it were possible for us to join an early seventeenth-century audience watching a production we would encounter two codes that would mean far less to us than they would to the rest of the audience. There first is the system of ritual poses and gestures which depicted certain emotions and states, perhaps partly

The Globe Playhouse,
1599–1613

A CONJECTURAL
RECONSTRUCTION

KEY

AA   Main entrance
B   The Yard
CC   Entrances to lowest gallery
D   Entrances to staircase and upper galleries
E   Corridor serving the different sections of the middle gallery
F   Middle gallery ('Twopenny Rooms')
G   'Gentlemen's Rooms' or 'Lords' Rooms'
H   The stage
J   The hanging being put up round the stage
K   The 'Hell' under the stage
L   The stage trap, leading down to the Hell
MM   Stage doors
N   Curtained 'place behind the stage'
O   Gallery above the stage, used as required sometimes by musicians, sometimes by spectators, and often as part of the play
P   Back-stage area (the tiring-house)
Q   Tiring-house door
R   Dressing-rooms
S   Wardrobe and storage
T   The hut housing the machine for lowering enthroned gods, etc., to the stage
U   The 'Heavens'
W   Hoisting the playhouse flag

FIGURE 4.1 C. Walter Hodge's reconstruction of The Globe playhouse

G (Position of)

G (Position of)

Position of Staircase

C.Walter Hodges
1965

Box 8: Playhouses

In 1576 James Burbage erected the first purpose-built permanent playhouse in Shoreditch, and called it The Theatre. His rival Philip Henslowe opened The Rose across the river in Southwark in 1587. The Swan was built nearby in 1595, then The Globe in 1599. The earliest companies had performed in the yards of galleried inns. A scaffold was put up, with a curtained booth behind as a backstage area. The audience would stand around the scaffold in the 'pit' or, in the case of the more wealthy, sit in the galleries above. These gallery balconies still exist at pubs like *The Eagle* (Cambridge) or *The George* (Southwark). The same arrangements were no doubt made when, in times of plague in London, the companies went off on regional tours. It was difficult, however, to collect money for a performance, since any passer-by was able to observe. Playhouse design reflected the yard-and-stage arrangement, but no-one could get in without paying.

The theatrical experience was not as it is today. As it was performed in full daylight, spectators could see one another as clearly as they could the actors, and vice versa. Audience reactions to events on stage would have been an integral part of the spectacle. Wealthier spectators in the galleries could not avoid seeing those in the pit, who were in fact clustered at the focal point of the building. Standers could see those in the galleries. There was no one privileged position for viewing (today the centre of the stalls) and you could move around the pit during the play to get different perspectives. The experience would have been much more communal and democratic than that of later centuries.

In 1608 the first professional indoor theatre with all-year-round candlelit performances was opened: the Blackfriars Theatre. Shakespeare was one of the shareholders. Basically a large rectangular room, this was a very different type of playhouse, aimed at a more aristocratic audience. To stand at The Globe or The Swan cost a penny; access to the galleries cost a further penny and it was threepence to sit in the highest gallery of all. A curtained-off lord's room cost sixpence. In contrast, just to get into the Blackfriars Theatre cost sixpence. This paid for a place in one of the three wooden galleries that ran along three sides of the auditorium. For twice that, a shilling, you could have a bench in the pit – this was an all-seater playhouse. For two shillings you could sit on the stage itself, which was twenty-five feet wide, the whole theatre being only sixty-six feet from the back of the stage to the auditorium. The Civil War in 1642 closed the public theatres, but the Blackfriars had provided a model for the theatres that would open after the Restoration (1660).

derived from the formal gestures taught in schools and colleges as part of rhetoric. These poses would not have been slavishly followed (even by the very worst actors), but they constituted an effective shorthand and so offered a basis from which to develop a performance. They seem to have featured in the so-called 'dumb-shows' (like that in Act III Scene 2 of *Hamlet*), which summarised the plot of the play or demonstrated some action which moves the plot along. The stage direction for the Player Queen to make 'passionate action' (III 2 135, stage direction [sd]) will have meant something specific to the boy playing the role. There are plenty of clues to some of these conventional gestures. Pulling your hat down over your face, as Macduff does when he hears the news of his slaughtered family in *Macbeth* (IV 3 208), seems to have indicated extreme grief. Having your arms wrapped around your chest in a 'sad knot', like Ferdinand in *The Tempest* (I 2 224), seems to have indicated melancholy. Good acting and subtle drama clearly would have played on these conventions in a knowing way. According to Ophelia's account of Hamlet's behaviour after he has burst into her chamber, he was displaying via the conventions of gesture and dress the emotions of a thwarted lover. She seems convinced by them, but because the audience would recognise these *theatrical* conventions, Hamlet's sincerity is clearly called in doubt at this point:

Ophelia My lord, as I was sewing in my closet,
   Lord Hamlet, with his doublet all unbraced,*   75
   No hat upon his head, his stockings fouled,
   Ungartered, and down-gyved* to his ankle,
   Pale as his shirt, his knees knocking each other,
   And with a look so piteous in purport
   As if he had been loosed out of hell   80
   To speak of horrors – he comes before me.
Polonius Mad for thy love?
Ophelia My lord, I do not know,
   But truly I do fear it.
Polonius What said he?
Ophelia He took me by the wrist, and held me hard,

Then goes he to the length of all his arm,   85
And with his other hand thus o'er his brow,
He falls to such perusal of my face
As 'a* would draw it.

(II 1 74–88)

* [75] *his doublet all unbraced* his jacket all unfastened [77] *down-gyved* hanging around his ankles like leg-irons (shackles which connected prisoners' ankles with a chain) [88] *'a* he

The other convention we would probably miss are the stage formations that refer to emblems (see p. 29). Sometimes the shape the actors' bodies made on stage, combined with their dialogue, would add a level of meaning by reminding the audience of one or other of these proverbial images. The English theatrical

Box 9: Homosexuality in Shakespeare's time

In the ancient Greek tradition, love between men was seen as a pure and noble thing. While sexual acts between men were capital offences in Shakespeare's day, individuals were hardly ever prosecuted. Homosexual acts occurred, of course, both between men and between women. There was at this time, however, no notion of an individual whose identity was 'homosexual'; indeed, historians believe that it was only in the last 100 years or so that people have begun to found their personal identity upon their sexual preference. Having sex with another man, or loving another man in a sexual way, did not make a man 'gay'. When plague struck London in 1592, the theatres were closed and Shakespeare went into the employment of the Earl of Southampton (doing what?). Many scholars believe that his sonnets were written to this man. If they are taken as sincere (some critics have just regarded them as a merely literary exercise), they suggest he had very strong feelings for Southampton, and may well have had some sort of sexual experience with him. This was a time, though, when love for another man was not regarded as strange and while having sex with another man was strictly illegal and considered sinful, if men wanted to do it they would.

scholar Martin White has identified one such moment in Thomas Kyd's play *The Spanish Tragedy* (1592), where two lovers embrace in way that would remind the audience of the emblem of the vine supporting the elm and keeping it upright, even in extremities. The Latin motto for this emblem (*Amicitia, etiam post mortem durans*) translates: 'Love, enduring even after death'. This is both appropriate and grimly prophetic, as the male of the pair, Horatio, is about to be murdered and hung upon a bower (White 1998: 140–1). We would miss this reference and others like it, which are hard to reconstruct today. They belonged to the semiotics (sign system) of the theatre of the time and to its art in general. Another example is afforded by the colours of costumes, which had a symbolism nearly lost to us now. Black, white, gold and red seem to have been the most common colours; green could suggest happiness and blue honesty; yellow a jealous character.

If we could go back to a public playhouse in 1600, the aspect of the staging of a play we would find strangest would be that all the female parts were played by males, usually teenage boys. What was the reason for this practice?

Women may well have appeared on stage in the guild plays of the Middle Ages; and actresses performed publicly in Italy, France and Spain in Shakespeare's time. We know also that when visiting Italian companies appeared at court women took their places on stage alongside the men. So why were they banned from the public theatres? And what was the attitude of the audience watching these boys in women's clothes, often playing high-tragedic leading roles?

The evidence can be confusing, and considerable academic controversy abounds here. Some contemporaries of Shakespeare clearly disapproved of the practice. Puritan opponents of the theatre (see Box 6, p. 63) quoted biblical injunctions against cross-dressing (e.g. Deuteronomy 22:5). Following the idea then common that a man was a more developed type of being than a woman – because his sexual organs were on the outside rather than still hidden within his body(!), and also because he possessed reason and emotional control – the Puritans argued that such transvestism was forcing the male to regress to an inferior state.

Worse, it encouraged lustful thoughts among men, who would, through their confused perception of them as women, become sexually attracted to boys. The British feminist critic Lisa Jardine has suggested that this is actually *why* it was popular. This gender confusion was particularly evident when boys playing women then disguise themselves as boys, as Viola does in *Twelfth Night* and Rosalind in *As You Like It*.

There is certainly evidence that some men found erotic this casting of boys as emotionally dependent creatures. The licensing of homosexual desire in this way was one of the attractions of the theatre. Figures like Viola dressed as Cesario 'are sexually enticing *qua* [in as much as they are] transvestied [*sic.*] boys, and that the plays encourage the audience to view them as such' (Jardine 1983: 29). Jardine means that watching the boy playing Viola as Cesario allowed men who perhaps liked looking at young men to feel they were *really* attracted to a woman, even though they knew they were actually fancying a boy.

The American critic Steven Orgel points out, however, that homo-sexual desire, and even homosexual acts, were not regarded as sufficiently scandalous to necessitate such an indirect and surreptitious route to these pleasures. He sees the culture's refusal to countenance women on stage as evidencing a more deep-seated fear: that of the public unleashing of female desire (Orgel 1996a: 49). The reason usually given at the time for all-male casting was that only a 'whore' (that is, a woman who behaves promiscuously, but not necessarily a prostitute) would want to display herself on stage, showing emotion freely, for all to see. Men were scared that their authority would be compromised by their wives' infidelity. Such a representation was regarded as a provocation and encouragement to women to pursue socially unacceptable desires; the free expression of female sexuality on stage might seem to many men to be the public broaching of a range of ideas and emotions whose eventual outcome would be female adultery (see Box 7, p. 69). They did not want to let women publicly express sexual desire because such behaviour invites a male response.

But, Orgel points out, this wasn't how women saw it. The

theatre's popularity among women of the time may well have stemmed, in part, from the theatre's capacity to question – by means of such conventions as males playing female roles – what were held to be fixed gender divisions in society (Howard 1994: 128). Gender roles were shown to be *performed*, not God-given or natural. Women might, at the end of a play, end up back under male control, but an alternative, a liberating suggestion, was present in the very casting of a play. Women in the audience watching an actor who was *biologically* male being taken for a woman because of the particular ways in which he talked, moved and behaved *might* have been seen here the suggestion that the restrictions on women's lives were actually *also* a matter of male-imposed *convention* (just as this one was on the stage). Such restrictions, then, might have no *necessary* connection to the female anatomy. If a woman could be represented convincingly by a male actor, it was possible that the way society defined women was as un-God-given as were the conventions which governed the way characters were created on stage.

Such a political reading was certainly present at some level, but the limited evidence we have of how audiences responded to boy actors on stage seems to indicate that they were often convinced by the convention and seemed to forget that the role was being played by a boy rather than a woman (Dawson 1996: 35; White 1998: 84–5). In any case there must have been considerable variety in the levels of female impersonation executed by the boys, ranging from a studied naturalism to a camp sending-up of stereotypical 'feminine qualities' (White 1998: 87–8). As with other conventions, it seems to have been the language and the action that established the dramatic effect – in this case femininity – not the appearance of the actor's body.

This is perhaps borne out by a remarkable passage in *Antony and Cleopatra*. Finally defeated in battle by Octavius Caesar, the Roman general Antony has committed suicide and his lover, the queen of Egypt, is contemplating her fate. If taken prisoner, she may be paraded in Octavius' triumph through Rome while the people perform satirical plays about her:

> *Cleopatra* The quick* comedians
> Extemporally* will stage us, and present
> Our Alexandrian revels: Antony
> Shall be brought drunken forth, and I shall see
> Some squeaking Cleopatra boy my greatness   220
> In the posture* of a whore.

(V 2 216–21)

* [216] *quick* lively [217] *Extemporally* Improvising [221] *posture* role

Of course, in 1608 these lines would have been spoken by a boy. The character Cleopatra is pointing out that she is too feminine and sophisticated a person to be portrayed by an adolescent male – and yet that is exactly the status of the person playing her and speaking these lines. At this point Cleopatra *imagines* the boy who will be playing her, rather than the actor imagining the character (Dusinberre 1996: 53). In this reversal we can perhaps see that the language , the role itself, does not depend on the physical body of the actor to create the sensual, playful and powerful role which dominates the play.

The feminist critic Juliet Dusinberre points out that, in modern times, actresses who have relied too much on their physical attractiveness in the role of Cleopatra have been less successful than those, like Judi Dench at the National Theatre in 1987 (see Figure 4.2), who have allowed *others* to make as important a contribution to her irresistible aura – in the way they describe and react to her – as the actress's own performance (Dusinberre 1996: 54). This might provide a clue to the original portrayal of Cleopatra, suggesting that physical appearance was not as significant to the role on stage as it is now.

Another interesting point to emerge from Dusinberre's discussion invokes a fascinating contrast between the play today and the play then; it may also explain some of *Antony and Cleopatra*'s impact. The role of Antony is sometimes seen as a thankless task for a leading actor: Cleopatra continually upstages him, in terms both of the play's action and of the lines she speaks. She gets the fifth act, with all its energy and poetry, to herself. The famous

FIGURE 4.2 Judi Dench as Cleopatra and Anthony Hopkins as Antony in the 1987 Royal National Theatre production of *Antony and Cleopatra*

twentieth-century Shakespearean actor Laurence Olivier said of the role of Antony:

> It's a wonderful part. But just remember, all you future Antonys, one little word of advice: Cleopatra's got you firmly by the balls.
>
> (Quoted in Dusinberre 1996: 60)

In the original production, a boy, presumably a teenage apprentice, would have upstaged and dominated the company's leading actor, the famous Richard Burbage, in the role of Antony. The youth will come across as more sexually potent and powerful within the theatre company, and the humiliation of Antony–Burbage, in thrall to the boy–Cleopatra, will be all the greater. This is a dimension to the performance obviously lost today, and it underlines yet again how the meaning of the play is tied to the specific circumstances of its production and its reception by the audience.

Performance *now*

I want to illustrate this last point by looking at three twentieth-century productions. I have chosen the first two because of their obvious political engagement with issues of race, gender and sexuality at the times when they were performed. The presentation of these themes on Shakespeare's stage, in a society in which white heterosexual men enjoyed power and authority over all others, is of particular interest to contemporary critics. My third selection is a recent Royal Shakespeare Company production. My reading of this third production is also political. I will look briefly at how, in each case, production choices – including the time and place of performance – underlined the political significance of these theatrical events.

Of course, the analysis of Shakespeare in performance need not be framed by an explicitly political agenda. Exciting and significant productions can produce their meanings for particular audiences without being primarily engaged with any of these issues (though I feel that they are always present in *some* form). Two of the three productions discussed below were in contexts in which race, in one case, and gender and sexuality, in the other, were certain to be in the foreground. The third production ignored political issues, only for them to emerge for at least some of the audience. I have chosen these productions because they allow me to illustrate how the concerns of contemporary criticism – issues of power and social justice – can intersect with close readings of 'performance texts'.

Paul Robeson's Othello

How relevant is skin colour to the casting of a Shakespeare play? What effect will the casting of black actors in particular roles have on the meaning the play has for its audiences? The answer seems to be: 'It all depends on the roles, the audience and the moment at which the performance takes place.'

The casting of Othello, the black general in the service of Venice whose colour is so important to the play, is a particularly interesting issue. Othello the Moor marries the white Desdemona, and is then falsely persuaded by his lieutenant, Iago, that she has been unfaithful to him (see p. 66). Othello kills her, and then himself when he discovers the truth. He is very much a black outsider in a white world. Ira Aldridge in the nineteenth century was, so far as we know, the first black actor to take the role. Aldridge, an American who came to Europe to escape the racially segregated theatres of the United States, was never engaged by either of the principal London theatres, Covent Garden and Drury Lane, though he had been acclaimed as the 'African Roscius' (Vaughan 1994: 181). The first black Othello in a major theatre was Paul Robeson, at the Savoy in 1930.

The son of a former slave, Robeson had made his name at Drury Lane in 1928 in the American musical *Showboat*. He remains a controversial figure. A fighter for civil rights and a socialist, he lost his US passport for 'un-American activities' during the 1950s and spend his later life in exile. The casting of

Robeson as Othello was not, however, motivated by anti-racism. Racism had developed slowly throughout the nineteenth century. By the early twentieth century it was felt by many 'educated' people – particularly in the United States, where black slavery had been completely abolished only in 1865 – that blacks and whites were intellectually and emotionally so dissimilar as to belong to different species. This racist view was, of course, strenuously opposed by many others. But it came to be thought that a rational, civilised, white man who was in control of his emotions was temperamentally unsuited to the role of Othello. A theory of racial difference, then, not an egalitarian principle, underlay Robeson's casting.

Although Robeson was at first very self-conscious (Vaughan 1994: 183) about playing love scenes with a white woman (Peggy Ashcroft as Desdemona – see Figure 4.3), there was no obvious opposition from London audiences to the casting of Robeson (though Ashcroft did receive hate mail, and Robeson himself was not made welcome at the Savoy Hotel that adjoins the theatre! [ibid.]).

Even so, Robeson saw the project as political in his own terms. He saw the Moor not as in any sense 'primitive', but simply as having come from a different culture – and it was as a defence of that culture's dignity that Robeson intended his own performance. He later told a theatre historian:

> [Othello] is intensely proud of his color and culture; in the end, even as he kills, his honour is at stake, not simply as a human being and as a lover, but as Othello. The honour of his whole culture is involved.
>
> (Quoted in Vaughan 1994: 196)

The production did not, however, allow him to realise this aim. The sympathy and humanity that an audience may have seen in the performance were undermined by crucial directorial decisions: the set, created by an inexperienced designer, ensured that most of the action took place right at the back of the stage, itself separated from the front of the audience by an orchestra pit; the lighting was often very dim; and Desdemona's death at Othello's hands was hidden by bed curtains. Much of the emotional impact of the playing, then, was muffled by the distance, or otherwise obscured, and the audience was unable to experience the characters' feelings at close hand. It was as if the director had been worried about exposing the audience too closely to inter-racial love. Furthermore, all reviewers seem to have agreed that Maurice Browne's Iago lacked any real wickedness, cunning or energy. His lines were cut to the extent that he had neither rapport with the audience nor presence as a demonic tempter.

Iago had been told by the director that his hatred of the Moor sprang from frustrated homosexual lust, but did not involve racial feeling. This made Othello's emotional outbursts appear all the more irrational and overblown – perhaps what was expected of what one reviewer, James Agate, called 'nigger Shakespeare' (Vaughan 1994: 188). Robeson's tight costume, European rather than Moorish, detracted from his dignity. Again Agate gave expression to gross racial stereotypes: 'his hands appeared to hang below his knees, and his whole bearing, gait, and diction were full of humility and apology: the inferiority complex in a word' (quoted in Vaughan 1994: 188). Some reviewers lamented Robeson's inability to speak the verse adequately. Others praised his performance because he fitted the stereotype of the simple, trusting, emotion-driven black man expected by the white middle-class audience. The literary critic John Dover Wilson later wrote of the performance that 'trustfulness and simplicity ... seem [Othello's] by nature when he is played by a Negro gifted with all the winning integrity of that race' (quoted in Vaughan 1994: 190).

Perhaps Robeson's political ambitions for the project would always have foundered on the prejudices of West End audience in 1930. The point remains, however, that decisions involving casting, cutting, design and directorial approach undermined whatever chance the production had of emphasising the humanity the black Othello shared with white people, both on and off stage.

Fear of racist opposition prevented Robeson playing Othello in America until 1943. Indeed, no financial backers could be

Figure 4.3 Paul Robeson as Othello and Peggy Ashcroft as Desdemona in the 1930 production at the Savoy Theatre, London

found, and a new director, the British actor Margaret Webster, got the project going eventually by casting unknown actors in the main parts and opening the run before liberal audiences at Harvard and Princeton universities. Stars were unwilling to risk taking part and no Broadway theatre would back the project. Though Webster saw the role in academic and racial terms, this time the production allowed the power and dignity of Robeson's performance to come through. *Othello* was a great success. It transferred to Broadway and completed a national tour, becoming at that time the longest running Shakespeare production in US history (Vaughan 1994: 193). Robeson was very proud of his achievement and considered it a blow against racial prejudice in general (Vaughan 1994: 192). Wartime America, her citizens black and white fighting side-by-side (albeit usually in different units!), was clearly a more receptive audience than the London of 1930, and the production allowed sympathy to develop for the Moor.

Laurence Olivier wore black make-up as the Moor in 1964, as did Anthony Hopkins for the BBC Shakespeare video. Both were controversial castings. Such make-up is too redolent of the racist stereotype of the 'nigger minstrel' to be acceptable today; moreover, there are in Britain today too many black actors capable of excelling in the role to justify a white Othello on the professional stage. Yet we are used now to seeing black performers in 'white' roles in Shakespeare, and even 'siblings' and 'sons' of different colours on stage, which audiences seem to accept without demur. At time of writing, there has yet to be a black Hamlet, Macbeth or King Lear at the Royal Shakespeare Company or Royal National Theatre, but it can be only a matter of time, and such casting would not crucially affect audience response. Yet a white Othello?

Othello is, for us, a play about race and colour. These are very much live issues in Britain today, though they would not have been (at least, not in the same way) in 1604. Consequently I think audiences will be more critically aware of the casting than they would be in a production of, say, *Hamlet*. Perhaps there is a clue here to how early modern audiences saw transvestite casting:

often, they ignored it, but when sexuality or gender was at issue in the text an awareness that they were watching males dressed as females would have been very much to the fore in their minds.

Cheek by Jowl's As You Like It

How significant is the gender of an actor to the casting of a Shakespeare play? It seems to depend upon the audience response it produces in a particular production. It also, of course, depends on the play itself.

The main action of *As You Like It* requires the heroine, Rosalind, to disguise herself as a boy, Ganymede, while she is in exile in the Forest of Arden. There she comes across her lover Orlando, who does not recognise her. As Ganymede, she tells Orlando that his love for Rosalind is 'madness' and that she can 'cure' him of it (III 2 399–405), if he pretends to court her as if Ganymede really were Rosalind. To prove his love he agrees, and engages in witty banter with the 'youth' as if he were 'her' lover (IV 1 38–196). So in a conventional modern production the actress playing a woman pretends to be a boy pretending to be a woman. But if a *male* plays Rosalind, of course, then in this scene a male impersonates a female impersonating a male impersonating a female!

In scenes like this, the way in which *gender* is represented on stage is clearly going to be the substance of the comedy. The humour would be expected to arise from the caricature of 'male' and 'female' qualities and behaviour.

Cheek by Jowl was probably the 1990s' most imaginative and successful group of British performers of classical drama. (By 'classical drama' I mean the plays which are traditionally regarded as of 'enduring value'.) When the company chose to stage the play at the Lyric Theatre (at Hammersmith in west London) in 1991 with an all-male cast (see Figure 4.4), some critics were cynical. Director Declan Donnellan and designer Nick Ormerod are gay, and in the general climate of hostility towards homosexuality, which was encouraged by certain individuals in the Conservative government and the tabloid press at

FIGURE 4.4 Adrian Lester (Rosalind) and Patrick Toomey (Orlando) in Cheek by Jowl's
As You Like It, Lyric Theatre, Hammersmith, London, 1995

the time, there was some suggestion that the casting was an excuse for transvestite camping. ('Camp' is usually understood to mean, in this context, an ironically self-aware, over-theatrical, parody of effeminacy, often accompanied by an acerbic wit.) This had been the case in an earlier production of the play: in the very different climate of sexual politics that followed the decriminalisation of homosexuality, Clifford Williams had in 1967 produced a 'coy and camp' (Holland 1993: 128) version of the play for the National Theatre. It was a liberal – 'swinging sixties" – response which saw homosexuality as an amusing and harmless comic subject for a 'straight' audience. Almost twenty-five years later, Benedict Nightingale writing in *The Times* (5 December 1991) did not think Donellan's production had moved on very far. He declared the production to be 'lively if limited'. The effect of the casting was 'no more, if no less than to give the play a strong homoerotic feel'. Tom Hollander, as Rosalind's friend Celia, affected 'the slightly camp, mincing voice only seldom to be found among gay men, let alone women'. Over three years later in the same paper (27 January 1995) Jeremy Kingston *did* admit that the production was 'marvellously funny, though the sight of men playing women is usually the source of it'.

But between these two dates the play had been enormously successful both in Britain and all over the world. *The Australian* (according to Michael Billington in the *Guardian*, 16 March 1992) called it the best Shakespeare seen in Adelaide since 1970. The production played to excited audiences on both sides of the Atlantic. They didn't see it as arch and camp; rather they found it 'marvellous' (Alan Sinfield in the *Guardian*, 27 April 1992), 'exhilarating' (Holland 1994: 128) and, indeed, 'as the audience liked it' (Bate 1996: 6). Donnellan's 'directorial conception was deeply and committedly ... [an] unabashed celebration of gay desire' (*ibid.*).

Its success was doubtless due in part to the direct simplicity of its staging and costumes, and the energy and irreverence of its style of popular theatre. The famous speech beginning 'All the world's a stage,/And all the men and women merely players' (II 7 139–40) was put at the beginning. On the second line the cast divided into their gender roles, and at this point Adrian Lester became Rosalind merely by donning a shapeless dress and granny specs. He removed them whenever he became Ganymede. The forest was produced by clever lighting effects and some strips of green cloth. A tuba and trombone accompanied the songs and some energetic dancing.

The play did more than just provoke laughter, 'pathos and tenderness', as the *Guardian* (6 December 1991) put it. The 'exhilaration' seems to have been produced by the way the casting and the acting explored the nature of love as it is depicted in the text: 'The problem of love and desire was defined as lying beyond gender, simply coming into being, irresistibly and unaccountably' (Holland 1994: 128). Homosexual desire between men playing men in the text wasn't hidden but clearly depicted (Jaques; Le Beau and Orlando); there were also different representations of female desire as played by men – or by men pretending to be women pretending to be men. But instead of being caricatured or mannered these representations were seen to be at once *conventional* and yet *still* moving. The audience heard the words and saw the gestures of these different lovers; but the play was performed to suggest that love is something *different* from the gender or sexuality of those who have that feeling. When, at the end, Rosalind revealed to Orlando that she was Ganymede all the time, there was no glib, conventional, smiling acceptance. It took time for Orlando to overcome his shock and shame to come downstage to claim her, his love having overcome all. The production had a commitment to lived experience and emotion despite its play with the sign language, theatrical and otherwise, of love and gender.

Two academics, Jonathon Bate and Peter Holland, were among those who saw the production. Bate (1996: 6–7) said this:

> The extraordinary thing about Adrian Lester was that, with his beautiful voice and grace of movement, when he played the female Rosalind playing at being the male Ganymede he seemed more like a woman playing a man than a man playing a woman. And when he played at Rosalind playing

> Ganymede playing Rosalind, one simply gave up trying to work out in one's mind whether one thought he was a woman playing a man playing a woman or a man playing a woman playing a man playing a woman.

Holland (1994:128) observed that the

> play-acting of Rosalind–Ganymede was both more intriguing and simpler than it usually is when a woman plays Rosalind but the tremendous erotic charge between Rosalind and Orlando had nothing glibly homoerotic about it. Instead one enjoyed the gaps of gender action as when Orlando playfully punched Ganymede's arm and Rosalind awkwardly and tentatively returned the male gesture, though the actor could clearly have made the gesture with ease.

As literature professors, Jonathan Bate and Peter Holland are very aware of the debates about whether gender is something we are born with or something that is socially constructed (see pp. 205f.). They located the play's power, in this production, in its ability to lay bare the common human emotion, love, which is beyond how we talk, how we dress, what we do in bed – or even with which sex organs we are equipped, even though that love can be sexually expressed only by those organs. The production's distinctive celebration of *love* accounted for its extraordinary impact. And, of course, university English departments are not, I am sure, usually centres of overt discrimination against homosexuality. These two academics brought with them to the performances they watched an attitude towards sexuality that, in either case, proved receptive to what Donnellan was doing.

I am not arguing that the play teaches a universal and 'timeless' message about love. But I am arguing that this production found in the text a meaning which in performance had a particular impact at a time of shifting attitudes towards love and sexuality.

At the same time there were feminists who objected to the 'bimbo-like' portrayal of Audrey, the 'lascivious goat-girl', and did find it a homosexual romp. More conservative reviewers, confident that Shakespeare's original audience 'cannot have thought of the Rosalinds, Violas and Portias as male at all' (*The Times* 5 December 1991), seemed to have similar opinions. But what Cheek by Jowl demonstrated – at least to those who at that time were disposed to see the production *both* in and out of its gay context – was that the all-male casting *did* change the meaning of the play and in doing so took it to a more profound level. Such a reading, whether the director intended it or not, was not available in 1967, when acceptance of the 'naturalness' of homosexuality was much less widespread. The political–social outlook on sexuality was at that time far more restricted in its scope and sophistication. Productions of Shakespeare's plays are the products of times in which they are conceived and performed. But they also act *on* those times to change the people who see them. Cheek by Jowl's *As You Like It* did not, I am sure, make very many of its audience more narrow-minded about love and sexuality.

The RSC in action: Adrian Noble's The Tempest

The two productions already discussed were, of course, controversial and unusual. They merited discussion because they underlined social and political issues which have been important in the performance of Shakespeare throughout the twentieth century. My third selection, a more typical example of Shakespeare in performance today, is a recent (1998–99) production of *The Tempest* by the Royal Shakespeare Company (RSC).

The RSC is the world's largest theatre company. It was formed in 1964 out of the festival organisation that performed every summer at the Shakespeare Memorial Theatre in Stratford-upon-Avon. The RSC now runs three theatres in Stratford and two in London, and stages other productions both on tour and in the West End. Its range of work is very wide, but the core of its activity remains large-scale productions of Shakespeare plays on the main stages both at Stratford and at the Barbican Centre in the City of London. Some RSC productions have been radical, even experimental, in approach – in particular those in the smaller, more intimate, performance spaces like The Other Place and The Pit. In recent years, however, its leading directors have been deliberately conservative in their readings of the major plays. This is not to say that the productions have actually set out with a particular agenda; in fact they often claim to have no particular agenda beyond letting a play speak for itself.

In 1993 Adrian Noble, artistic director of the RSC, said in an interview in the *Independent* that he was 'a classicist, a tradition-alist', who saw his role to be that of 'conducting tutorials for the country's leading directors on how to speak the verse'. In an earlier interview he had complained about 'this dreadful reduc-tion of the English vocabulary by those who taught the Bard as an anti-feminist imperialist' (quoted in Wilson 1997: 59). As the RSC has been dependent on corporate sponsorship since 1979, this apparent avoidance of 'politics' can perhaps be understood as a refusal to bite the hand that feeds it.

Adrian Noble's 1998–99 production of *The Tempest*, like his popular 1995–96 *A Midsummer Night's Dream*, used very bright colours in its design and simple but spectacular staging. The aim apparently was to tell the story as straightforwardly as possible: perhaps to produce theatre as a ' "social and emotional experi-ence" to counteract "the voices of [political] dissent, phrase it how you like" ' (Wilson 1997: 58). Given that a substantial number of those attending performances of these two produc-tions were either school students or foreign tourists, their narrative focus is understandable.

There is, of course, no such thing as a production which simply presents the text as a story, or an 'emotional experience', without engaging in the political issues of the play, as they are related to the time and the place of performance. *The Tempest* is a play whose very content makes it controversial in the early twenty-first century. Prospero, the rightful Duke of Milan, has been deposed by his brother Antonio, aided by Alonso, the King of Naples. Twelve years prior to the events of the play Prospero, accompanied by his daughter Miranda and his books of magic, had been exiled to the island on which the events unfold.

Prospero is a student of 'white' sorcery, and has learnt to control spirits which do his bidding. He has brought under his control Ariel, a spirit of the air, and also Caliban, the only other mortal inhabitant of the island. At first Caliban had been friendly with the new arrivals; but after they had taught him their language, he sought to rape Miranda (see pp. 258f.). Caliban is now Prospero's slave, and is tortured if he does not carry out his master's commands. When a ship carrying Antonio and Alonso appears off the coast of the island, Prospero seizes his chance for revenge. He starts by shipwrecking its passengers on his shore. He ends by forgiving all who have harmed him, having secured his daughter's marriage to Alonso's son Ferdinand.

For many years now the play has been seen as a representation of colonialism, with Prospero and Miranda as the European invaders and Ariel and Caliban as the indigenous inhabitants (though, of course, neither had been born there). Some productions, like Jonathan Miller's at the Mermaid Theatre in 1970, have been explicitly colonialist. In Miller's African setting, Caliban became the black victim of imperialism who refused to accept his new masters, whereas Ariel was willing to become a servant in order to learn to exercise power himself (Orgel 1987: 53–5). Even if a director, for whatever reason, chooses to ignore the colonialist aspect of the play, a piece of theatre about some Europeans who enslave the inhabitants of an island is obviously going to have certain resonances in Britain today, whether the director intends it or not. How the colonised and the colonisers are depicted will have a political meaning. With whom will the audience sympathise – Prospero, Caliban, or both or neither?

In Noble's production Ariel was played by a tall, muscular, shaven-headed man clad only in a white loincloth. His body was covered in a white make-up that shone eerily when under blue light. He moved slowly and gracefully, and always stood very erect. His appearance may have suggested a baby, or even the crucified Jesus – either way, his innocence and unearthliness were clearly evoked. Caliban also was dressed only in a loincloth – but his body was covered in a thick brown mud. He dragged himself around the stage, usually on all fours, and growled his lines. Most strangely, his mouth and eyes were red. Had he not emerged, for his first scene, mollusc-like from a giant sea-shell, it would have seemed that he was being depicted as an ape. Only the shackles around his wrists asserted his status as a prisoner.

At the end of Act II Scene 2 Caliban sings his wine-induced song of freedom. He thinks he has cast off Prospero for two new masters: Stephano and Trinculo, the butler and the jester of the King of Naples. In this production the drunken Italians stand behind him, mimicking his dance and inviting the audience to laugh at him (II 2 180–5). Later, the beautiful speech in which Caliban praises the beauties of the island, with its vision of what might be (III 2 135–43), was growled out like the rest of his lines – albeit accompanied by some vaguely African-sounding music.

It is interesting to compare this depiction with a 1995 touring production by the RSC, directed by David Thacker. Thacker's touring production was performed in sports halls, often in localities not served by theatres. There seemed to be a much clearer desire in this production both to connect with the audience and to explore the themes of power and inequality. In Thacker's production Caliban was recognisably human, wearing tattered clothes of North-African appearance. He had burst explosively from out of a chest for his first entrance. He, too, dragged himself around; but for his song and his speech about the island he differed markedly from Noble's Caliban. When singing he possessed a dangerous power and energy, the effect of which was to scare Stephano and Trinculo; for the speech he rose to his full height and spoke very lyrically, with tears in his eyes. Thacker's Caliban had a capacity for power and an articulate appreciation of beauty that Noble's seemed to lack. Noble's sub-human Caliban needed to be controlled for his own good. Thacker's Ariel was an acrobatic and dreadlocked young woman whose energy seemed to be cramped and limited by Prospero – quite different from Noble's content, pure and statuesque Ariel, the elegant, if occasionally moody, servant of a wise master.

In Thacker's 1995 production Stephano and Trinculo spoke to the audience directly and often as individuals, Trinculo ad-libbing where necessary to explain the jokes which are no longer accessible to the modern play-goer. Thacker acknowledged that there are contemporary references and allusions in Shakespeare which are the point of certain jokes. At these points his jester sent up the text's impenetrability and lack of universality, either by trying to explain the joke in his own words, before camply giving up, or by shrugging massively and adding a Frankie Howerd-like 'Please yourself!' or 'I didn't write this stuff, you know!' That Shakespeare's humour is *not* for all times itself became the joke. Noble's 'purist' approach to these lines, by contrast, consisted in letting the text 'work for itself' – which, of course, it didn't. Trinculo and Stephano had to fall back on the RSC's usual method of getting a squeal of laughter from audiences: for instance, pretending that the hand-props – in this case, bottles – were their penises.

As Thacker's production played in sports halls, in the round, the audience were very close. For Noble's production the distance between the vast Barbican stage and the audience was increased: the front rows of the stalls had been taken out and across the gap a bridge into the stalls had been built. Some actors made their entrances via this bridge. Prospero watched the on-stage action from this position at a time when he was supposed to be invisible. If the idea had been that he would be seen as part of the audience, it didn't work: he was still too distant from the audience for this. It was hard to see what real purpose the bridge served. Contact between the actors was often inadequate in this production. All of them were so keen to belt out their speeches to the back of the stalls that they rarely seemed to listen to one another. The gap between audience and actors was only emphasised by this bridge.

Noble's Prospero was weary and very human. He clearly had great powers, displayed in the spectacular effects of sound and lighting, and acres of blue silk. His mystical difference was signalled by his oriental robes, which contrasted with the Jacobean costumes of the Italians whose presence on the island he had ordained. Nevertheless, because the actors did not appear to listen to one another (no matter how clearly and *slowly* they spoke their lines), I found it hard to become sufficiently involved in the play. Consequently I didn't find Prospero's decision to forgive, rather than to take revenge, either affecting or thought-provoking. The production didn't seem to know what it thought about the play. The programme contained lengthy extracts from Anne Barton's 1968 Introduction to the New Penguin edition, which stresses the mysterious and bewildering qualities evoked by the play's myth-like features. Yet the production's uncertainty of direction failed to provide even an 'emotional experience'.

Noble's production was not deliberately pro-imperialist. It failed, like so many modern institutional productions, simply because it did not engage those themes of the text which today it must if it is to make real contact with its audience: the play's questions of race, gender, power and authority. Performance must also acknowledge that the period for which the play was written is not the present: Shakespeare is not our contemporary in the literal sense. In not making these acknowledgements, the production revealed assumptions about these very issues, which it did not want to examine. This was a production of a 'classic' high-status play about a white man taking over an island and enslaving its inhabitants, which had been written at a time when the City of London was funding this very process in several parts of the world. This performance was by an organisation that is funded by the government and sponsored by the monarchy. It was being staged in a capital city the wealth of which had been founded on the exploitation of foreign countries. Millions of the descendants of the very people once enslaved by the London merchants who had exploited their countries now live in this city. If a production of the play chooses to pay no attention to this context, then some people, whatever their family history, will wonder about that decision and question the assumptions that *license* the production to ignore that context. These people may then analyse the features of the production that indicate those assumptions, whether the director or designer intended them or not.

As soon as the play is put into performance by voices; as soon as it is clothed and embodied on a stage, the meaning of the text changes: it becomes a performance text. This should to be borne in mind through the chapters that follow. One of my aims there is to demonstrate how contemporary criticism finds important political notions in the plays – whether a production wishes to acknowledge them or not.

Summary

- This chapter has emphasised an approach that regards the plays as blueprints for stage performances.
- When we read them we must always be aware that any realisation on stage will produce a fuller meaning than will mere reading. The conditions at time and place of staging also can be powerful factors in the production of meaning.

Further reading

A good reconstruction of how an original performance may have gone can be found in Thomson (1983: Part II) and in White (1998: Chapters 4 and 5). Bate and Jackson (1996) include very interesting accounts of the many ways in which Shakespeare has been performed and understood in performance over the centuries. Look also at the introductions to the New Arden editions of particular plays. Finally, at a more advanced level, there a good introduction to performance theory in Bulman (1996: Chapter 1).

Videos

Watching Shakespeare on video is an excellent way of understanding the notion of a performance text. The medium, through freeze-frame and replay, also allows close analysis of particular moments, which is not possible in the theatre.

There are considerable differences, of course, between the theatre and the film/video experience: the film director chooses the composition and angle of each shot for us; a 'complete' text is rarely performed, and the order of what is included usually differs from the sequence of lines and scenes in the printed versions. Nevertheless, as performance texts they are as valid as any others, and have probably had more widespread influence on audiences than have modern stage productions.

A personal recommendation of notable productions would include the plays mentioned below:

1   It is very interesting to compare Laurence Olivier's 1944 version of *King Henry V* with Kenneth Branagh's 1989 version – particularly with the text of the play in front of you. There is a good discussion of both films in their historical contexts in Holderness (1992).

2   Three versions of *Hamlet* can also be very usefully contrasted. Olivier's very psychological 1948 production is interesting to read against Franco Zeffirelli's much cruder 1991 film, with Mel Gibson as the prince. The Zeffirelli goes overboard on the imputed 'Oedipal' relation between Hamlet and his mother (Glenn Close). Fortinbras is missing from both these films, though he is important in Kenneth Branagh's 1996 film version, which unusually presents a 'complete' text in the surroundings of Blenheim Palace. There is an excellent video produced by the British Film Institute (Shakespeare Cinema Study Video 1993), which contrasts scenes from the Olivier and Zeffirelli versions of *Hamlet* as well as including film extracts from Toby Richardson's 1969 controversial London production and a Russian production directed by G. Kozintsev (1964).

3   Roman Polanski's well-known 1971 version of *Macbeth* is set in an obviously feudal Scotland. There is, I think, a 1960s' feel to it, produced as it was at a time when film-makers were taking advantage of the relaxations of censorship which occurred in this period: there is both nudity and plenty of blood – indeed, the film was produced in association with the publishers of an international 'girlie' magazine, and it certainly shows! John Turner makes excellent use of Polanski's

film to give a critical perspective on the text (often in comparison to the video of Trevor Nunn's 1976 production) in his book *Macbeth* (Buckingham, Open University Press, 1992).

4   Equally distinctive and famous is Baz Luhrmann's 1996 *Romeo and Juliet*, set in a hyper-modern California. The film sets out to appeal to a mass teenage audience in the 1990s and does it with great style and energy, staying in my opinion remarkably close to the spirit of the original, too.

Part II

The genres

Chapter 5

What is genre?

A legacy of Romantic thinking is the belief that when a writer sits down to create he or she is free to go wherever the imagination may lead. If this were ever true, it is certainly not true of writing that seeks to succeed commercially. Shakespeare and his fellow writers depended for their livlihood on writing plays that they knew a theatre company would buy; and they were aware that what a theatre company looked for was a play that built on the elements of other successful popular plays. I am not denying the brilliance and originality of many of Shakespeare's plays; but the plays were generally written to please a paying audience whose tastes were known.

One of the most popular plays throughout this period was Thomas Kyd's *The Spanish Tragedy*, first produced in its original form around 1582, just as the theatre was becoming a commercial and professional venture. In this play Kyd had drawn

119

Box 10: Theatre companies

The appearance of the first professional secular theatres in Elizabethan London was a remarkable feature of the age. Key figures in the respect were Philip Henslowe and James Burbage, entrepreneurs who put up the capital and managed the companies of actors.

Each company was named after its aristocratic or royal patron. A company's core comprised eight to ten 'sharers': performers, and sometimes writers, who bought into the company and shared its profits. Another ten or so actors, musicians, costume managers, a prompter, front-of-house staff, and so on were hired on contract, and paid very little. Some of the hired back-stage staff were female. Companies were rather unstable, with actors moving from one to another, and back again. When Burbage built The Globe in 1599 Shakespeare became a shareholder, making the sharers of his company – the Lord Chamberlain's (subsequently the King's Men) – majority owners of their own playhouse. Clearly this was a more stable arrangement, and it was copied by other companies. With up to 2,500 play-goers a day at The Globe, there was much money to be made. The company was later able to expand into the Blackfriars Theatre.

Companies performed six days a week in the public playhouses, putting on a different play each day. A new play would be added every two weeks or so, with more popular plays repeated and others abandoned. Henslowe's company offered thirty-eight plays in its 1594–5 season, of which twenty-one were new. The demand for new plays was high and playwrights often collaborated in teams or reworked others' material.

Playwrights sold individual plays to company managers. Additional payment seems to have come from 'benefit days', when the dramatist took all profits from a performance. The plays were usually considered the property of the company which bought them, but Shakespeare seems to have kept ownership of his early plays and to have taken them with him when he changed companies in 1594. A few established writers were put under contract to produce a certain number of plays in a specified time, receiving a 'salary' on top of the usual payments. Shakespeare's 1594 contract with the Lord Chamberlain's Company, probably for one 'serious' and one 'light' play during the year, was so far as we know the first of these rare arrangements.

When King James came to power in 1603 he and his family became patrons of London's three main companies. The Lord Chamberlain's Company became The King's Men, alongside the Queen Anne's Men and Prince Henry's Men. For the companies this meant regular and lucrative performances in the royal palaces, but it also gave the court influence over the theatre.

upon elements of Roman tragedy, but the parts of his play which were most popular with audiences included the appearance of a ghost, the actions of a character who pretends to be mad in order to conceal his plans for revenge, and a conclusion in which a public spectacle turns to vengeful murder and mayhem. These and other elements are to be found in *Hamlet* (1600) and also in a large number of similar plays of the period. Middleton's *Women Beware Women* (*c.* 1623) and Webster's *The Duchess of Malfi* (1614), for example, share many of the same conventions, as also does *The Atheist's Tragedy* (1607, attributed to Cyril Tourneur). They all belong to the genre of *revenge tragedy*.

A *genre*, then, is a type of play, book, film and so on, each example of which has certain characteristic features or *conventions*. A *soap opera* wouldn't be a soap opera without a strong mother-figure and an attractive-but-villainous-man, or if all the storylines concluded at the end of each episode. A conventional *Western*, similarly, would not be set in suburban England. So, in the same way, a *tragedy* in Shakespeare's time has to end with the stage littered with corpses; a *comedy* has to end with marriage. Such was the nature of theatre then – and in some respects still is, now. The stories in Shakespeare's plays had, by and large, set paths on which to run – or, rather, along which the audience expected them to run; any deviation from those paths would be measured in terms of the effectiveness of the difference from the expected path taken.

Classification by genre

John Hemmings and Henry Condell, editors of the First Folio of 1623 (see Box 2, p. 25), divided up Shakespeare's plays into Comedies, Histories and Tragedies. There has been considerable critical debate over the years about these terms and their use as classifications for particular plays. The 1997 Riverside Shakespeare uses a fourth category: Romance. This fourfold division seems to make sense – but there are still plays which do not neatly fit *one* of these four because, for particular effects, they combine elements characteristic of one or more of the other three genres.

Here are some typical examples of the four genres:

1   Comedies

- *The Comedy of Errors* (1592–94)
- *The Taming of the Shrew* (1593–94)
- *A Midsummer Night's Dream* (1595–96)
- *As You Like It* (1599)

The conventions of Comedy include: disguise, often involving cross-dressing; thwarted love; mistaken identity; marital and romantic misunderstandings. Comedies end in multiple marriage.

2   Histories

- *King Richard III* (1592–93)
- *King Richard II* (1595)
- *King Henry IV Parts I and II* (1596–98)
- *King Henry V* (1599)

Among the conventions of History are: conspiracy; fighting; prominent sub-plots involving non-noble characters; a large number of characters; a decisive on-stage battle.

3   Tragedies

- *Hamlet* (1600)
- *Othello* (1604)
- *King Lear* (1605)
- *Macbeth* (1606)
- *Coriolanus* (1607–8)

The conventions of Tragedy include: a single heroic main character (the protagonist); some dreadful dilemma or wrong decision; conspiracy; fighting; (often) madness; many deaths at the end.

4 Romances

- *Pericles* (1607–8)
- *The Winter's Tale* (1611)
- *The Tempest* (1611)

Romance conventions include: natural disasters; remarkable adventures; unlikely coincidences; conflict between generations and within families; an unforeseen conclusion in which forgiveness and reconciliation are achieved against all the odds.

Two plays that exploit genre conventions while defying neat classification within those genre categories are *Troilus and Cressida* (1601–2) and *Measure For Measure* (1604). There is, then, a fifth classification – *mixed-genre* (or genre-defying) plays.

In these texts, which used often to be called 'problem' plays, conventions from several genres sit – more or less uneasily – together. *Measure For Measure*, for example, features disguise and ends with a multiple marriage. The darkness of its mood and grimness of its plot, however, make it hard to classify it as a Comedy.

Shakespeare is not afraid to play with genre, and does so in many plays. For example, the second half of what would seem a typical History, *King Henry V*, features several comedic conventions (disguise, a practical joke, a comic wooing ending in marriage). Why Shakespeare incorporated within one play conventions from distinct genres is a question to which I return later in the book (see pp. 179–80)

Part II discusses each of the genres in turn. I provide an approach to understanding the nature of each, according to the interests and ideas of contemporary critics. In the process, I aim to show the limitations of criticism that is based predominantly on character, theme and plot. The critical approach employed here, it is important to add, is not the *only* way of reading Shakespeare. What follows is a sample of modern critical ideas for you to use as a springboard in your own work. Influential though these ideas are, they are not rigid principles that cannot be challenged or developed.

I tackle the genres roughly in the order in which the plays were written. Broadly speaking, Shakespeare started with Comedies, and moved on to Histories and then Tragedies. After the more experimental *cross-genre* plays, he concluded his career as a writer of Romances.

Chapter 6

Understanding comedy

*The Taming of the Shrew,
A Midsummer Night's Dream
and The Merchant of Venice*

Comedy could be simply defined as a dramatic presentation which makes us laugh. Literary and cultural critics, however, tend to regard something as a comedy not so much because it makes us laugh – laughter may be evoked in tragic circumstances – but because a certain set of conventions is being followed. The very act of breaking with these conventions is an acknowledgement that they remain in place.

Those of Shakespeare's plays called comedies are so designated primarily because they adhere to a particular set of expectations (see pp. 122f.) – not necessarily because they are funny. Some are, of course – but the history plays – even the tragedies – can, in my experience, get more laughs in performance than productions of *All's Well That Ends Well* or *The Two Gentlemen of Verona*. Thus, although *The Merchant of Venice* is usually regarded as a comedy because of the conventions it deploys, the subject matter of its main plot is not particularly a laughing matter. It is worth considering, however, that it *might* have been for some or all of its original audience.

What all the comedies seem to have in common is their pre-occupation with the journey of young women (and sometimes men) from the state of virginity to that of marriage. Whereas tragedy works towards death, that moment which gives a particular meaning to the actions of the protagonists, comedy traces the passage of young people out of their parents' control and into marriage. Thus Portia in *The Merchant of Venice* has to endure the ritual of the caskets prescribed by her father and simply hope that it will produce a man she can love; Hermia in *A Midsummer Night's Dream* has to run away into the woods with her lover Lysander in order to avoid marriage to Demetrius, the husband chosen for her by her father. It is, of course, clear why death in a tragedy is regarded as the end of the story (though it isn't for the *survivors*). It's less obvious why marriage should be regarded as an end: if anything, it is the beginning of a totally new story. It is the point, however, where sexual desire becomes legitimised (approved of by those in power), socialised (accepted by society at large) and channelled in a particular direction. In other words, comedy is often about one or more young persons whose love meets an obstacle of some sort.

Often some sort of resistance to this obstacle, be it parental disapproval or the apparent refusal of the loved one to return that love, is shown. The central plot of a comedy often requires the young people to disguise themselves (usually with women cross-dressed as men, like Portia in *The Merchant of Venice*, Viola in *Twelfth Night* or Rosalind in *As You Like It*), or to abscond into the woods (like Hermia and Helena and their lovers in *A Midsummer Night's Dream*, or Rosalind in *As You Like It*, or to undertake a journey (like Petruchio and Katherina in *The Taming of the Shrew*). When they emerge on the other side of the experience, something will have happened to make their love a social reality in some way, and the play ends with an apparently happy union.

Now it has to be borne in mind that a woman was not supposed to have the right to choose for herself a suitor or spouse: that was the male's prerogative. Comedy can therefore be seen as challenge of sorts to the authority of fathers or husbands-to-be, which is played out in some imaginary world – the magic wood, or a place where women in male disguise are never recognised as women until they wish to be. The whole play is itself, of course, a make believe world, too.

Contemporary critics, feminist and otherwise, seem very concerned about the question of prerogative when it comes to comedy. Two alternatives seem possible:

1   Are these plays to be seen as acting out a fantasy of female independence through some kind of symbolic revolt against the power and authority of fathers? And is this revolt shown only to demonstrate in the end the rightness of the inevitable progression from youthful desire to the socially approved institution of marriage? In other words, Hermia may think she is choosing for herself and going against her father's wishes, but she still ends up *married*, and with the approval of the Duke of Athens himself. She learns that it is best for a woman to control her desires and obey someone – if not her father, then her husband and the duke.
2   Might they, on the other hand, show that the world need not be as it is? Do they show women escaping the descriptions and identities which society imposes on them *so* dynamically that when the ending of the play comes they do *not* become fully reabsorbed into society? Does the ending suggest that in fact after the wedding ceremony there is another story to be told – one of the kind of male–female relationship in which there is the potential for power to be more evenly distributed?

The first position tends to be associated, very broadly speaking, with the *new historicist* critics; the second, with the *cultural materialists* (see pp. 240f.). Any question of the possible subjugation or liberation of women in these plays is naturally a matter of concern to feminists.

There is considerable disagreement among historians and critics about the position of women in English society in

Shakespeare's time. Some feminists are keen to stress the utter oppression of women in all domains of life: economic, domestic, sexual, familial and personal. Others point out that while it is certainly true that women were in no way regarded as the equals of men in official aspects of life, the Puritan doctrine of 'companionate marriage', which stressed the spiritual equality of man and wife in a loving relationship, was related to a kind of feminist flowering in this period among the sort of middle-class women – those whose Protestant beliefs encouraged them to consider themselves the spiritual equals of their husbands, but who did not hold anti-theatrical views – who would have attended the London theatres. What is more, there is considerable evidence that women were far more active in economic life as skilled workers, managers of large domestic organisations and small businesses (Orgel 1996a: 73–4) than has often been assumed. Of the Puritans, the British feminist critic Juliet Dusinberre has written:

> Their reforms were aimed at men and women equally, but their effect was greater for women because they alleviated the exploitation made possible by the economic dependence of the woman. Thus the agitation for women's rights and for changed attitudes to women which was a vital aspect of the society for which Shakespeare wrote was to a large extent set in motion and furthered by the most powerful pressure group, both numerically and morally, of the time, and one which had the moral support of the most talented and creative of Shakespeare's contemporaries. This was the climate … in which Shakespeare took root as a dramatist.
> The drama from 1590 to 1625 is feminist in sympathy.
>
> (Dusinberre 1996a: 5)

After this period writers were more committed to writing for the indoor theatre and the court rather than for the public playhouse. The way women were then presented, she argues, changed for the worse.

Other contemporary feminists see this period as one of male backlash against the freedoms which, they say, women had in fact enjoyed in the late medieval period (Davies 1995: 14). Since Dusinberre first published her views in 1979 they have been challenged and qualified by other feminist writers. Whether this was a period of relative freedom for women or one of an oppression totally unacceptable by modern standards remains a moot point among critics and historians. For example, the novelist and feminist critic Stevie Davies has pointed out the legal realities of life for a married woman in Shakespeare's time:

> Possessing no civil or civic functions, she was debarred from office in camp [the army], council [government], bench or jury-box [the courts]. She could neither vote nor be a candidate, nor (generally) give evidence in a lawcourt. She could not make a contract, sue or be sued. The reason for this was that a married woman did not, in law, exist. ... Furthermore she could not own property because she *was* property. She owned neither the dowry she brought with her, nor the roof over her head, neither the jewels, if any, round her neck, nor the very clothes in which she stood up.
>
> (Davies 1995: 10)

Whatever the true situation was – if we can ever know it remains the case that in this debate the plays themselves stand as important pieces of evidence about the status of women in this period. They are not separate from their background, but part of our understanding of women's lives at this point in history.

Comedy and gender: *The Taming of the Shrew*

If there is a play from this period that seems unequivocally misogynistic (expressing a dislike of women) it is surely *The Taming of the Shrew*. Katherina is a young woman who always speaks her mind and is not afraid to be rude and aggressive when she needs to be. She wants a husband – but not the one approved of by her father. She is courted against her will by Petruchio, who openly admits that he has come to Padua in search of a wife with a rich dowry, no matter what she is like (I 25–76). Katherina's father is very happy to get her off his hands, even though she positively refuses the match. In this comedy, the desire of a woman to reject all suitors who are not to her liking is the female need which is to be brought under male control. It is done in the most domineering way possible, short of actual violence. That act of control might be seen either as exposing the injustice of male definitions of what a woman should be or as simply reinforcing those definitions. That seems to be the matter at stake for critical study of the play.

Petruchio's courtship and marriage seem designed to humiliate Katherina and break her spirit. His behaviour is calculated to embarrass and degrade her as much as possible. After the wedding he takes her off to his house where he refuses to let her eat or sleep, pretending that he is doing it for her own good (IV 1 197–211). Eventually she seems to accept that his authority over her is complete, even to the point where she will agree that the sun is the moon if he says it is (IV 5 18–22), or that an old man is a young woman (IV 5 37–41). In the final scene Katherina wins for her husband a dinner-party wager according to which she is the most obedient of those wives present, as she stoops in a gesture of submission to place her hand beneath Petruchio's foot. In the longest speech of the play she offers the other wives a series of well-worn traditionalist reasons why man should have authority over woman:

Katherina Thy husband is thy lord, thy life, thy keeper,
　　Thy head, thy sovereign, one that cares for thee,
　　And for thy maintenance; commits his body
　　To painful labour, both by sea and land;
　　To watch the night in storms, in day the cold,　　　　150
　　Whilst thou liest warm at home, secure and safe;
　　And craves* no other tribute at thy hands
　　But love, fair looks and true obedience -
　　Too little payment for so great a debt.
　　Such duty as the subject owes the prince,*　　　　　155
　　Even such a woman oweth to her husband;
　　And when she is froward, peevish,* sullen, sour,

And not obedient to his honest will,
What is she but a foul contending rebel,
And graceless traitor to her loving lord?   160
I am ashamed that women are so simple*
To offer war when they should kneel for peace,
Or seek for rule, supremacy and sway,*
When they are bound to serve, love and obey.

(V 2 146–64)

* [152] *craves* asks for [155] *prince* monarch [157] *froward,
peevish* pushy, obstinate [161] *simple* foolish [163] *sway* power

This speech is so unambiguous a statement of women's subservience that feminist critics who wish to argue that the play is no simple story of just male triumph over a foolishly rebellious woman have much work to do. The *Guardian*'s theatre critic, Michael Billington, famously asked 'whether there is any reason to revive a play which seems totally offensive to our age and society' (6 May 1978) – and looking at the way the play ends his question seems a perfectly reasonable one.

Many critics and directors have sought to interpret the play as ironic, making its suggested deeper meaning (implicit rejection of the way Katherina is treated) much more significant than its surface meaning (women must learn to obey men no matter what). This may stem from a refusal to admit that Shakespeare could write a play as sexist as this appears to be. After all, other outspoken female characters are treated with far more sympathy: Emilia in *Othello* (see pp. 209f.) and Paulina in *The Winter's Tale* (see pp. 248f.), not to mention Beatrice in *Much Ado About Nothing*.

At the same time, however, if the portrayal of Katherina seems so 'out of character', it should be remembered that, as one of his earlier plays (1593–94?), the lack of sophistication in this regard is perhaps explicable in terms of Shakespeare's immaturity?

Some of the arguments which have been advanced in order to reinstate this text emphasise the play's subtlety. What is unusual about *The Taming of the Shrew* is the framing – or, actually, half-framing – of the action by the Christopher Sly plot. The play begins with an 'Induction', in which a drunken tinker, Christopher Sly, is thrown out of a pub and falls asleep outside. Found by a lord who is out hunting, Sly is taken back to the lord's house and as a practical joke treated as if he were its owner. His 'previous life', he is told, was just a dream. The household members even provide him with a 'wife', who is actually a page dressed as a woman (Induction I 1 105–35) The play *The Taming of the Shrew* is staged by a group of players for the entertainment of Sly, the lord and his household. It is a play within a play, and so is not presented to its audience as a 'reality' in which they are to believe. It is not just self-confessedly fictional, but actually presented as part of a conscious deceit. (In fact, the other side of the frame is missing: the Folio text forgets about Sly and the lord, and the play ends without their reappearance. Modern directors often add on the conclusion of the Sly framing-plot from a play called *A Shrew*, a Quarto text which seems to be an earlier version, of some sort, of Shakespeare's play. For an explanation of 'Folio' and 'Quarto' see Box 2, p. 25.)

The point is that the play itself does not invite us to take seriously Petruchio's actions and Kate's submission: the play becomes a kind of fantasy of male wish-fulfilment, while consciously admitting that this view of the male–female relationship exists only in fiction. We are, then, free to see it as a demonstration that the gender roles played by men and women in society are in fact 'constructed' (see pp. 205f.) and do not form part of their essential natures. The comic swapping of identities among the other characters also underlines the idea that all of what we observe on stage is only role-play. None of those we see has any 'fixed' nature: Tranio pretends to be Lucentio; the pedant pretends to be Vincentio; and Lucentio is in disguise as Cambio. What we are seeing in this part of the plot is not real, even within the context of the fiction in which it is set. That so many of the characters seem drawn from the stock types of the Italian *commedia dell' arte* (Davies 1995: 50) also undermines any confidence the audience might have that they are supposed to regard these characters as a representation of the world as it is. Consequently Katherina's submission is very much an *imaginary* resolution of the conflict with her husband. Her final speech holds up the conventional reasons for male supremacy, as advanced by Renaissance writers, as fictions that are no more to be believed than the reality of Tranio or Lucentio's characterisation, whether as *themselves* or as someone else. The speech's doctrines are so at odds with the experienced needs of men and women, then and now, that it is only in a make-believe world that they could bring domestic harmony. The ending, argues Juliet Dusinberre (1996a: 108), is, to say the least, ambiguous and equivocal. The clinching last line of the play expresses the incredulity of the other characters that Katherina really has been 'tamed' at all (V 2 189).

In what may be a clue to how the play was understood at the time, Dusinberre (ibid.: 105–6) points out that in John Fletcher's sequel, *The Woman's Prize, Or The Tamer Tam'd* (probably written between 1604 and 1617) – about Petruchio's second wife – Katherina, now dead, is reported to have remained resistant to taming until the end of her life

The American feminist critic Karen Newman (1986: 46) has argued that to show gender relations on stage as 'natural' in a fantasy play such as this (especially in a theatre where boys play women) is to reveal the artificiality of those relations by exposing their contradictions. She sees Katherina's behaviour, right up to the end of the play, as a refusal to be categorised and controlled by the power structures by which men subordinate women. She refuses either to be silent or to submit herself as a passive public object for the male gaze. In this period obedient women were praised for their appearance. Disobedient women, especially those who 'talked too much', were publicly shamed by being ducked in rivers or ponds. In some cases a vicious metal gag, called 'the branks', was clamped around the mouth. Katherina, according to Newman, refuses to be seen and not heard. She takes on the male language and undermines it in two ways.

The first is her riddling wordplay with Petruchio, through which she refuses to accept that he has a right to decide on the meaning of his own words. In fact, her puns expose marriage as an (unequal) sexual exchange in which women are exploited to produce offspring for men with no benefits (such as respect or affection) for themselves. Her wordplay emphasises the transparency of Petruchio's interest in her as a mother to his children, irrespective of whether she wants him or not. Her language emphasises his unworthiness to be her partner:

Petruchio Myself am moved* to woo thee for my wife.
Katherina Moved! In good time!* Let him that moved
   you hither   195
   Remove you hence. I knew you at the first
   You were a moveable.*
Petruchio Why, what's a moveable?
Katherina A joined stool.*
Petruchio Thou has hit it; come sit on me.*
Katherina Asses are made to bear, and so are you.
Petruchio Women are made to bear,* and so are you.   200
Katherina No such jade* as you, if me you mean.
Petruchio Alas, good Kate, I will not burden* thee,
   For knowing* thee to be but young and light.*
Katherina Too light* for such a swain* as you to catch,
   And yet as heavy* as my weight should be.   205

                                 (II 1 194–205)

* [194] *Am moved* desire [195] *In good time!* Indeed! [197] *a moveable* a piece of furniture – she means a dumb object, but also a mere household item (which he would make her) – also means fickle, unreliable emotionally [198] *A joined stool* a low stool that was proverbially easy to overlook. Petruchio's inferiority to her as a potential partner is the focus of her punning in what follows [198] *sit on me* a crudely sexual proposition [200] *bear* i.e. 'have me on top of you', but also 'bear my children' [201] *jade* a horse that soon tires – Petruchio wouldn't be able to satisfy her in bed, perhaps [202] *burden* 'bother', but also 'accompany' (in a song), and a reference back to 'bear' [203] *For knowing* 'Because I know you are'; *light* 'delicate', but also in the sense of 'promiscuous' [204] *light* quick, elusive; *swain* country bumpkin [205] *heavy* serious, worthy of respect; there

is also the sense that she is *true* coinage, not a coin that has been clipped or is counterfeit: she means what she says!

She may be the object of his sexual innuendo, but she retains her dignity and has the last word about what the language of the exchange actually means.

Throughout the trials of her wedding day and night, Katherina insists on her right to have her voice heard (III 2 207–21; IV 3 73–80). Petruchio deliberately mishears her, distorting what she says to suit his meaning. Female speech in the play is associated with female independence; it is not to be listened to.

Newman (1986) reads Katherina's apparent capitulation in the final scene as too knowing and blatant to be accepted at face value. After all, the only language available for a public statement like her final speech is male language; the only rhetoric she is allowed to deploy is male rhetoric. As a woman capable of 'miming' the male role to such effect, she exposes its contradiction. She has *not* in the end been silenced. The comedy genre's resolution requires a 'happy' union. This is the speech to which the plot has been leading; it is the only way in which the comedy can end. But it is not Petruchio who speaks it. If she is tamed, how is it she holds the stage at the end, unsilenced? Newman says that the effect is to put the speech 'in italics' (Newman 1986: 51). Katherina is quoting someone else in order to bring to attention that person's mistake. Newman sums up the argument like this:

> Kate's having the last word contradicts the very sentiments she speaks; rather than resolve the play's action, her monologue displays the fundamental contradiction presented by a female protagonist, between women as sexually desirable, silent objects and women of words, women with power over language who disrupt, or at least italicize, women's place and part in culture.
>
> (ibid.: 51)

Petruchio's actions produce not a mute beauty, the object of his taming, but a female version of himself.

For some feminist critics, this is all too much – 'manifest evasion', Stevie Davies (1995: 62) calls it. The play is a blatant and offensive metaphor for man as the tamer of an unruly horse or a wayward hawk. Men are masters and women are their animals to be tamed. If at the end two shrews (Bianca and the Widow) remain, that just shows how never-ending the task is.

When Petruchio describes his wife as 'My household stuff, my field, my barn,/My horse, my ox, my ass, my anything' (III 2 231–2), it is not intended to shock; it is a simple statement of the legal realities of marriage (see pp. 129f.). Katherina's language doesn't quite escape Petruchio's control through its wit and word-play. Instead he often makes it appear as if she is only repeating what he wants her to say (see, for example, the exchange with the tailor in IV 3 103–5). It's not that he wilfully mishears her throughout the play, either. If she won't be silent and speak only at his bidding, then her language is not worth listening to. He knows what she really means, even if she is saying the opposite (see, for example, the scenes at his house in IV 1 and IV 3). She must learn this. When Katherina at his bidding calls the sun the moon (IV 5 2–22), it is not exposing the absurdity of Petruchio's demand for total domination. Rather it shows her realisation that nature itself is turned upside down if she insists on turning the equally natural social order of male supremacy upside down (Davies 1995: 11).

At the end Katherina is allowed the play's longest speech, even though a woman, because it is her husband speaking through her at last. Her voice, too, is now fully his – and there is no irony intended. No other evidence within the play suggests that the speech is not sincerely meant. Indeed, the idea that Katherina will have some sort of power by publicly going along with Petruchio's wishes while getting her own way at home is, as Davies argues, 'demeaning to both parties' (ibid.: 55). Students sometimes suggest that once she realises her love for him she discovers that social expectations don't actually matter: they are silly conventions to be played out in public, but which are absurd from the perspective of their life together as lovers. The final speech is a knowing pretence at conformity, to be delivered with a wink. Their lives as lovers have nothing to do with such social conventions. Such an interpretation has indeed been attempted in production. The problem is that there is not a single line in the text to support such a reading.

The play can also be seen, then, to be a plain statement of the right of men to control and dominate their wives. It can be argued, moreover, that the play itself has actually operated over the years to reinforce that domination, no matter what Shakespeare may or may not have said in other plays.

Comedy and power: *A Midsummer Night's Dream*

If Davies is right, *The Taming of the Shrew* is a crude but theatrically energetic statement in support of the rights of the powerful. Other critics have found Shakespeare's comedies to be more subtle reinforcements of ruling-class values.

In the Athens of *A Midsummer Night's Dream* the rule of the father over a daughter is enforced in a savage way. Duke Theseus is about to marry the Amazon queen Hipplolyta, whom he wooed, he boasts, 'with my sword' (I 1 16). A nobleman, Egeus, insists that his daughter Hermia marries Demetrius, rather than Lysander, the man she wants. By the law of the state her refusal will be punished either by death or banishment to a convent. Theseus gives Hermia until his own wedding day to make up her mind. Once alone, the lovers plan to elope to stay with a favourable aunt outside the city where they can marry. They arrange to meet that night in a wood. They tell Hermia's friend Helena, who is in love with Demetrius, of their plans. She tells the audience that she will inform Demetrius of their escape. He will then pursue them, and she him, into the magic wood. There the four undergo various transformations at the playful hands of the woodland fairies, led by their quarrelling monarchs Queen Titania and King Oberon. When their nocturnal adventures are over Hermia and Lysander and Helena and Demetrius will be happy together, and will marry with the blessing of Theseus himself, overruling the wishes of Egeus (IV 1 179–81).

Their experiences in the wood not only untangle the knot of their conflicting desires, but Demetrius' account of his transformation from 'sickness' to 'health' (IV 1 160–76) seems to win over Theseus to the cause of true love and all is resolved happily for the young people.

Once in the wood the lovers seem to think that they can choose for themselves, free from state and patriarchal authority. But, argues the American Marxist critic Elliott Krieger, this is an illusion. What the play demonstrates is that state and patriarchal power is enforced not only physically, by law and punishment, but by aesthetic means (*aesthetic* means concerned with art and beauty). In this play sexual passion and the need for individual liberty in defiance of Duke Theseus' power are always transformed to an imaginary artistic level on which violence can be glossed over in beautiful language, and in a purely make-believe world rebellion can be played out to the satisfaction of the players inside that world, but never actually challenges those who hold power in the real world.

The Amazons were a race of warrior–women who rejected men altogether from their lives. Theseus' defeat of Hippolyta is firmly reinforced by her marriage to him – a marriage for which, in the first scene, she notably expresses no desire. (In some productions she is made to be obviously hostile; and in a famous 1966 production she was even brought on stage in a cage [Holland 1994: 51].) But the violence of his conquest is to be turned into beauty, aestheticised, by its represention as public spectacle:

Theseus Hippolyta, I wooed thee with my sword,
   And won thy love doing thee injuries;
   But I will love thee in another key,
   With pomp, with triumph and with revelling.

(I 1 16–19)

The festivities of the wedding are only a shift in musical 'key'. Violence is swiftly transformed into art. In the same way, Theseus relishes the musical sound of his hunting hounds' baying (IV 1 105, 110, 124–5) and their physical appearance (IV 1 119–23), rather than any actual ability they have to perform their proper function: the capture and killing of gentler creatures (Krieger 1979: 48–9). The court performance of *Pyramus and Thisbe* by Bottom and the other craftsmen is another example of how tragedy and thwarted desire are turned into a safe aesthetic experience to be enjoyed by an aristocratic audience. Normally the weaver, the carpenter and the tailor transform nature into something useful. In Theseus' court they can transform only themselves into useless *representations* of nature for aristocratic approval.

The wood appears to the lovers to be a place of pastoral escape, safe from the power of Theseus and Egeus; that is why they agree to meet there. It was, after all, the place wherein the two women used to feel free to tell each other their youthful dreams (I 1 214–16). But it is actually full of Theseus's power. Quince calls his rehearsal at the 'duke's oak' (I 2 110) in the 'palace wood' (I 2 101). The fairies who rule there are a kind of aristocratic fantasy, blessed with magic powers and enjoying the happy service of a crowd of retainers, in a parallel power structure to that which obtains in Athens. Titania's dispute with her husband over possession of the Indian Boy is resolved happily through Oberon's magic powers (IV 1 71ff.). Oberon wants the child to enter his service; Titania had promised a close female friend, now dead, that she would not part from him (II 1 119–37). Meanwhile in Athens the desire of women to express solidarity with one another without the intervention of male power is crushed through military action in Theseus's victory over the Amazons. In the wood, on the other hand, male art–magic resolves conflict in ways that please and amuse.

The fairies themselves are a literary creation, a transformation of the actual world. As a fantasy expression of a ruler's power, they can control nature itself through their actions. The fiction of the magic potion is a metaphorical expression of the power of society to make people love in a way approved by the state. In the fairy world, the world of the wood, the love of the four young people is in fact confirmed as love expressed via the literary conventions of courtly and pastoral poetry. In this kind of poetry, often written by aristocrats, the young man writes, in elaborate language full of mythological reference, of his unfulfilled desire. The sought-after woman is said to possess a physical beauty way beyond that of any real woman; the man's love has a power and intensity which can be expressed only in powerful and often dense metaphor. Thinking and speaking in this literary language, the lovers in the wood cease to communicate directly with each other, for they are living in a world whose language is the creation of an external literary–aristocratic authority, and not an expression of their own authentic subjective desires: 'while in the forest', writes Krieger, 'they reiterate, in a different form, the authoritarian social system that controls Athenian love' (1979: 43). In Athens, sexual desire is controlled through the conventional language in which it is expressed. Before they went into the wood Lysander had talked of love in terms of a right justified through social status (I 1 99–102), or as a process following certain literary expectations (I 1 132–5); Hermia's promise of true love to him is in accordance with mythic and literary notions of what love is (I 1 169–74).

But in the wood the language of the lovers doesn't actually change. When Lysander wakes up from his sleep, affected by the potion, he sees Helena and falls in love with her. It's not her beauty he loves, says Krieger (1979: 45), but the *story* of beauty in a love-fiction:

Lysander Reason becomes the marshal to my will, 120
   And leads me to your eyes, where I o'erlook
   Love's stories written in Love's richest book.

(II 2 120–2)

When Demetrius falls in love with Helena, his feelings for her are expressed in the language of the most conventional love poetry.

These are clichés, not sincere words. That's why they often get a laugh in the theatre:

> *Demetrius* O Helen, goddess, nymph, perfect, divine!
>   To what, my love, shall I compare thyne eyne?*
>   Crystal is muddy. O, how ripe in show
>   Thy lips, those kissing cherries, tempting grow!   140
>   That pure congealed white, high Taurus'* snow,
>   Fann'd with the eastern wind, turns to a crow
>   When thou holds't up thy hand.

>   (III 2 137–42)

* [138] *eyne* eyes – an old-fashioned, literary form [141] *Taurus* a mountain in Turkey often referred to in classical poetry

Even the violence threatened between them is literary rather than real: Lysander wishes to stab the word 'Demetrius' with his sword, not Demetrius himself (II 2 106–7). Passion and desire are socialised; not freed from constraint. No matter what they themselves think, the untangling of the lovers' relationships has happened in a space and in a language under the control of Theseus. He licenses their desire, and makes it part of his own wedding celebrations. Egeus doesn't get his way – but Theseus' own patriarchal power is enhanced, not diminished. And, indeed, during the rule of the Tudors and Stuarts, state and church control over marriage and the family increased; and the controlling power of individual men over their families, particularly among the aristocracy, correspondingly decreased.

The threat to established power of youthful sexuality, which tends to disregard authority and social convention, is, Krieger argues, defused by giving it literary rather than authentic expression. But *A Midsummer Night's Dream* is itself both a literary expression of certain desires and anxieties and an attempt to tell its audience that these desires and anxieties can be satisfyingly resolved. The American critic Louis Adrian Montrose, for example, suggested (1983) that the play represented, and itself influenced, certain Elizabethan social anxieties about the relations between men and women. Here was a country in whose men had a near-monopoly on power, but whose symbolic and political head was a woman. Whether looking at Hermia or Hippolyta or Titania, the play shows again and again women's disruption of male bonds – but ultimately male power regains ascendency. Montrose, in one particularly subtle reading (1983: 127), gives an explanation of Oberon's story about Cupid's dart. Cupid aimed his love-dart at a beautiful virgin, but it was deflected on to a 'flower/Before milk-white, now purple with love's wound' (II 1 166–7). Montrose says that this story can be seen to represent Queen Elizabeth's own virginity paradoxically keeping in place a social system in which men had power over the virginities of all other women. The Queen is the 'fair vestal throned by the west' (II 1 158); other women are the 'little western flower' (II 1 166). This flower's juice is, of course, used by Oberon's servant Puck to control who loves whom in the wood (II 2 26 sd; II 2 78–9; III 2 453 sd).

Comedy for critics like Montrose, then, is about the containment of challenges to the symbolic and actual power of men over women. But, as we have seen, it can also be read as a manifestation of women's potential to burst the bounds of that power. Feminist readings of *The Merchant of Venice* are a very good example of this.

Comedy and utopia: *The Merchant of Venice*

The story of the defeat and humiliation of Shylock, the vengeful and 'inhuman' Jew, would seem an unlikely place to look for egalitarian sentiments about the rights of those who are denied full expression of their humanity. But contemporary critics have argued persuasively that it is precisely here that such sentiments are to be found.

The heroine of this play, the wealthy Portia, has two obstacles to overcome before she can marry the man whom she loves, Bassanio. The first is her father's will, a legally binding document which requires her to marry the man who solves the riddle of the three caskets. He who correctly interprets the words inscribed on the gold, silver and lead boxes, and consequently chooses aright, will become her husband – whether she wants it or not. The second is that Bassanio's friend Antonio has managed to acquire the money for Bassanio's wooing of Portia only by borrowing from Shylock the Jew. (Antonio loves Bassanio and will do literally anything for him. It seems to be a same-sex love which is not returned [III 2 318–22]) Apparently as a joke, for 'merry sport' (I 3 145), at first, Shylock requires Antonio to forfeit a pound of his flesh if he fails to repay the 3,000 ducats on time. Antonio's ships are supposedly lost at sea, and Shylock, now enraged at his daughter Jessica's elopement with Lorenzo, a Christian, demands his 'bond' in full. Refusing all pleas for mercy, and even three times the original sum in compensation, Shylock knows that the laws of Venice cannot deny him the forfeit, which he demands. He is about to make the fatal cut when Portia, appearing in disguise as a young (male) lawyer, points out that while the law will allow him to take his pound of flesh, any Jew who sheds Christian blood, will, by another law, forfeit all his goods to the state. Furthermore, there is another law decreeing that any 'alien' who seeks to take the life of a Venetian will lose all his property and have his life put at the mercy of the duke. Dispossessed and forced to convert to Christianity, Shylock leaves in despair. The disguised Portia then tests Bassanio's loyalty by demanding a ring he wears as payment for her work as his lawyer – she had previously given Bassanio this ring, telling him that it would be the end of their love were he ever to give it away (III 2 171–4; see below). The reluctant Bassanio is eventually persuaded, and gives her the ring. It is possible that she feels prompted to put Bassanio to this test, having heard him say during the trial that he'd rather his wife were dead than that Antonio should lose his life (IV 1 282–7).

The play's final scene was seen by some earlier critics as a light-heartedly romantic resolution of the comic plot in the aristocratic surroundings of Portia's Belmont, away from the commercial values of Venice. But this is to gloss over the uncomfortable atmosphere of the play's ending. Shylock, though clearly having sought savage revenge on a man who had long despised him for his race and religion (I 3 106–13), has just left the stage to vicious Christian abuse. Shylock's daughter Jessica and her husband Lorenzo begin the scene by saying that the night reminds them of many other famous love affairs: Troilus and Cressida, Dido and Aeneas, Medea and Jason – all of which, though they don't mention it, ended disastrously. A large part of the scene (V 1 142–270) is taken up with Portia and Nerissa berating their husbands for giving away their rings; they suggest that it was a kind of symbolic giving of their own wives to other 'men' (258–65) (see below). Though Nerissa promises faithfulness (282–3), Portia does not address her husband with real affection at the end. And it is Portia who remains in charge, inviting all the others to leave the stage. It can be argued that this is a play that ends with a woman very much empowered, while the men have been embarrassed and outwitted.

Karen Newman (1987) has argued that the exchange of goods (including women) between men characterises the play's action. In patriarchal society men have rights over women that are not reciprocated. In the world of the play, Portia's father has the right to choose her husband; the women, however, cannot propose to the men. In fact, Newman argues, anthropologists have noted that men establish their relationships and their pecking order by the granting of gifts. But, Newman says, in this play Portia's rhetoric makes it clear that *she* is making a gift of herself to Bassanio – one which *she* can withdraw. When Bassanio chooses the right casket and claims her as his wife, she talks of herself impersonally, in the passive voice (III 2 166–7), acknowledging herself as a property which at a particular moment is 'converted' to another's legal possession:

Portia Happiest of all, is that her gentle spirit
    Commits itself to yours to be directed,
    As from her lord, her governor, her king.   165
    Myself, and what is mine, to you and yours
    Is now converted.

                                (III 2 163–7)

This material transaction is not represented as 'naturally' binding, however: it may be undone again. Its material and arbitrary nature is symbolised by a token, her ring, the significance of which can change just as any representational token, be it a word or a picture or a coin, may have its reference altered. You own me now, she says; but lose my ring and you lose me.

Portia This house, these servants, and this same myself   170
Are yours – my lord's! – I give them with this ring,
Which when you part from, lose, or give away,
Let it presage* the ruin of your love,
And be my vantage* to exclaim* on you.

(III 2 170–4)

* [173] *presage* foretell [174] *vantage* opportunity; *exclaim on* denounce

Bassanio's response to such a bold assertion, so untypical of a woman's love-pledge in romantic comedy, is to liken the confusion in his head to the experience of one who has just heard a 'beloved prince' (179) speak. He acknowledges that she has made him a gift of herself and her wealth, which is so great that he is effectively in her power (she seems like *his* lord) because he can never repay it (Newman 1987: 124–5). Maybe it is her wealth, vastly superior to his own, that gives her the right to assign meaning to the ring – now and in the future – if he betrays her love. There is, however, another source of power in the text.

Once Bassanio has given the ring to a woman dressed as a man, it ceases to be the token of the husband's possession of the wife and instead becomes associated with an unruly woman who wears men's clothes. Cross-dressing was a subversive breaking of the rules. Fashionable, or adventurous, poor, young women who did it in Shakespeare's time, found it both empowering and sexually liberating – which made it all the more condemned by moralists. Some were pilloried or whipped for it (Orgel 1996a: 119; see also Howard 1994: 96). (It is interesting to note that men taking part in acts of violence against their employers or lords would sometimes adopt female dress. Cross-dressing was a mark of subversion. [Howard 1994: 105]). Portia also triumphs in the male profession of lawyer – a profession founded on the very qualities of reason and skill at public speaking that women were supposed to lack. Bassanio thinks he is engaging in a bond with another man, but Portia's identity, as both woman and man, as both his 'prince' and yet his possession, changes the meaning of the ring as a token. The ring comes to mean female self-expression, female sexuality (V 1 307), changeability and unruliness. The symbol of male possession of women is transformed into a symbol of women slipping out of male power. Portia's successful refusal to be bound by the rigid category of femaleness exposes the truth that women are more than commodities to be exchanged.

It is characteristic that the means by which Portia defeats Shylock is the riddle, or quibble. Shylock can have his pound of flesh only if he doesn't shed a drop of Antonio's blood (IV 1 305–12). The same kind of riddling wordplay is used by Portia and Nerissa to baffle their husbands in the final scene, when they assert that they have slept with the lawyers to whom the rings were given (V 1 258–62). To understand the riddle is to grasp that women can be taken for men. If women can thus escape their 'nature', they can escape the definitions and restrictions which men and their language place upon them.

Some critics have felt that Portia surrenders to her husband's power at the end of the play. That this is highly debatable, even on the surface of the text, I have argued above. In fact she can be seen to become a person who has escaped male control through her slippery and riddling disguise and language. 'Unruly' women who can be taken for men don't ever actually become men: they're neither men nor women, but both at the same time. They become something that slips out of the control of male language and control, like the ring that no longer fits the category of symbol which it was assumed to have done when first given. Because a riddling language can't be pinned down, nor its implications refuted, it is a challenge to those who seek to exert power. As Catherine Belsey puts it:

> Riddles demonstrate that meaning is neither single nor transparent, that words can be used to conceal it. They show that language itself seduces and betrays those who believe themselves to be in command of it …

> (Belsey 1991: 144)

In the final scene Portia and Nerissa, like the audience, know the answers to their riddles. But there is another meaning which is at work here once this language gets to be spoken. The riddle asserts a kind of equality between men and women. Portia's teasing of Bassanio in the fifth act (for example V 1 224–34), like the sexual pun of the last line of the play, asserts the difference between men and women (or does it?). But the riddles suggest that the women are *both* the 'other' that inspires desire in the men *and* the equal of the men – in as much as they were treated as men by the men. As Portia says: 'If you had known … / … half her worthiness that gave the ring' (V 1 199–200) – 'The lawyer Balthazar was your equal, at least because he saved Antonio and you'. Women are very different from men but actually the same. Perhaps this ending hints at a utopian sort of marriage, when husband and wife treat each other as equals. At that historical moment of Puritan ascendancy, writes Belsey, 'the meaning of marriage is unstable, contested, and open to radical reconstruction' (1991: 149). Could a woman be the sort of friend (/lover?) to a man that Antonio was to Bassanio? That is the possibility posed by the riddle at this moment.

I have focused here on two feminist critics' readings of the play. It is interesting to note that the same arguments about the need for equality of treatment between men and women could be applied to the even more obvious issue of anti-semitism, as it is displayed by many of the Christians in the play. Shylock famously asserts his own right to equal treatment, after all: 'Hath not a Jew eyes? Hath not a Jew hands, organs, dimensions, senses, affections, passions … ' (III 1 59–73). Because the two feminist readings focus on questions of sexual equality, they are clearly *partial* readings of the play. It is however, in the nature of Shakespeare's plays that the very richness of the material often makes it hard to provide in a critical reading the means with which to comprehensively discuss a whole play.

Katherina is 'tamed', but perhaps this 'taming' exposes the injustice of the social system that regards women as objects of exchange; Hermia's and Helena's experience in the wood, on the other hand, may be seen to demonstrate the complex system of ideas which keeps social inequality in place. Portia concludes her play, however, with a demonstration that women can and should be the social equals of men.

Summary

- In comedy, young people, and women in particular, are commonly seeking union with a lover, often against the wishes of their fathers. In the end they do marry those they sought.

- Given that Shakespeare was writing in a very male-dominated society, some critics read these plays as a kind of playful rebellion in sexual matters by young people against the authority of parents. That rebellion is, however, always absorbed by those in authority. At the end passionate love is transformed into safe, socially sanctioned, marriage.

- Other critics argue that although a kind of social order is imposed by the event of marriage at the end, the subversive comic energy of the 'rebellion' is such that it demonstrates that a more equal kind of relationship between men and women is possible, and indeed desirable.

- How could you apply these ideas to the female characters who marry in *Much Ado About Nothing* and *As You Like It*? Are they applicable at all to, say, Viola in *Twelfth Night*, or Luciana in *The Comedy of Errors*?

Further reading

A good place to start is Ryan (1989), which gives a reading of the comedies that is both accessible and radical. There's a good introduction and a useful collection of essays in Waller (1991). Davies (1995) is both readable and well written, and clarifies some complex matters of theory. The Macmillan New Casebooks, edited by Dutton (1996) and Coyle (1998), are valuable resources for the student, particularly in their summaries of a wide range of important criticism.

Chapter 7

Understanding history

King Richard II,
King Henry IV Part I
and King Henry V

During the early part of Shakespeare's career – roughly until about 1600 – many plays about English history in the fourteenth and fifteenth centuries were being staged. Some were popular romps, mixing comic working-class characters with idealised portraits of jovial monarchs who were at one with their subjects. Shakespeare's plays were, however, much more closely based than were these popular offerings on serious records like the Tudor chronicles. Even so, they did not deal solely with kings, queens and lords. They generally gave some sort of portrait of the nation as a whole, with peasants, workers and soldiers having roles to play – often in a comic sub-plot of some sort.

It was during this period that the idea of England as a *nation* was beginning to emerge. The history books and the plays themselves were part of a process by which people came to see themselves as belonging first and foremost to 'England' rather than to family, household, village community or lord's retinue.

When discussing Shakespeare's history plays, scholars generally talk about two *tetralogies* (a tetralogy is a group of four works). The plays that comprise the first tetralogy would have been written in the earlier years of his career; they tell the stories of the civil wars between the two noble houses of York and Lancaster in the mid-fifteenth century, known as the Wars of the Roses. The first tetralogy comprises the three *Parts* of *King Henry VI* and *King Richard III*. The second tetralogy, which is the concern of this chapter, comprises *King Richard II*, *King Henry IV Part I*, *King Henry IV Part II* and *King Henry V*. The first two and the last of these plays are dealt with in this chapter, these being plays commonly studied at school, college and university. The three plays cover a period of roughly twenty-five years, from the late 1390s through to Henry V's peace treaty with France in 1420.

Richard II (reigned 1377–99) was a weak and vain king, deposed (removed from the throne) by his cousin Henry Bolingbroke, Duke of Lancaster, who became King Henry IV. Once in power Henry fell out with the noblemen who had helped to put him on the throne, and his reign (1399–1413) was marked by civil war and factional fighting. The two parts of *King Henry IV* tell the story of those years. Henry V (reigned 1413–22), Bolingbroke's son, achieved some measure of national stability, uniting the English armies to wage a war against France that culminated, in 1415 at the Battle of Agincourt, in an unlikely English victory against great odds. In so doing, Henry V became a national hero. After his death in 1422, at the age of 35, the peace with France broke down as the French fought to reconquer territory possessed by the English king. England meanwhile was plunged into a long and bloody civil war as two aristocratic factions sought control of a weakened throne.

Of our more recent history, there are certain periods that, for different reasons, have been of particular interest to novelists, dramatists, script-writers and even historians. The Second World War and Victorian England, for example, seem more popular than, say, the First World War or the Restoration period. In the

England of the 1590s, it was the period covering the deposition of Richard II and the wars which followed that interested people greatly. The reasons for this particular interest in Shakespeare's time are discussed next.

History and history

We are constantly aware that the society in which people lived centuries' ago was very different from our own society, today. Similarly, we expect that society in a couple of hundred years' time will not much resemble the one we know today. But throughout the medieval period people wouldn't have though along such lines. In a period when the population was growing very slowly – or, in some areas, even declining – and technological progress was minimal, the past was thought to have been very similar to the present. The future was expected to be little different.

The economy was based on agriculture, and at not much more than a *subsistence* level. This term means that people grew what they needed and didn't usually work to produce a surplus with which to trade. Society was organised in a rigid hierarchy. It was very difficult in practice (and, in theory, impossible) to rise above the class or 'estate' into which you were born. Indeed, it was quite rare to leave the village where you were born. Society was held together by bonds of loyalty (*fealty*) between individuals. The lords owed loyalty to the king, and were in turn owed allegiance by their knights. The knights were supported by their yeomen, who were the lords of the peasants. People's identities were defined largely by these bonds of loyalty, rather than by their occupation, gender, political feelings and aspirations. The theory, as it applied to the ordinary people (the 'peasantry'), was that the lord of your locality would protect you, and grant you the right to hold land, and in return you would serve as a soldier in his army. Notice that women, who weren't soldiers, could fit into this picture only as the possessions of the men. The lords ruled by birth, but their right to rule had been originally established by their ancestors' prowess as mounted warriors. Consequently the values of the warrior were taken very seriously by the rulers. This society valued loyalty to the lord's family as a central virtue; bravery and skill in battle were similarly important. To simplify a little, these two values together became generally known as 'chivalry'. Chivalric loyalty towards the king often came into conflict with loyalty to the family and one's own honour. These conflicting loyalties contributed significantly to the constant state of war there seems to have been between the medieval barons. This system, known as 'feudalism', had long seemed unchangeable; but by the fourteenth century it was already in transition.

The universal Catholic Church (see Box 11, p. 155) was organised in a hierarchy parallel to the social, and belief in its authority in all matters of religion was widespread. Culture tended to be based around the calendar and ritual of Catholicism.

By 1600, however, the people could recognise that feudalism was clearly past; but they missed it. They were uncertain about the new society which had evolved from it: 'modernity' or 'capitalism'. There is much debate about how and when the transition began, but by Shakespeare's time social mobility – the movement of individuals from humble status to power and rank – was an obvious fact. Merchants and industrialists were already building up wealth, power and influence that were not based on the possession of land. The absolutist Tudor monarchy, with its centralising tendencies, succeeded in doing away with the private armies of individual lords and in concentrating taxation and legal powers in a government bureaucracy based in London. In other words, kings no longer ruled with the co-operation of their armed fellow-lords, but claimed the God-given right to rule exactly as they pleased. They relied on the law and an emerging civil service to see that their will was carried out all over the country. The capital grew very rapidly into a recognisably modern city, based on trade and commerce, where rich and poor existed side-by-side. Professional infantryman – pikemen and musketeers in combination – made the heavily armoured noble knight obsolete on the battlefield. Explorers opened up a world way beyond the traditional maps of Greek and Roman writers

Box 11: Religion

In 1600, religion continued to provide the focus in which people saw the world. The two poles of belief were Catholicism and Protestantism.

Roman Catholicism was officially banished from England by Henry VIII's Reformation in the 1530s, only to be restored when Mary took the throne (1553–58) and then banished again under her sister Elizabeth's rule (1558–1603). English monarchs became Supreme Head of the Church of England, the state-run Protestant Church.

The Catholic faith had dominated western Europe since the time of the Roman Empire. Authority and obedience were the key ideas, reflected by the hierarchy of deacons and priests, bishops and archbishops, and the cardinals who reported to the Pope. The Church had the ultimate right to interpret scripture and throughout the Middle Ages most believers had no access to the bible, which anyway was available only in Latin. Its stories were revealed, but the sacred text was never read to Catholic congregations in their own language. The Mass was conducted behind a perforated screen, in Latin, with the celebrant priests facing away from the congregation. At the moment when they believed that the bread and wine *became* Christ's body and blood, the church's bells would ring and the congregation would kneel down in prayer. Salvation was offered to all who took the sacraments of baptism, confirmation, marriage, confession, communion and the last rites, conferred only by priests. All people were born in a state of sin, but baptism took that sin away. After that, offences could be forgiven through confession, provided that the sinner was truly sorry. 'Good works' were also required. The Church became closely linked to mystery, magic and ritual.

By the late Middle Ages many felt that its accumulated power and wealth had corrupted the hierarchy of the Church. The incumbent Pope was a major prince; he had his own army, and often sired children. Monasteries were seen as places of ease rather than havens devoted to the contemplative life. All this had been true for some time, but in the fourteenth century a new way of thinking was beginning to make its mark. A new class of essentially secular-minded intellectuals celebrated the application of reason rather than simple obedience to authority. One of their key ideas was that through careful reading of Greek and Roman texts they could recover the understanding of the world which, they thought, made ancient times superior to their own. It soon became apparent that critical reasoning should be applied to the bible itself. And if reading the bible was the route to Christian knowledge and virtue, then it should be made available in the languages people actually spoke. In these ideas was the beginning of the Protestant Reformation.

Protestantism is usually traced back to the teachings of the German monk Martin Luther, in the early sixteenth century, although similar ideas had been circulating for roughly 200 years. Luther taught that the individual had a personal relationship with God and found his or her own truth through close study of the bible, without priestly intervention. Furthermore, you could go to heaven 'through faith alone', or simply by believing that you were saved. You didn't need any sacraments, and 'good works' were a sign of being saved, rather than the means of achieving it.

By stressing the importance of revelations of divine truth to individuals, Protestantism fostered the splitting of the Church into different sects, each convinced of the authenticity of its own version of Christianity's message. In a country with one state-established Church, headed by the monarch, such diversity could not be tolerated. The more 'extreme' of these sects would not tolerate any ministers at all and it was a short step from denying religious authority to denying royal authority. The Church of England kept its hierarchy of priests and bishops and defended its position.

The most influential form of Protestantism in England in 1600 was Calvinism, named after Jean Calvin, who set had up a model Protestant community in the Swiss city of Geneva. While Mary, a Catholic, ruled England, leading religious opponents of Protestantism were under threat of imprisonment and execution. Many Protestant clergymen fled to Geneva. There they produced the Geneva translation of the bible into English, which was the version Shakespeare used. When these Protestants returned at Elizabeth's accession they were very influential in the settlement which brought limited religious toleraance to England (although this did not extend to Catholics).

A key to Calvinism is the doctrine of predestination. If God is all-knowing and all-powerful, he must know from the beginning of time who will go to heaven and who to hell. Our fate is already decided and cannot be changed. If we look into our souls and find a calm confidence in our own salvation, then we are members of God's 'elect'. If we find there doubt, then we are probably 'reprobate' and destined for damnation. Good deeds will not save the damned, but the most apparently wicked individual could through divine grace become one of the saved.

The terrors and contradictions of such a belief system were such that by the 1620s predestination was giving way to the idea of free will. However, at the time Shakespeare was writing Calvinism was the official position of a great number of people in London. As many Protestants held that wealth and power on earth were signs of God's favour and proof of election, Calvinism proved attractive to the merchant class. Poverty, by the same token, could be proof of reprobation.

Because the Calvinists and other serious Protestants regarded their teachings as a pure version of the original form of Christianity, they came to be known as *Puritans*. Today the word is associated with a disapproval of sex, drinking and taking pleasure in general. This was not the attitude of all Calvinists, but some did regard this life solely as a place of contemplation of the joys to come. It was a mark of the elect not to value the pleasures of the flesh. Many traditional festivities that involved drinking, dance, laughter, and indeed fornication, were regarded as expressions of superstition or else as 'Popish', and the Puritans sought to stamp out such diversions. The theatre became a target, and some London preachers regularly denounced the playhouses in their public sermons. The playwrights retaliated by satirising Puritans as hypocrites, like Angelo in *Measure for Measure* and Malvolio in *Twelfth Night*.

Between leaving Warwickshire and arriving in London, Shakespeare may have been in the service of a Roman Catholic family in Lancashire, completing his education – or perhaps teaching (Honan 1998: 60–5). Evidence existed that his father was a Catholic, and gossip soon after Shakespeare's death asserted that he 'died a Papist' (Williams 1933: 232). We cannot know what Shakespeare actually 'believed'. Perhaps he didn't know himself. In such a time of changing beliefs, many held a mixture of Catholic and Protestant beliefs. Still, the endings of *The Winter's Tale* and *The Tempest* might be seen to reflect a particularly Catholic attitude towards the Christian doctrine of sincere repentance.

and exposed Europe to new continents and new ways of living. The universal authority of the Catholic Church was challenged by Protestantism (see opposite page). Powerful nation-states arose and fought wars for overtly religious and economic reasons, not just for the honour and rights of the monarch. That monarch, however, increasingly aimed at absolute power in the state and argued for his or her 'divine right' to rule as God's representative on earth.

In a world of rapid social and technological change, early modern writers tended to look back at an idealised version of the Middle Ages in which everyone knew their place and the future was secure and certain. Those same men of influence whose wealth and power depended on the destruction of feudalism looked back on it with nostalgia, insecure as they felt in the world of the emerging modern, market-based, capital-led economy. This is a world where a speculator can be rich today and ruined tomorrow, and profit is regarded as more important than personal loyalty. To many, the reign of King Richard II seemed to have been the last time when the old world-order was completely present.

There was no doubt that Richard's was a true claim to the throne by descent from the great warrior-king Edward III. When Henry Bolingbroke usurped the throne, he introduced kingship based on political effectiveness rather than birth, even if not explicitly. Furthermore, as Queen Elizabeth grew older and the question of who would succeed her grew more vexed, many feared the arrival of a cunning and unprincipled Bolingbroke-like figure – perhaps the Earl of Essex – who would take advantage of her physical infirmity and seize power. A supporter of the Earl of Essex published a history of the reign of King Henry IV only to have it banned by Elizabeth's government. 'I am Richard II, know ye not that?' she is believed to have once exclaimed. Like the idealised Richard, Elizabeth encouraged her people to see her reign as a golden age of stability and national glory. She had always known her weakness as a woman in a turbulent political situation otherwise dominated by men. She feared threats from all quarters, but particularly from men of political and military cunning.

Shakespeare was, it appears, acutely aware that the world he described in his history plays was one that had passed away; yet he seems sometimes to write as if his characters were actually living in the England of the 1590s not the 1390s. The plays contain many anachronisms (references to items that were not available in the time the play was supposed to be set). Douglas has a pistol (*King Henry the IV Part I* II 4 345–6), even though pistols hadn't been invented in Henry IV's day; Falstaff drinks 'sack', a sweet wine popular in the 1590s but unknown in England 200 years' earlier. Falstaff's soldiers at the Battle of Shrewsbury are decimated by musketfire (V 3 29–39), not the arrows and crossbow bolts of the actual battle. The presence of anachronism is not, as some early critics thought, explained by supposing Shakespeare to have been ignorant. In fact these anachronisms work to ensure we have a kind of double perspective on the action. We're reminded that we are watching a play whose ideas and concerns are relevant to the present day, yet they also depict a past which has really gone, and can be reproduced only by representing it as a product today, upon the stage. That this is a retrospective view on the world from the perspective of the 1590s and not a timeless commentary on human affairs is constantly signalled by the contemporary language of the working-class characters and the up-to-date weapons, artefacts and information which litter the plays (Rackin 1990: 95).

Medieval paintings in lavishly illustrated ('illumined') books will often show historically successive events on one page as if they were happening simultaneously, with the same characters repeated next to one another. This is because, to the medieval mind, all events seem to happen at once as far as God is concerned; God sees everything from the perspective of eternity. The ways of the past are the ways of now. Society and history are static. When we see a Shakespeare history play, however, we are made aware that the text self-consciously demonstrates an awareness that these events are over and cannot come back again – except in the counterfeit form of today's actors impersonating figures of the past. A *secular* (i.e. non-religious) modern idea of time is emerging in these plays, moving forward from the past to the future in a progressive way: tomorrow will be different from today; the world can be changed. When we watch a history play in the theatre today, of course, we need to add a further perspective – that of the contemporary present! Any reading or interpretation of these plays will have to operate at these different levels.

King Richard II is the play which is most explicit in its demonstration that feudalism has passed away. Indeed, the drama seems to concentrate very carefully on the internal forces which destroyed it. It begins with a ritual of justice long out-dated by the time Shakespeare was writing: trial by combat. In the fourteenth century a man accused of treason could prove his innocence by challenging his accuser to ritual combat. God, in the form of 'divine providence', it was believed, would ensure that justice was done (see pp. 187f.). Henry Bolingbroke, at this time Duke of Hereford, has accused Thomas Mowbray, Duke of Norfolk, of treason (plotting against the king) and with involvement in the murder of the Duke of Gloucester, who was uncle to both the king and Bolingbroke. He accuses him also of embezzling the king's money (I 1 87–100).

That we are in a distant world where feudalism applies is apparent even in the play's opening lines; and yet there is still a subtle emphasis on the fact that Shakespeare's audience were seeing the action from a time in the future:

King Richard Old John of Gaunt, time-honoured Lancaster,
  Hast thou, according to thy oath and band,*
  Brought hither Henry Herford thy bold son,
  Here to make good the boist'rous late appeal,*
  Which then our leisure* would not let us hear,   5
  Against the Duke of Norfolk, Thomas Mowbray?

Gaunt I have, my liege.*

(I 1 1–7)

* [2] *band* duty owing to your superior [4] *make good the boist'rous late appeal* justify the shocking recent accusation [5] *leisure* or, rather, the lack of it [7] *liege* the term used to address the superior to whom you owe feudal loyalty

This is an old-fashioned formal language, with its explicit emphasis on the bonds of loyalty which held feudal society together. Respect for the chivalric virtue of bravery is made apparent by the king calling Henry Hereford 'bold' (line 3), a word which by Shakespeare's day had begun to acquire some of the connotations of rudeness and rashness which it has today. In the fourteenth century 'bold' was a term simply of praise. But notice also that John of Gaunt, a hero of English history for his valour and virtue, is both 'old' and 'time-honoured' (line 1). 'Old' in the sense of 'aged' he literally is; and he is 'time-honoured' in the sense that he is respected for his acquired wisdom. But he is old also in as much as he is an historical character, and 'time-honoured' because future generations still hold him in esteem. The double-time perspective of the text is immediately made apparent.

The contradictions within feudalism and the new forces which will destroy it are similarly made quickly apparent. Each participant in this ritual combat prefaces his challenge by protesting loyalty to the king (I 1 20–4, 31–2, 54); but it soon becomes clear that the sense of personal honour and loyalty of each to his family is more important still. After long speeches full of the archaic (old-fashioned) terms and concerns of chivalry, the king asks them both to forgive and forget in a 'modern' joky sort of speech which draws on the distinctly unknightly trade of surgery. Here Mowbray is admitting that he once set an ambush for Bolingbroke:

Mowbray But ere* I last received the sacrament*
    I did confess it, and exactly begg'd   140
    Your Grace's pardon, and I hope I had it.
    This is my fault. As for the rest appeal'd,*
    It issues from the rancour of a villain,
    A recreant* and most degenerate* traitor,
    Which in myself I boldly will defend,   145
    And interchangeably* hurl down my gage*
    Upon this overweening* traitor's foot,
    To prove myself a loyal gentleman
    Even in the best blood chamber'd in his bosom,
    In haste whereof, most heartily I pray   150
    Your Highness to assign our trial day.
King Richard Wrath-kindled* gentlemen, be rul'd by me,
    Let's purge this choler without letting blood.*
    This we prescribe, though no physician;*
    Deep malice makes too deep incision.   155
    Forget, forgive, conclude and be agreed,
    Our doctors say this is no month to bleed.

                                   (I 1 139–57)

* [139] *ere* before; *sacrament* the Catholic rite of the Mass. This, like the mention of confession (1 140) is a reminder that the play is set before the Reformation of the 1530s that officially abolished Catholic practices [142] *appeal'd* charged against me [144] *recreant* faithless – by Shakespeare's time, already an archaic term, but there were many such old words to do with loyalty and disloyalty; *degenerate* having declined from a once noble family – a typically feudal insult [146] *interchangeably* in turn; *throw down my gage* hurl my glove down, the traditional chivalric gesture of challenge [147] *overweening* impertinent, going dangerously beyond the bounds of what a subject owes a king [152] *wrath-kindled* literally, set ablaze by anger [153] *purge this choler without letting blood* it was believed that an angry disposition or fit was caused by an excess of a 'humour', or fluid, called 'choler'. The natural balance of one's body and disposition could be recreated by bleeding – letting blood and draining off some of this excess fluid [154] *physician* doctor

Richard doesn't seem to realise that the feudal notion of 'fealty' is a two-way thing. He has to respect *their* honours, not cast them aside so lightly. His attitude does not prove persuasive. They will not obey his command, so he gives in to them and ordains their trial day at Coventry.

In I 3 there is a grand heraldic spectacle, and plenty more archaic feudal language and ritual. But just as they are about to fight, both on-stage and off-stage audiences are denied that dramatic spectacle by Richard intervening to prevent the combat. He sentences both challengers to exile: Mowbray for life; Bolingbroke for ten years, though this is immediately commuted to six – almost, it seems, at the king's whim. Soon after, Bolingbroke's father, Gaunt, dies, and Richard acts in the most unfeudal and tyrannical way: he seizes all of Gaunt's possessions in order to finance his Irish war, rather than let them be inherited by Bolingbroke.

In this he behaves like a divine-right monarch rather than a feudal lord. The 'absolutist' monarch of Shakespeare's day and later recognised no controls on his power from anyone else in the country, because he saw his authority coming directly from God ('divine right') and therefore not to be opposed. Richard's behaviour here exposes the contradictions within the feudal system and lays the foundations of the process which will destroy both himself and the feudal kingship itself.

In theory a feudal king was both God's anointed representative on earth – who must therefore be obeyed in all points – *and* himself a warrior-lord who must respect the honour of the other warrior-lords of the kingdom. Richard's motive for depriving Bolingbroke of his incomes and titles is to provide resources for his own personal war, as Lord of England, against Ireland. He thinks he is behaving in a way appropriate to his honour and position, but a feudal monarch cannot actually behave like an absolutist monarch of Renaissance times, demanding absolute obedience from all. After all, as Richard's uncle, the Duke of York, points out to him, it is only the principle of inheritance through birth which gives him his right to the throne:

York Take Herford's rights away, and take from Time   195
     His charters and his customary rights;
     Let not tomorrow then ensue today;
     Be not thyself; for how art thou a king
     But by fair sequence and succession?

                                        (II 1 195–9)

York thinks that the right of succession from father to son is so central to nature itself that Time itself cannot move from tomorrow to today without it. But it isn't *natural*; and, once it has been violated, that violation both absolves everyone of their duty of allegiance to Richard as hereditary monarch and reveals the true principle that justifies the possession of absolute power: force.

Richard believes that power, both natural and supernatural, resides within himself simply because he is the king:

King Richard Not all the water in the rough rude sea

> Can wash the balm* off from an anointed king;   55
> The breath of worldly men cannot depose
> The deputy elected by the Lord;
> For every man which Bolingbroke hath pressed
> To lift shrewd steel* against our golden crown,
> God for his Richard hath in heavenly pay   60
> A glorious angel: then if angels fight,
> Weak men must fall, for heaven still guards the right.

(III 2 54–62)

* [55] *balm* the sacred ointment used in the coronation ritual
[59] *shrewd steel* a dangerous sword

He soon discovers that this a fantasy. Power resides in the material, in troops and weapons. The ceremonies and rituals are not the granters of power, but merely its markers. A king is really no more than a man (see III 2 173–7).

The early modern notion of absolute monarchy can be seen, then, in this play as emerging out of feudalism – and destroying it. Richard may be defeated, but the principle of absolute monarchy – which was always one of the forces threatening to destroy feudal society – is seen being unleashed by him. His successors waged constant civil war to secure the final victory of that principle over the feudal notion of mutual loyalty owed between king and lords. It is only at the end of the Wars of the Roses that the first Tudor monarch, Henry VII, establishes peace through absolute monarchy. *King Richard II* dramatises the death of feudalism as its internal contradictions burst it open. At this moment we see the emergence of the early modern principle of absolute monarchy.

The way in which money operates to destroy feudalism is clear, too. In medieval society loyalty between social unequals is the glue which holds society together; Richard replaces it with a modern financial relationship between king and subjects. Richard sells to individuals the rights of tax-gathering in his kingdom in order to finance his wars, rather than rely on the military support of his own nobles. In this way he imposes on his problem the solutions of the free market, rather than co-operate in the traditional way with those warrior–lords whose chivalric gallantry in battle had always secured the sacred fame and glory of Old England – or so the dying John of Gaunt says:

Gaunt This blessed plot, this earth, this realm, this England, 50
This nurse, this teeming womb of royal kings,
Fear'd by their breed,* and famous by their birth,
Renowned for their deeds as far from home,
For Christian service and true chivalry,
As is the sepulchre* in stubborn Jewry*   55
Of the world's ransom, blessed Mary's son;*
This land of such dear souls, this dear dear land,
Dear for her reputation through the world,
Is now leas'd out – I die pronouncing it –
Like to a tenement* or pelting* farm.   60
England, bound in with the triumphant sea,
Whose rocky shore beats back the envious siege
Of wat'ry Neptune, is now bound in with shame,
With inky blots and rotten parchment bonds;*
That England, that was wont to conquer others,   65
Hath made a shameful conquest of itself.

(II 1 50–66)

* [52] *Feared by their breed* because of their war-like qualities over the generations [55] *sepulchre* the tomb of Jesus; *Jewry* Palestine [56] *blessed Mary's son* notice again explicitly Catholic and pre-Reformation devotion to the Virgin Mary [60] *tenement* farm let to a tenant [60] *pelting* petty, paltry [64] *bonds* legal documents

Both the breeding and the acts of violence of the knights and kings of England had made it a country as famous as the very tomb in which Jesus was laid, and for which the crusaders fought. Even nature itself, in the form of the sea-god Neptune, cannot capture this stronghold of valour. Yet this king has sold the country for money, a filthy ('inky' and 'rotten') paper transaction that has abolished the sacred glory of yesteryear. Money can do this alone; the old, chivalric England is gone because it is no match for the values of the marketplace.

In the second half of the play chivalry and feudal loyalty are actually parodied – copied in a mocking way. As the old system is breaking down, what was once admirable now seems absurd. The noble and heraldic challenges to combat we saw delivered by Bolingbroke and Mowbray in the first scene, with their ritual throwing down of gloves ('gages') in an act of challenge, are turned into an absurd spectacle in Act IV Scene 1 (Rackin 1990: 132). In the space of fifty lines (IV 1 25–76), Aumerle, Fitzwater, Percy, Surrey and 'Another Lord' have thrown down their gloves in challenges, one after the other. Bolingbroke is not interested in all this nonsense, and curtly puts them all off until his old opponent is forgiven and returned (IV 1 86–9). In Act V there is a farcical scene where Aumerle, who has been discovered by his father, the Duke of York, to be in possession of a document implicating him in a conspiracy against the king, pleads for forgiveness of Henry Bolingbroke and easily gets it. Aumerle's father – who has just been seen, like some aged buffoon in a comedy, calling for his boots and arguing with his wife – then rushes in. He demands his own son's death. Before King Henry can get much of a word in, however, the Duchess of York enters, and soon she too is on her knees pleading *against* her husband for the king to spare her son. Eventually he convinces them all, but the tone is one not of life-or-death high drama but of domestic comedy. Even treason has become a subject for laughter in the fallen feudal world of Henry's court after Richard's self-induced demise.

History and power

King Henry V believes, or certainly seems to believe, that he is the rightful King of France (II 2 193). The righteousness of his cause both justifies his invasion of France and authorises the death and devastation that will follow. To the medieval mind, Henry's power would seem to flow through this sense of Providence – of God being on Henry's side. He is always keen to stress that he needs God to ensure his success (e.g. I 2 307; II 2 189–90); and when the English forces win so comfortably at Agincourt, it seems that divine intervention really must have played a part. He says of the victory: 'Take it, God,/For it is none but thine!' (IV 3 111–12).

Providence, however, is the necessary *ideological* cover to the actual operation of power in this play, and elsewhere in the histories (by 'ideology', I mean here the widely believed stories propagated by the powerful which justify their exercise of power; see pp. 194f.). Shakespeare makes clear in the writing of these texts that it is not in fact divine approval, gained because of a ruler's essential virtue, that ensures victory in battle. These plays show, first, that royal power is actually not very different, either in content or in execution, from the actions of thieves and fraudsters; and, second, that such power is very often exercised not through wisdom, or valour in battle, but simply through the convincing performances, the rhetoric, of the rulers, who get their way because of their skills as speakers, not as warriors. This idea has something interesting to say about modern politics and the political role of theatre.

Many readers and audience members are puzzled by the character of Ancient Pistol in *King Henry V*. Boastful and cowardly, he speaks a strange language which seems entirely made up of bad blank verse taken from other plays. Yet there is also something vaguely familiar about his grindingly heavy-handed rhetoric.

In the first scene we discover that he has married Mistress Quickly, the landlady of the Eastcheap tavern where he and his companions spend most of their time. His claim to her is not unchallenged, however. Corporal Nym claims that she was previously engaged to *him*. Nym draws his sword on Pistol. Mistress Quickly, the 'hostess', intervenes, but Nym spurns her:

Nym Will you shog* off ? I would have you solus.*   45
Pistol 'Solus', egregious* dog? O viper vile!
   The 'solus' in thy most merveilous* face,
   The 'solus' in thy teeth, and in thy throat,

And in thy hateful lungs, yea, in thy maw,* perdy;*
And which is worse, within thy nasty mouth!   50
I do retort the 'solus' in thy bowels,
For I can take,* and Pistol's cock is up,*
And flashing fire will follow.

(II 1 45–53)

* [45] *shog* move; *solus* alone (Latin) [46] *egregious* remarkable, a word usually used as praise [47] *merveilous*
marvellous: astonishingly ugly [49] *maw* stomach; *perdy* by
God [52] *take* strike; *cock is up* the cock of a pistol was the
hammer holding the flint which, struck against steel,
produced the sparks to fire the gunpowder: he means he's
ready to kill, but no doubt Pistol's *double entendre* here is
deliberate

But on stage only about five minutes previously, King Henry had
been engaged in a dispute over France – often referred to as
female in the text (e.g. I 2 227) – and had responded to a rude
challenge in a passage of strikingly heavy repetition and obscene
innuendo. The dauphin, the King of France's son, has sent Henry
some tennis-balls to play with, because, he says, they're more the
kind of thing which Henry is fit to be concerned with than are the
affairs of state. King Henry responds to the French ambassador:

King Henry And tell the pleasant prince this mock of his
    Hath turned his balls to gun-stones,* and his soul
    Shall stand sore-charged for the wasteful vengeance
    That shall fly with them; for many a thousand widows
    Shall this his mock mock* out of their dear husbands;   285
    Mock mothers from their sons, mock castles down;
    And some are yet ungotten* and unborn
    That shall have cause to curse the Dauphin's scorn.

(I 2 281–8)

* [282] *turned his balls to gun-stones* converted his tennis-balls

to bullets, but there is the innuendo that he'll shoot him in the
testicles [285] *mock* mock here means both to laugh at and to
cheat [someone of] [287] *ungotten* unconceived

The parallels between Henry and Pistol are picked up in other
places, too. The boy says of Pistol that he 'hath a killing tongue
and a quiet sword' (III 1 34). Henry captures the port-town of
Harfleur, not by assaulting it but by promising terrible rape and
slaughter if the French governor does not surrender the town (III
3 1–43). It turns out to be a good thing that he did surrender, for
Henry's army was in fact in no condition to make the assault (III
1 55–6) (see pp. 174f.). In the same way Pistol captures the French
soldier in Act IV Scene 4 because of his ferocious *threats* and
brutal *manner*. Pistol is no real threat to anyone, of course. He
won't charge into the breach at Harfleur – all he can do is sing a
song about the glory of war (III 2 8–11). (But maybe war is
glorious *only* in song. Those who do charge into the breach
clearly don't come out again.) Pistol leaves London for France
with these words:

Pistol Let us to France, like horse-leeches my boys,
  To suck, to suck, the very blood to suck!

                                                    (II 3 55–6)

A few minutes later the King of France uses the same word to
describe Henry, even if he is using a different metaphor:

French King For England* his approaches makes as fierce
  As waters to the sucking of a gulf.*

                                                    (III 4 9–10)

    * [9] *England* the King of England [10] *gulf* a whirlpool

Why these connections? Pistol is a thief. He is going to France
to make what personal profit he can (II 1 111–12). He is able to
get his way – up to a point – by his boastful language. At first he

impresses both Fluellen (III 6 12–16) and Henry (IV 1 62); but he remains a braggart and a thief. The question which seems to arise from the comparison is this. Henry is an English king who has a dubious claim to France that he can enforce only by violence, because its rulers and people don't want him. How is he different from a thief like Pistol? Henry's war is a war fought for personal glory: it's a war of aggression, not a war of national defence. He's seeking to pocket up what isn't his. In addition, the very theatricality of Pistol's language draws attention to the way Henry uses rhetoric so effectively to get what he wants: and Henry is a king as performer (see below).

The same use of the subplot to emphasise this notion of rulers being morally comparable to criminals is built into the early structure of *King Henry IV Part I*. In Act II Scene 2 Falstaff and his gang rob some innocent pilgrims on their way to Canterbury. No sooner have they seized their booty but they are robbed in turn by the disguised Prince Hal and his friend Poins. The point of the jest is to see what preposterous lies Falstaff will tell about the incident that night in the tavern: as Hal expected, Falstaff extolls his own bravery when in fact he ignominiously ran away (see pp. 73f.). In the previous scene, however, we had seen Worcester and Northumberland reveal their plot to depose the usurper Henry IV from the throne – the very throne which they had helped him seize in *King Richard II*. The same narrative motif, of thieves being robbed by thieves, recurs here first as serious action, then as comedy. But the comic repetition undercuts and de-heroicises the noble characters in their original playing of the actions.

Now one could read this scene in a very conservative way. I have a 30-year-old school edition of this play, the editor of which states with full confidence that '[Shakespeare] wrote to demonstrate that rebellion and usurpation were sinful in the sight of God and unmitigated disasters to the countries that experienced them' (Reese 1965: 5). You could argue that the montage effect here reveals the moral turpitude of the usurper Bolingbroke: authority must never be resisted, even when it's dangerous or tyrannical. But one can also read this scene as a dramatic deflation of all the pretensions of monarchs and nobles who steal and murder but dignify their acts by calling them other things. Power in the history plays comes down to one of three things: first, having the military force to take what you want; second, being able to persuade people; or, third, being able to put on a convincing performance which makes effective use of the most powerful beliefs of the time. Talk of 'divine right', 'just claims' and 'providence' mystifies these unattractive alternatives; but the dramatic structures of main plot and sub-plot in these plays hint perceptively at the bald truths of power in medieval and early modern England.

Many writings about politics in Shakespeare's time use theatrical metaphors. It was widely recognised that a monarch's actions and demeanour should be such as to inspire belief and obedience. The monarch's speech and costume must have what writers called 'decorum': appropriateness to the circumstances in which he found himself. This is at the heart of what Machiavelli wrote about politics (see pp. 200f.). Public events – like the entry of King James I into London for the first time as monarch in 1604 – were intricately staged, with painted triumphal arches, specially written poetry and carefully costumed courtiers. King James' court mounted expensive dramatic entertainments – masques – extolling a particular royal virtue or teaching some lesson about loyal obedience. Members of the royal family and the court themselves acted in these plays.

Prince Hal and Henry IV are very aware of the theatrical element of kingship in the world in which they live. They talk openly about the king having to be a performer (actually, of course, *performers* playing kings and princes talking about kings and princes having to be performers). Theatricality was very much at the cultural and political heart of early modern England. Power and the theatre interact closely (Howard 1994: 145).

At the end of the very first scene of *King Henry IV Part I* Prince Hal explains to the audience the nature of his part, his *act*, in this play. He is associating with Falstaff not because he necessarily enjoys it – though his behaviour might well lead one to suspect that this is one of his reasons. Rather, he is making himself look a very unlikely candidate for monarchy, so that when he abandons his old companions he will *appear* to be totally different from people's expectations. He will therefore be all the more admired as a monarch because his virtues will be so unexpected:

Prince Hal So when this loose behaviour I throw off
    And pay the debt I never promised,
    By how much better than my word I am,   210
    By so much shall I falsify men's hopes,
    And like bright metal on a sullen ground
    My reformation, glittering o'er my fault,
    Shall show more goodly and attract more eyes
    Than that which hath no foil* to set it off.   215
    I'll so offend, to make offence a skill,
    Redeeming time when men think least I will. (*Exit*)

                             (I 2 208–17)

    * [215] *foil* the metal 'housing' of contrasting colour to that of the jewel which it holds. Hal means that if he had always been well behaved there would be nothing with which people could compare his conduct when he became king. As it is, the future contrast with his present behaviour will make him look all the more impressive when he changes his lifestyle

It is a common dramatic technique to satisfy an audience by making a morally wayward character suddenly turn out to be the hero we all hoped he would be. Here this dramatic technique is used for a blatantly political end. Now you may find this an example of at worst duplicity, and at best deviousness, but kings and politicians in general have a public identity which is not necessarily the same as their private one. King Henry explains very carefully to his son that it was the *image* he presented to the lords and the people that made him preferred to the vain and foolish Richard, who had allowed his *presence* to become too familiar and common. Consequently people tired of him, as his faults, instead of being concealed, became all too clearly revealed (III 2 39–84).

Hal and Falstaff's acting out of two different versions of this scene in the tavern the night before it actually happens (II 4 374–480) underlines, in the sub-plot, the centrality of ideas of performance in the politics of the play; and the very fact that this satirical improvisation takes place twice, with two different 'non-scripts', indicates the theatre to be not only no respecter of the dignity of monarchs but capable of showing that the world need not be as it is. If monarchs are performers who keep their power by pleasing their audiences, theirs is an act that can always be changed: no unchangeable divine law governs their actions and decisions. If the world as it is is unjust, it really can be changed. The humanity of monarchs beneath the essentially hollow stage conventions and rituals of the institution is also stressed by this focus on kings as performers. As King Henry V Hal learns this all too well (IV 1 238–69). 'Ceremony' makes a man a king, but he is still a man like any other in every other way. Yet the king must still play his part well and establish his unique claim to the role. When Henry IV dresses up several lords in a copy of his armour at the Battle of Shrewsbury (V 3; V 4), to make it appear as if the king is fighting everywhere, it seems as if Henry is cheating. He devalues his own presence, as well as revealing that it doesn't really matter who is king – that as long as the performance is convincing anyone can do it. Hal makes it clear when he confronts Hotspur at the play's climax that only *he* is truly qualified to play the role of Prince of Wales (V 4 63–7).

Hal surpasses his father in theatrical skill. When he invades France to claim the throne of France for himself, his very first objective is the port town of Harfleur. He meets with very little success, however. One of his greatest talents is to clothe his own personal ambition in the mantle of nationalism in his great public speeches, such as the one he makes in order to persuade his men to go 'Once more into the breach, dear friends, once more' (III 1 1). But this attack, too, fails. So the king summons the governor on to the walls of the town and makes a series of startlingly bloodthirsty threats. Unless they surrender now, he cannot promise to control the behaviour of his men once they get into the town. The dire consequences which follow will then be the governor's fault for not surrendering, while Henry still has the English army securely under his command. Surrender, he says:

King Henry If not – why in a moment look to see
    The blind and bloody soldier with foul hand
    Defile the locks of your shrill-shrieking daughters;   35
    Your fathers taken by their silver beards,
    And their most reverend heads dashed to the walls;
    Your naked infants spitted upon pikes,
    Whiles the mad mothers with their howls confused
    Do break the clouds, as did the wives of Jewry   40
    At Herod's bloody-hunting slaughter-men.*
    What say you? Will you yield, and this avoid?
    Or guilty in defence, be thus destroyed?

                                           (III 3 33–43)

> * [40–1] In Matthew's Gospel (2:16–18), just after Jesus' birth Herod, King of Judea, ordered all the first-born babies of the Jews to be killed in an unsuccessful attempt to kill Jesus, the new 'King of the Jews'

The governor does open the gates of his town. He has heard that no reinforcements are on their way, and is convinced by Henry's speech that the English really do have the power to take the town and the will to commit these awful atrocities. It is immediately revealed, however, that it was all a bluff on Henry's part. The English army has taken so long to take the town that winter now approaches. What is more, the soldiers are so enfeebled by sickness that they must abandon the whole campaign and march for Calais, and home (III 3 55–6). Even in war, Henry wins as much through virtuoso performance as through combat.

It is interesting that the Chorus in *King Henry V* paints an idealised picture of Henry and his army that is not supported by what we see in the dramatic scenes which follow. The Chorus to Act III depicts a mighty and heroic fleet full of 'culled and choice-drawn cavaliers' (III 0 24). But in the scenes that follow we see only the cowardly Pistol and his cronies or the squabbling officers who discuss the siege: the pompous Fluellen, the taciturn – not to say dim – Gowar; and two men – Jamy and Macmorris – who, since they come from countries normally at war with England in this period, can only be mercenaries (III 2). The Chorus to Act IV describes how, on the night before the Battle of Agincourt, Henry goes among his troops offering vital encouragement and personal inspiration (IV 0 28–47). Yet, in the scene following, Henry actually adopts a disguise so that he can be alone. When he does meet his men he seems either to quarrel with them (Pistol, Williams) or to actively suggest that their situation is desperate (IV 1 97–8). In a first long soliloquy he appeals to the sympathies of the audience regarding the difficulties that beset a king (IV 1 269–84) – his peasants have it easier, he says!

Why is this? It can be argued that the heroic and theatrical language of the Chorus offers a *poetic* version of history specifically crafted for presentation; the dramatic scenes may be seen as a more prosaic reality with which the poetic version is deliberately juxtaposed. In doing this, the myth-making – which is part of all historical writing – is held up to the audience's gaze. In the same way, Shakespeare's own histories are self-consciously crafted versions of 'real events', and it is the *internal* contrasts of these histories that reveal political ideas and attitudes.

This is not *necessarily* to argue that Shakespeare's exposure of the theatrical pretence of kings constitutes an attack on the very idea of monarchy. Shakespeare demystifies monarchy though without at the same time suggesting a considered alternative. It can be argued that the plays in fact reveal the workings of monarchy while showing also the desirability, indeed the necessity, of the institution in the world of 1600. Nevertheless, it can be shown that the very structure of these plays recognises the voices of the politically excluded, so that the plays raise more questions than they settle about the way power was distributed in early modern England. And of all those groups which at this time could have claimed to be excluded, none has an apparently stronger claim than did women.

History and women

Where are women in Shakespeare's histories? Of the 135 named characters in the *dramatis personae* of the second tetralogy in the 1997 Riverside edition of Shakespeare only ten are women – but they are crucial to the action, even so. In the world of military conflict and male honour presented in these plays, women stand both physically and symbolically as the forgotten centre, or unregarded 'other', of their ideologies.

A crucial issue in these plays is genealogy. Power and property in medieval society is passed down through the principle of *primogeniture*: everything goes, on the death of the father, to the first-born legitimate son. (At time of writing this is still the principle governing the transference of the British crown.)

Richard II has produced no male heir; the question of which of his cousins is to succeed him then becomes vital. The Archbishop of Canterbury in *King Henry V* (I 2 32–95) goes to great lengths to query the reasoning behind the principle (called 'Salic Law' in the play) that prevents princes of France inheriting the throne through female succession. Exeter later presents to the French king a carefully written genealogy to validate Henry's claims, showing his descent from earlier French kings through the male line (I 4 84–95). 'Female succession' means, for example, a claim to the throne based on descent from a king's daughter rather than from his legitimate male heir

The key word in all this is *legitimacy*. Prior to the development of the kind of scientific testing now available, how could a man ever be absolutely certain that the son to whom his wife gave birth was actually his own? Unless he literally had his wife under constant surveillance how could he be sure that another man had not fathered the child who was now his heir? He would have only his wife's word, and the words of women were not regarded as having the same weight as men's. Female sexuality and female sexual desire consequently have the power to undermine and destabilise the very basis on which male power and property is built. A woman's desire to have sex with another man can destroy the 'house' and thence the honour and family line of her husband. This anxiety keeps surfacing in the plays, and, interestingly, it is here to be put to rest by the display of male violence in battle. The display of fighting by men both impresses and abashes female sexuality. Female qualities are seen as a threat to the male qualities of the warrior.

When Henry V is seeking to motivate his troops before Harfleur, he issues this challenge:

King Henry Dishonour not your mothers; now attest
That those whom you called fathers did beget you.

(III 1 22–3)

If the English soldiers do not fight bravely, it will suggest that their mothers had been unfaithful and allowed lesser warriors than their valiant fathers to breed by them. They are fighting, then, in what seems a chivalrous way, to demonstrate their mother's chastity; but there is certainly a subtextual worry about the capacity of English women to have sex with other men, whether they are valiant warriors or not. Furthermore, The British critic Lisa Jardine suggests (1996: 12) that female sexual susceptibility to other (foreign) men actually undermines the notions of national purity and stability, blurring the very distinctions between the English and the French that are at the heart of the play. Women must be controlled if war between *true* nations is to be possible at all.

As the English army marches unhindered through France, the dauphin, spoiling for a fight, argues that his soldiers must prove their manhoods to French women in battle against the English or the women will turn to the invaders for sexual pleasure:

Dauphin By faith and honour,
Our madams mock at us, and plainly say
Our mettle* is bred out, and they will give
Their bodies to the lust of English youth   30
To new-store France with bastard warriors.

(III 6 27–31)

* [29] *mettle* heroic quality

In *King Henry IV Part I* Hotspur is so appalled by the effeminacy of King Henry's messenger – a man who wears perfume, who is scared of cannons and finds dead bodies distasteful (I 3 23–69) – as to forget himself and fail to pay attention to the messenger of the king himself. Womanliness is an affront to the warrior: its caring and nurturing values must be shunned because they damage the hero's willingness to kill at close quarters. Indeed, a real warrior like Hotspur seems to get a strange kind of thrill from blood, and, indeed, from breathless physical contact with his male opponent. Look at the way he describes his prospective encounter with Prince Hal at the Battle of Shrewsbury:

Hotspur The mailed Mars shall on his altar sit
    Up to the ears in blood. I am on fire
    To hear this rich reprisal* is so nigh,*
    And yet not ours. Come let me taste my horse,
    Who is to bear me like a thunderbolt   120
    Against the bosom of the Prince of Wales.
    Harry to Harry shall, hot horse to horse,
    Meet and ne'er part till one drop down a corse.*

(V 1 116–23)

* [118] *reprisal* prize; *nigh* near; [123] *corse* corpse

And, of course, violent soldiers can abuse women's sexuality and actually control their bodies when they turn to rape. Rape is threatened disturbingly often in King Henry's speech prior to Harfleur (III 3 11–14, 21–2, 34–5). Hal and Falstaff look forward to 'buying' the scores of maidenheads that will be made available to them as the war reduces desperate women to prostitution (II 4 361–5).

A common belief at this time was that a woman was an 'incomplete' man. She had been created without the faculties of reason and self-control. Men in Shakespeare's plays are constantly in fear of losing these qualities and so falling back into a state of *womanhood* (Sinfield 1992: 135). But it is not reason that is used in the attempt to control female sexuality: it is military violence, or its modern variant, effective performance. Mortimer, the apparently legitimate heir to King Richard in *King Henry IV Part I*, loses his qualities as a warrior because he so loves his wife (III 1 263–4). Hotspur is so keen to demonstrate that he is not effeminized by love for his wife that he gracelessly and jokily puts her off and mocks her, even when she is upset at not being part of his life (II 3 90–5). Neither of these men shows the ability to win over a woman with the convincing manliness displayed by King Henry in the last scene of *King Henry V*. While claiming to be a bluff soldier, Henry is so charming that he wins Katherine, his wit and apparent affection making him seem the obvious and appropriate bridegroom for her. In fact, as Katherine's reply makes clear, she has no say in the match at all:

King Henry ... wilt thou have me?
Katherine Dat is as it shall please *de roi mon pere**
King Henry Nay, it will please him well, Kate; it
    shall please him, Kate.
Katherine Den it sall also content me.

(V 2 246–50)

* [247] *de roi mon pere* 'the king my father'

In fact, Katherine had been offered to Henry as a way of buying off the invasion even before Henry reached Harfleur (III 0 29–30). By concluding a dynastic marriage Henry declares his wish to produce a son who will have genealogical claims to the thrones of both France and England (V 2 206–9). He has, however, to persuade the audience that the courtship succeeds through his and Katherine's mutual affection, and this indeed is the way the scene is usually played. The text, though, would allow the actors to play the scene so that Katherine's lack of choice and, indeed, lack of real power of assent are made obvious. He dominates the conversation, often turning her words back wittily on her (V 2 109–10, 169–73, 195–8). He assumes the right, since he has the power, to decide the meaning of her language in their conversation. The stark reality of power is once more dressed in the pleasing costume of the performer, and the facts of the case almost escape us (Howard 1994: 150).

I say *almost* because following the wooing of Katherine there is a passage, often cut from performance, in which Henry and Burgundy, in Katherine's presence, exchange crude and public innuendoes about the shyness of virgins in their first sexual encounter (V 2 291–314). Once the wooing is over, Katherine is immediately treated by Henry as an object of his pleasure, not as an individual woman. She is another French city 'girdled with maiden walls that war hath never entered' (V 2 321–2). This tends to be lost among the general good humour of the scene in performance. As already stated, France has been the female body for which the men have fought; but it has also become the background against which they have sought to prove their masculinity through acts of violence. The skilful monarch is able to justify his power by making his violence appear appropriate and required. That is Henry V's great victory.

History plays were popular throughout the 1590s not just because they gave a clear sense to their audiences that their world was indeed different from what it had been, but because they were in tune with a developing sense of national identity and distinctness. England was an embattled Protestant country with its own Anglican Church, faced by an array of Catholic continental enemies. The plays seem to want to draw clear divisions between past and present, England and France. It is perhaps not surprising that the differences between men and women are much less loosely drawn than they seem to be in the comedies (see pp. 145ff.)

Summary

- These plays show an awareness that the old feudal world had gone and that in its place was a new world in which monarchs, with the backing of their armies, demanded absolute power.
- The plays also can be seen to show royal power to be fundamentally self-serving. While claiming God's support, in reality these kings justified their authority by their more or less convincing performances in the monarch's role.
- Women's potential for undermining men's right to inherit is in these plays kept in check by the threat of violence.
- Consider these ideas in relation to the actions of both Prince John and Hal in *King Henry IV Part Two* (Act IV Scene 2 and Act V Scene 2, respectively). Do they help explain why Falstaff has to be banished at the end of this play (V 5 41–96)? You might also like to consider the idea of the king as performer in relation to *King Richard III* (look, for example, at Act I Scene 2 and Act III Scene 7).

Further reading

Holderness (1989c) is a good introduction to the perspective on feudalism contained in *King Richard II*. Ideas relating to feudalism in the play are dealt with also in Rackin (1990). Howard (1994) gives a very thorough exploration of the idea of monarchs as performers. Connections between sexuality and nationalism in the history plays are interestingly discussed in Sinfield and Dollimore's 'History and ideology, masculinity and miscegenation: the instance of *Henry V*', in Sinfield (1992) and also in the Introduction to Jardine (1996).

Chapter 8

Understanding tragedy

Hamlet, King Lear and *Othello*

Literary criticism uses the word *tragedy* differently from the way we use it in normal conversation. In normal use, any untimely death is 'tragic'; colloquially, an own-goal in the last minute of injury time in an FA Cup match is also described, by one team and its supporters, as 'tragic'. This use of the word demeans its literary use, however. In literary criticism it is used with a specific, one might say technical, meaning – and it is not simply that a play has a sad ending.

The first tragedies were written by the ancient Greek dramatists, most notably by Aeschylus, Sophocles and Euripides, who wrote in the fifth century BC. They were imitated by the Roman writer Seneca, whose plays were studied in Elizabethan (1558–1603) schools. The conventions of classical tragedy had been identified by the Greek philosopher Aristotle in his *Poetics*. For Aristotle, a tragedy has a main character, a protagonist. This protagonist must be 'noble': not only rich, powerful and strong but possessing certain admirable personal qualities. The play will tell the story of their fall. In order for such a fall to have its effect on the audience it must be from a position of eminence and must affect other people – perhaps a whole country – who depend on the protagonist. Though fate plays a strong part in these plays, the downfall of the protagonist must be due to some personal error of judgement (*hamartia* is the Greek word). The tragic spectacle depends on the audience being aware of the capacity of even the most powerful of individuals to destroy themselves through their imperfect understanding of our human condition. The experience of this insight, which Aristotle believed conferred moral benefits upon the audience, would not occur if the protagonists were wicked, or if their fall came about by accident. In the first case the audience would feel no regret at their fall, and in the second no perception into mortal frailty would be granted. The point of tragedy, then, was to provide some form of moral and philosophical education for the audience about the ways of human life.

There is no evidence that Shakespeare had a direct acquaintance with the *Poetics*. Early modern English tragedies on the public stages of London took the name and an approximation of the tragedic form. These plays had no moral or philosophical intention as the Greek writers did. They set out to tell a story in a recognised dramatic genre that would be attractive to London theatre-goers, only a small minority of whom would have come across classical tragedy in its Senecan form. There was no contemporary idea of what tragedy would be, even if aristocratic writers like Sir Philip Sidney recommended going back to the classical rules.

In telling these stories within the genre of tragedy the playwrights made statements about the nature of political power and the problems of the powerful in the world they knew. They were aware that the feudal society of the fairly recent past had been very different in its organisation and in its ideas about how life should be lived. They could see a new world coming into being, a world in which individuals had much more opportunity to make their own way; where new forms of power were competing with old ones; where the role of women was changing.

When powerful historical forces come into conflict, individuals are sometimes the site of that conflict and are destroyed by it. A protagonist who is living within one system of ideas or beliefs has to struggle to come to terms with the forces of another system. But he can't understand this other system (usually) because he can see the world only from where he is. Yet, standing outside of the drama, as members of the audience, we can see how things could have been different; from the outside we can see that men and women can transform society because the conditions that produce tragedy are shown to be man-made, not divinely ordained as many critics thought in the past. Some critics find the experience of watching the end of a tragedy to be a gloomy confirmation of human powerlessness; others see there a pointer to a more just world which is perhaps the product of, but separate from, the conflicting forces which have just destroyed the protagonist. There is death, waste and destruction at the end of a tragedy, but there is always some hope.

Tragedy and history

It is important to understand the way in which the historical moment of transition between the medieval and modern worlds creates the nature of Shakespeare's tragedies. I want to explain this idea by referring to *Hamlet* and *Othello*.

Just after Shakespeare had written *Hamlet* there occurred a serious political disturbance in London. On Sunday 8 February 1601 Robert Devereux, Earl of Essex, ex-general of the Queen's forces in Ireland, and one-time royal favourite, seems to have made an attempt to seize power by force. That was certainly the way the old Queen's government saw it; Essex was beheaded for treason. Six of the other 140 rebels were executed. Shakespeare's former patron, the Earl of Southampton, had taken part but was reprieved and released from the Tower after two years. The reasons for Essex's desperate attempt are complex; but the mind-set of the aristocratic warrior seems to have played some part. In previous centuries heroic men of noble birth and skill in combat were regarded as their country's natural leaders. The king himself was supposed to embody these qualities; indeed, the ability to kill all your challengers must have been one of the essential qualifications for kingship in the earliest days of that institution. Kings of England were leading their armies into battle until as recently as the 1740s. Essex certainly had these qualities. He was an accomplished swordsman and a fearless warrior, and he had a very high opinion of his own qualities as a general. The fact that he saw himself as a knightly warrior is suggested by his curiously old-fashioned behaviour. When abandoning the siege of Rouen in 1592 he rode up to the city wall and flung a lance into the wooden gates, bearing on it a challenge to single combat to anyone who claimed their mistress was fairer than his lady Queen Elizabeth. (The figure of the monarch as military adventurer also haunts Shakespeare's history plays; see Chapter 6.)

By 1600 the existence of men living this way of life was increasingly seen as a problem rather than an asset to the state. Elizabeth set about depriving the lords of their private armies and preventing them from settling their jealousies and grudges in bloody skirmishes on the streets of London. The government was effectively run by Robert Cecil. Short, hunchbacked and quietly spoken, his rank as secretary of state and his prestige at court were due to his political vision and administrative skills, not his military valour. That world had passed. At the time of his rebellion Essex was in disgrace and effectively under house arrest. He responded in the only way he knew.

In the first scene of *Hamlet*, we are told by Hamlet's friend Horatio that a border dispute between Denmark and Norway in the days of Hamlet's father had been settled by the kings of the two countries in single combat – a fight won by Old Hamlet (I 1 80–95). Now young Fortinbras, the son of that defeated Norwegian monarch, is secretly planning to recover by force the territory lost. Claudius' response to this renewed threat is very different from his predecessor's. He sends ambassadors to the current king of Norway, the defeated king's brother, with very precise diplomatic instructions (II 1 17–41). Their mission is successful – at least temporarily. We can see here that Old Hamlet belongs to the old world of heroic chivalry – even his ghost appears in full plate armour in Act I. His way of settling the question is the solution Essex might have chosen. Claudius, however, belongs to a recognisably more modern political system, one in which a rational approach is taken to a dispute between nations. Personal military prowess is not the decisive quality in a political leader.

In the Middle Ages trial by combat was a means by which justice was seen to be done. If one nobleman accused another of killing a member of his family, and the other denied it, single combat between the two would settle the matter. Shakespeare depicts just such a conflict between Bolingbroke and Thomas Mowbray, Duke of Norfolk, in Act I of *King Richard II*. It was believed that providence would ensure that victory lay with the true contestant (by *providence* was meant the belief that God would ensure that the good are rewarded, and the wicked punished, even on earth). Two things changed this. First, people began to rely on their own observations rather than on the decree of an authority. (A truly medieval mind would believe X to have been guilty in some way if he lost the combat, even though their own eyes may have assured them of his innocence.) Second, the state's courts and judges finally succeeded in taking control of *all* disputes, even those involving the aristocracy. Old Hamlet lived in the heroic–chivalric world of trial by combat – the medieval language used by Horatio to describe him reinforces that (I 1 83–95). But Prince Hamlet lives in Claudius' early modern court. What, then, is he to do when his father's ghost comes back from the dead demanding revenge?

To start with Hamlet, like his fellow student Horatio at the University of Wittenberg, doesn't even *believe* in ghosts. Denmark, like England, was an officially Protestant country where ghosts were regarded as a foolish Catholic superstition. The ghost can be seen as a manifestation of the old feudal values which Hamlet's father held. Hamlet loved his father, but he is a modern sceptical rationalist – he even doubts that there is life after death (III 1 55–85). He lives in a state where justice is not to be privately settled but publicly resolved. We can see the reasons for this in Laertes' behaviour. Hamlet kills the king's chief minister Polonius, by mistake. Laertes, Polonius' 'noble' son, returns furious at his father's death and threatens the safety of the king himself in his desire for revenge. Laertes' reaction reminds us that blood feuds lead only to further bloodshed: there will never be peace or justice while they are allowed to flourish.

And yet we can see also the problem with the modern system of state justice. What do you do when the state itself is corrupt and secretly carries out actions that its own laws define as crimes? How can Hamlet call on Claudius to arrest himself for the secret murder that only the two of them know Claudius committed? Once you step out of the framework of the rule of law – through revolution or assassination, perhaps – are you not back in the lawless territory of the blood feud and personal revenge? The character of Hamlet can be seen as tragic because he is caught in this double-bind between, on the one hand, the loved father whose ghost demands a medieval revenge that Hamlet's modern mind wants to, but cannot, accept; and, on the other, the modern state that he wants to believe in but knows to be corrupt. The Marxist critic Arnold Kettle described Hamlet as 'the first modern intellectual in our literature' because he realises that 'power is in the hands of a class whose values humane people feel they must repudiate' (Kettle 1964: 156). In the end, he has to fall back on letting events take their course. Despite his scepticism about matters of religious belief Hamlet falls back on the workings of providence. Let God decide when and how Claudius dies; Hamlet himself can't affect his fate:

> *Hamlet* If it* be now, 'tis not to come; if it be not to come, it will be now; if it be not now, yet it will come – the readiness is all. Since no man, of aught* he leaves, knows what is't to leave betimes,* let be.

(V 2 220–2)

* [220] *it* his death [222] *aught* anything; *knows what is't to*

leave betimes knows what he misses if he leaves early

Many critics don't like to talk about character at all. They take the view that both stage characters and real people aren't actually unified coherent individuals at all. We are never consistent enough to be talked about as if there were an essential core to our identity. We talk differently and act differently depending on who we are with and what we are doing – and that doesn't take account of our subconscious. Indeed, some critics believe that it is the *language* we use in these particular circumstances that creates who we are – and that language exists societally outside of the individual – we don't create it for ourselves. Such critics ignore character, and are more interested in looking at how a role in a Shakespeare play is constructed from the social and political relationships of the time in which the play was written. Hamlet's *subjectivity*, as they put it, is produced by the conflicts and stresses in his society. The play doesn't either approve of or condemn revenge – but it does present to the audience, both then and now, important problems with certain political principles. These principles are the underlying ideas about revenge in each of the conflicting ways of life in which Hamlet must live.

One of Hamlet's key concerns is his identity. He seems unsure whether he is a madman or coldly sane individual; a real avenger or an actor playing a role in a revenge play (II 2 571–87); a lover of Ophelia and his mother or a hater of women in general. But this may be because the tragic protagonist always goes through a process of losing his identity. In the medieval world social status was identical with political power. Your position within the feudal hierarchy at birth – as prince, duke, earl, knight or peasant – told you who you were, who you remained and how you should conduct yourself. It established your relationships with others, too. There is, however, in Shakespeare's time a new fluidity. It is possible to be a prince, as Hamlet is, but have no power because the cunning politician Claudius keeps him sidelined and under surveillance. He cannot see clearly who he is any more: that is another distinctly tragic feature of the role. Hamlet is an intelligent and perceptive man struggling to live among the deceptions, contradictions and stupidities of the only society he can know: that is what makes him a tragic figure. But he sees that the world could be otherwise. Claudius recognises this too, I think, but decides to accept the present situation for his own selfish advantage (III 3 3–72). It is the time in which Hamlet has to live that is actually 'out of joint' (I 5 188) – not the prince himself. That is why he has no stable identity in a disjointed and contradictory society.

Othello, on the other hand, has power but no status. Venice is happy to employ mercenaries to lead its forces. Noble Italian birth is not a qualification in this modern situation; military proficiency is what matters. Yet Othello is black and foreign, so he cannot be accepted in the hierarchy of the Venetian state. Brabantio, Desdemona's father, cannot accept him as a suitable husband for his daughter because of his colour. Yet Othello does not come across, in either his language or his attitudes, as foreign. His foreignness and blackness are, however, emphasised by others. There is a certain grand pomposity to his language, but this is to do with Othello's vision of himself: and he sees himself as a noble, almost legendary, warrior. Only a minute or so after he first comes on stage he tells Iago 'I fetch my life and being/From men of royal siege' (I 2 21–2), a most unusual –archaic – use of the word 'siege', meaning 'seat' and therefore social status. The story of his life, which he tells to the duke and the senators, is a story of desperate adventures straight out of a 'romance' – a medieval tall story of the unlikely adventures that a wandering knight ('knight-errant') meets on his quest. It was the same story that he had told to Brabantio and which had made such an impression on Desdemona:

Othello   Wherein I spoke of most disastrous* chances:
    Of moving accidents* by flood and field,*   135
    Of hair-breadth scapes i' th'imminent deadly breach,*
    Of being taken by the insolent foe
    And sold to slavery, of my redemption thence
    And portance* in my travel's history;
    Wherein of antres* vast and deserts idle,   140

Rough quarries, rocks and hills whose heads touch heaven,
It was my hint to speak – such was my process* –
And of the Cannibals that each other eat,
The Anthropophagi,* and men whose heads
Do grow beneath their shoulders.   145

(I 3 134–45)

* [134] *disastrous* unlucky [135] *accidents* events; *by flood and field* on sea and land [136] *i' th'imminent deadly breach* in the deadly danger of leading an attack through a gap made in a castle wall [139] *portance* conduct [140] *antres* caves [142] *process* proceeding [144] *Anthropophagi* man-eaters

In the romances it is a knight's feats that win the lady's love; chivalric prowess is actually inseparable from the love of the knight's lady who dignifies and sanctions his deeds. And it is for these very adventures that Desdemona loves Othello. He tells the duke and senators:

Othello She lov'd me for the dangers I had pass'd,
    And I loved her that she did pity them.

(I 3 167–8)

Desdemona's love for Othello is founded on his qualities as a warrior and his history of noble deeds. These heroic qualities even override his blackness(!):

Desdemona My heart's subdu'd   250
    Even to the very quality of my lord.*
    I saw Othello's visage* in his mind,
    And to his honours and his valiant parts*
    Did I my soul and fortunes consecrate.

(I 3 250–4)

* [250–1] *subdu'd / Even to the very quality* 'my heart has been conquered completely by his way of life and the character

that gives him' [252] *visage* face – here she means real face
[253] *parts* qualities

This is a love from the world of stories and legends – an idealised
version of courtly love in feudal chivalry. It is completely at odds
with imperialist, pragmatic, money-driven Venetian society
(Holderness 1989b: 58).

Both lovers become dupes of the worldly Iago: Othello is an
outsider in Venice and unsure of its ways; Desdemona is a young
noblewoman who has been kept apart from male society and
politics. Their love is not grounded in the reality of how their
society operates, and so it founders when it comes into contact
with that world in its most pure form: Iago. Not that the nature of
their love is shown to be admirable. Indeed, the contradictions of
this sort of courtly love are quickly exposed. If the warrior's qualities are dependent on the steadfast love of a woman, and that
woman proves unfaithful, then the warrior loses his status: once
Othello is convinced that his wife is having an affair with Cassio,
'Othello's occupation's gone' (III 3 357). The capacity for
violence which gives the warrior his suitability as an object of
love is then turned against the woman: 'I will chop her into
messes. Cuckold [i.e. be unfaithful to] me!' (IV 1 200). She must
be destroyed because she is a threat to male integrity: 'she must
die, else she'll betray more men' (V 1 6) For her part, Desdemona
cannot understand how a woman's love can be unfaithful, since
she understands love to be the complete surrender of the woman
to the warrior ('My heart's subdu'd/Even to the very quality of
my lord' [I 3 250–1]). This explains her naive question to Iago's
wife Emilia (IV 3 61–3), when she asks if there really are women
who are unfaithful to their husbands. It explains also her strange
claim to be responsible for her own death, and her continuing
love for her 'kind lord' at the moment of her death at his hands (V
2 124–5). If the woman loves a man because of his ability to use
violence against his enemies, she can only approve – crazily – of
that violence being turned against her should she become a suitable target in his eyes. Otherwise she betrays his love and deserves

his hatred. The man's love in this sort of relationship is all-subduing and allows no argument once you accept it.

Othello's tragedy is that he lives according to a set of stories through which he interprets the world – an ideology – but it is a world that has been superseded. He cannot see that this is so, and the contradictions within his ideology destroy him (Holderness 1989b: 58). He is living the life of a chivalric warrior in a world run by money and self-interest. A woman's love inspired by violence will itself fall prey to that same violence when, thanks to Iago, the chivalric code by which he once lived is of no use in providing him with an understanding of the real world of Venice in which Othello finds himself living.

Yet we can see, from our perspective outside of the world both of Othello and of the Venetians, that the play points forward to an order of living in which people should be free to love whoever they want; where marriage with anyone outside your country, class or colour is not seen as 'unnatural' (as Iago says III 3 229–31). Othello's tragedy can also be seen to be the product of being trapped in a period of history where such egalitarian values are unachievable – but the play *hints* powerfully to the audience at the possibility of such values, as Emilia's speech at the end of Act IV indicates (see pp. 209f.).

In a similar way *Macbeth* can be seen to dramatise the contradictions that lie within the feudal society (see pp. 153f.) of medieval Scotland. On the one hand, the language used to describe both the king (I 7 16–20) and his relationships with his loyal nobles (I 4 14–29) makes Scotland sound a gentle place, where social bonds rest on mutual affection and genuine respect (Holderness 1989b: 60–1). On the other, it is clear that violent challenges to the authority of the king are actually the normal state of affairs in this country. In the course of the play, Macdonald, Macbeth and Malcolm make violent attempts to seize the throne. But it is to be noticed that bloodthirsty violence (I 2 16–23, 35–40) in support of the king is praised in the highest terms (I 3 89–93); violence directed against the king is condemned utterly (I 2 9–14). As the British critic Alan Sinfield points out, Macbeth kills a rebel and a king at the beginning of the play and is condemned. Macduff kills a rebel and a king (who happen to be the same person) at the end and is to be praised (Sinfield 1986: 126). Critics often assume Malcolm to have been the legitimate king and Macbeth the usurper; but it is by no means clear that being 'Prince of Cumberland' ensured succession to the throne: kings in medieval Scotland, it seems, were sometimes elected (Sinfield 1986: 128).

The historical evidence would, in any case, indicate that it was usually violence which ensured succession. In the feudal Scotland of *Macbeth* violence is the means by which power is achieved and held; but the value system by which the nobles claim to live says that loyalty and faithfulness are what keeps the political order intact and functioning. The stories about their society told by Duncan and Macbeth are evidently at odds with how these men actually live their lives. There is, then, a second set of values – a cult of masculine military prowess – that is in conflict with the first one of steadfast loyalty.

Acts of valour and daring are what make a man worthy in this society. A real man, as Lady Macbeth successfully argues, keeps his word and is not afraid even to murder the king (I 7 39–59). The most worthy man is he who will challenge the strongest authority in the country – the king. Yet the king is the very man in whose interest Macbeth is supposed to use violence, the person to whom he owes ultimate loyalty. This contradiction within feudal society is what divides and destroys Macbeth. Macbeth cannot avoid living on the line of division running through his society; his fate is therefore tragic.

Tragedy and power

Because Shakespeare's tragedies are concerned with people who have a share in the power and authority in their societies, understanding these plays will involve looking at what they have to say about the nature of power.

Power may be simply defined as the means by which you get other people to do what you want them to do. Sometimes you achieve this by physical force, because those on whom your power works don't want to obey you, but must in order to avoid injury or death. Power exerted in this way at state level depends on the firm loyalty of the police and the armed forces, and is therefore expensive and of questionable reliability; and if loyal armed forces are the only means by which power is sustained, one's hold on it is unlikely to be a very long one.

In 1600 there was neither a police force nor a standing army in England, so that state power was not a real option for its rulers. It is not clear that rulers at this time would want such forces, either. A better way to exercise power is to convince people that it is in their interest to obey you, even if it actually is not. If people in a society believe a set of stories that explain and justify the exercise of power by one group over others in this society, then that power will be much more secure. This 'set of stories' is a better definition of the word *ideology*. The powerful themselves will no doubt believe these stories – unless, that is, they are 'machiavels' (see pp. 200f.).

The most secure exercise of power is that which is seen as *natural*, even by those who are exploited by that power. Shakespeare is very interested, it seems to many modern critics, in power that is exercised in this ideological way. He seems particularly interested in how power is connected with justice. In all the tragedies this is perhaps nowhere more evident than in *King Lear*.

Edmund is the character who at first glance has some very perceptive insights into how power operates. He is the illegitimate son of the Duke of Gloucester, and he has a grudge. All of Gloucester's property will be inherited by Edgar, the legitimate son and heir. Edmund realises that the law which denies the father's property to the illegitimate son is merely 'custom' (I 2 3) – it is a man-made rule; there is nothing *natural* about it. He is just as much a man as his brother. Why, then, should bastards be regarded as inferior people? (I 2 6–15) And indeed, rationally speaking, one can see the truth of what he says. His father's affection for him is the same as it is for Edgar (I 2 16–17), but the law will not permit that affection to be reflected in inherited property. Thus Edmund has seen that the relationship between affection and property is purely *arbitrary*: there is no natural or essential reason why the amount of love a parent holds for a child, or a child holds for a parent, should have any connection with how much property that parent passes on to his children. Love is love and property property. In a humane society, love is not love when it depends on external factors that have nothing to do with it – as the king of France remarks in the first scene of the play (I 1 238–40).

This is an insight that has certainly escaped Lear in the same scene. The aged Lear has decided to 'retire' and divide up his territory between his three daughters. He invites each of them to say how much they love him so that he can reward their affection accordingly. The two older sisters, Goneril and Regan, strive to outdo each other in their declarations of love; but the youngest, Cordelia, refuses to play along. She says she loves her father as much as she ought, in duty; she refuses to speak a great deal of words which she knows are bluster and exaggeration. Lear is furious, and disowns Cordelia, banishing her without a dowry to become the wife of the king of France, who is happy to accept her nevertheless. Thus he loses, simultaneously, that 'love' of his false daughters, which was his only for so long has he retained kingly power, and the company of his true daughter, who loves him simply because he is her father. Lear is trapped in a way of thinking that defines who he is but no longer fits the world in which he lives.

Edmund, too, is aware that we tend to hide the actual causes of events in the world behind abstractions and religious dogma and so lose sight of our ability to change the world for ourselves. Astrology is a typical example of this:

Edmund An admirable evasion of whoremaster* man, to lay his
goatish
disposition on the charge of a star! My father compounded*
with my mother under the Dragon's tail, and my
nativity* was under Ursa Major,* so that it follows,   130
I am rough and lecherous.* Fut, I should have been
that I am, had the maidenl'est star in the firmament
twinkled* on my bastardising.

(I 2 127–33)

* [127] *whoremaster* literally a pimp, but here it must mean someone who is 'always after sex' [128] *compounded with* slept with [130] *nativity* birth; *Ursa Major* the Great Bear – a constellation, like the 'Dragon's tail' [129] *lecherous* lustful [131–3] *I should have been … bastardising* 'I would have been just as I am had the most virginal star in the sky twinkled on the moment of my illegitimate conception'

If our natures were laid down by the position of the stars in the sky at the moment of our conception, there would be nothing we could do to change the way the world is. In that sense astrology is part of a distinctly conservative ideology. But Edmund sees that this is a story that we tell, like the one about 'legitimacy' and 'illegitimacy', to mask the real facts of individuals and groups seeking to exert power over others. They are just stories; and the more that those stories involve the mystical or the 'natural', the more powerful they are likely to be. Edmund sees all this; he sees the fact that justice in the world of the play is simply what the powerful say it is – the message that Lear is going to learn to his cost.

Lear thinks that he can give away all his property to his daughters Goneril and Regan and still retain the authority and respect due to a king and the affection due to a father. He has not seen that all these things are the direct product of the land he possesses, which gives him economic power. He does not realise that in the world of the play love and respect flow towards possessions, but do not belong to people as individuals. He is loved as a king because he is powerful. Without his power there is (apparently) nothing there to love. Cordelia tries to reveal this 'truth' to him, but the story he had told himself, that kings are loved and obeyed for their personal qualities – which he confuses with their power – makes him regard her statement as treasonable. Only on the heath, when he has been deserted by nearly everyone, can he see the truth about power.

Just before he is found by Cordelia's attendants, Lear meets Edmund's father Gloucester. Gloucester has been cruelly blinded by Regan's ruthless husband Cornwall for helping Lear to escape

from their clutches. He, too, is destitute and wandering. Lear tells
him that he does not need eyes to see the truth about justice in the
world:

> *Lear* What, art mad? A man may see how this   150
>   world goes with no eyes. Look with thine ears; see
>   how yond* justice* rails* upon yond simple thief. Hark
>   in thine ear: change places, and handy-dandy,* which is
>   the justice which is the thief? Thou hast seen a
>   farmer's dog bark at a beggar?   155
> *Gloucester* Ay, sir.
> *Lear* And the creature run from the cur?* There
>   thou mightst behold the great image of authority: a
>   dog's obey'd in office.*

                          (IV 6 150–9)

> * [152] *yond* that; *justice* judge; *rails* abuses, shouts at [153]
> *handy-dandy* a child's guessing game in which an object is
> hidden in one hand or the other. Lear means here 'You can
> take your pick – the same thing can be hidden in either hand.
> The same man could be either judge or thief' [157] *cur* dog
> [158] *a dog's obey'd in office* the authority of an official has
> nothing to do with the personal virtue or qualities of the
> person holding the office

Because the dog belongs to a landowner, a beggar will recognise
its authority even though it is only a dog. In the same way, Lear
has realised, a king is obeyed and loved only because of his position as monarch. Any man could be a king, in fact. Who is to say
that the man sitting in judgement hasn't himself at some time
robbed another? So long as the public remains ignorant of the
fact, his ability to pass judgement is, to the public mind, unim-
paired. He has no personal virtue just because he is a judge. Or
maybe stealing itself is socially defined: if I pay very low wages in
a time of high unemployment, am I not stealing my employee's
labour just as much as if I were to take one of their possessions
without paying for it ?

Yet Lear has to be stripped of all his office and power before he can see through the ideology of kingship – the idea that monarchs rule because they personally have the particular qualities that befit them to exercise power over the rest of us, or because God has chosen them to have this power. He sees now that monarchs are just ordinary men and as such need to pay attention to the basic humanity they share with the poorest of their subjects. As the rain lashes down upon him on the heath, he has this realisation:

Lear Poor naked wretches, wheresoe'er you are,
    That bide* the pelting of this piteous storm,
    How shall your houseless heads and unfed sides,   30
    Your loop'd and window'd* raggedness, defend you
    From seasons such as this! Take physic,* pomp,*
    Expose thyself to feel what wretches feel,
    That thou may'st shake the superflux* to them,   35
    And show the heavens more just.

                                                    (III 4 28–36)

* [29] *bide* suffer [31] *loop'd and window'd* full of holes [32] physic medicine; *pomp* the rich and powerful [35] *shake the superflux* redistribute your excess of wealth – the image is of a man shaking off something un-needed that has stuck to him

He would have had no idea that the redistribution of wealth from the rich to the poor was what needed to be done had he not experienced what it was to be destitute himself. There seems, then, to be a suggestion here that wealth and position prevent the powerful from ever understanding the lot of the poor. The society of the play is organised in such a way that the rich will never understand what needs to be done if social justice is to prevail. The poor are, it seems, more likely to have a clear idea of what justice is. This is emphasised by the fact that one of Cornwall's servants had earlier been prepared to fight his own master and die in an attempt to prevent the torture of Gloucester, simply because he saw it as wrong and cruel (III 7 72–82).

Edmund, as already observed, can see through the stories which are told to justify power, but so powerful is his desire for ownership of land and property that he is prepared to go along with what he knows to be purely conventional (I 2 1–22). People's relationship to land and property in the play defines their identity and establishes their power, irrespective of their personal virtue. That is clearly the power structure of the Britain of *King Lear*.

Characters in early modern English plays who see that the moral and political stories told by the powerful to justify their position amount to no more than a cover for their naked exercise of power, and act accordingly, are sometimes called *machiavels*. The teachings of the Italian statesman and philosopher Niccolo Machiavelli (1469–1527) were understood to advocate deception and ruthlessness in order to maintain a ruler's power, recognising Christian humility and truthfulness as qualities to be shunned by an ambitious and successful politician in the real world. Though officially demonised, Machiavelli's books were privately recognised by many intellectuals as a ground-breaking analysis of power that broke away from medieval pieties. As Edmund demonstrates, however, an understanding of how ideology works does not seem to lead to any radical desire to make the world a more just place for all (Dollimore 1984: 201). It should be pointed out also that Machiavelli believed 'the Prince' (the title he uses for the ideal ruler) had a right to rule because the mass of his subjects lacked the intelligence and virtue to ensure the general good. Only on stage, it seems, do the insights which escape the powerful get suggested to the audience.

Rituals, processions and plays themselves are of course also stories. An important way in which early modern – and indeed modern – rulers make their right to rule seem natural is by taking possession of the symbols that society regards as being the markers of valid power.

Crowns, thrones and rich robes on public display were of course important parts of this, but so were the rituals and the formal language of power. As a new ruler, Claudius in *Hamlet* has to establish his power by symbolic display as much as by any other means. His first entrance, in what is clearly a formal court occasion, is marked by a fanfare of trumpets. The actors would enter in order of their precedence in the hierarchy of the state:

> *Flourish.* * *Enter* CLAUDIUS, KING OF DENMARK, GERTRUDE THE QUEEN; COUNCIL: *as* POLONIUS; *and his son* LAERTES, HAMLET *cum aliis** [*including* VOLTEMAND *and* CORNELIUS].
>
> (I 2 0, sd)

> **Flourish* a fanfare of trumpets; *cum aliis*: Latin, meaning 'with others'

As discussed above (see pp. 78f.), Hamlet's position in the procession entering the stage is clearly different from that designated for his rank. It is also clear from dialogue later in the scene (I 2 68, 77–8) that his black mourning-clothes are not in tune with the bright and expensive ceremonial robes worn by the king and queen. This obvious symbolic dissent must be visually reconciled with the royal ritual or it will be apparent to any onlooker that Claudius' power over his court and kingdom is incomplete – and therefore in reality less effective. After a carefully crafted speech, the rhetoric of which seeks to justify his optimistic outlook in the face of the general mourning for his recently deceased brother (I 2 1–16; see pp. 24f.), he instructs his diplomats to deal with the threat from Fortinbras. Then he hears a request from Laertes, his chief minister's son, *before* addressing Prince Hamlet – a clear snub in terms of the Hamlet's rank in the court. The entreaties of both king and queen succeed in wringing from Hamlet a grudging promise to obey his mother's authority. Claudius, having re-established his authority, announces that he will celebrate by having cannons fired as he drinks that evening:

> *King* This gentle and unforc'd accord of Hamlet
> Sits smiling to my heart, in grace whereof,
> No jocund health* that Denmark* drinks to-day,   125

But the great cannon to the clouds shall tell,
And the King's rouse* the heaven shall bruit* again,
Respeaking earthly thunder. Come away. *(Flourish. Exeunt all
but Hamlet)*

(I 2 123–8)

* [125] *jocund health* joyful toast; *Denmark* the King of
Denmark [127] *rouse* a full glass drunk down in one; *bruit*
echo noisily

And indeed we hear the cannon firing offstage to mark Claudius'
drinking while Hamlet awaits his appointment with the ghost
later that evening. The public symbolism of this custom seems
clear. The echoing of the king's delight in the skies shows divine
approval of his happiness. The heavens concur with his power to
wish good health and fortune as he drinks. The king is a
consumer of goods on behalf of the people; in fact his unequal
consumption of goods is clearly marked as for their benefit . The
cannon-fire indicates his military power; the fact that the heavens
re-echo the noise shows that God's judgement, in its traditional
form of the thunderbolt, is completely in agreement with
Claudius. Privately, Hamlet says the custom is actually read by
other nations as proof that the Danes are drunks! But this sort of
subversive reading of ceremonial display is what the sheer spectacle is supposed to disarm.

The fencing match of the play's final scene is also part of a
formal display to validate Claudius' power. The fact that he can
stage a symbolic duel between two of the kingdom's most
powerful young men symbolises publicly his ability to control
and neutralise conflicts within Denmark. The same ritual of the
cannon and the drinking takes place during the duel, once more
showing who has the real authority (V 2 283, sd). However,
Claudius has distorted the ritual from a symbolic to a material
exercise of power by giving Laertes a sword tipped with a deadly
poison so that he can *accidentally* kill Hamlet. When we hear a
cannon announcing the entrance of Fortinbras it remains unclear
whether it is a symbolic ceremonial salute or a piece of artillery

fired in anger. The symbolic is here sliding into the actual. And indeed Fortinbras, whose name means 'strength in arms', seems to symbolise the supremacy of armed force in political conflict. Claudius might scheme and connive; Hamlet might put on a subversive play; but the man who rules Denmark at the end of the play is the man who has an army on stage to support his claim. Military ceremonial looks as though it will set the symbolic tone, too, of the new regime.

> *Fortinbras* Let four captains   395
>   Bear Hamlet like a soldier to the stage,
>   For he was likely, had he been put on,*
>   To have prov'd most royal; and for his passage*
>   The soldiers' music and the rite of war
>   Speak loudly for him.   400
>   Take up the bodies. Such a sight as this
>   Becomes the field,* but here shows much amiss.
>   Go bid the soldiers shoot.
>   *[(Exeunt [marching; after the which a peal of ordinance* are shot off]]*
>
>   (V 2 395–403)

> * [397] *put on* become king [398] *passage* i.e. death [402] *Becomes the field* would suit the battlefield [403] [stage direction (sd)] 'a peal of ordinance' means a number of cannon fired simultaneously

Although Hamlet has adopted several identities in the play; there's precious little evidence in the text to suggest that 'soldier' appropriately describes him. If the 'his' in line 398 is taken to refer to the dead Claudius, not the dead prince, the same consideration would apply. The point is, however, that it suits the aim of the military adventurer Fortinbras to portray the previous legitimate rulers as military men just like himself: it is a means now of securing the power.

An important question arises from all of this. If the plays show public display used to legitimise the power of monarchs, what then was the function of the *plays themselves* in the public theatres of London? There is an important school of criticism which argues that because the acting companies were licensed by the monarch, and indeed could exist only under the patronage of an aristocrat, the function of the theatre was always to affirm and consolidate the power of the monarchy. Of course, it is true that the plays shows monarchs acting unjustly; it also shows them overthrown and punished. Many of the theatre's Puritan critics argued that the plays actually taught their audiences disobedience and a willingness to defy authority through a sort of 'copy-cat' effect. But the American *new historicist* critics argue that, even though the plays do show authority challenged and overthrown, the drama always ends with monarchical power re-established; and indeed, all the more strongly established because it allowed subversion to flourish, but has contained it successfully. Monarchical power – the right of a king or queen to rule absolutely, without deferring to the authority of any other person or body in any area, like the Church, the landowners or parliament – was under threat right the way through the period in which Shakespeare wrote for The King's Men. Indeed, it collapsed altogether when war broke out between king and parliament twenty-six years after Shakespeare's death; and, of course, parliament immediately closed down all the theatres. Absolute monarchical power in the person of Fortinbras, argues Leonard Tennenhouse, an important American new historicist, has shown itself more secure than ever at the end of the play. Neither of the regicides (king-killers), Claudius and Hamlet, have shown, in the way they stage themselves and their concerns, the ability to be the rightful ruler of Denmark. Legitimate monarchy, when it is descended from royal blood and uses military force openly and effectively, is irresistible. Neither Claudius nor Hamlet uses force in this way, and each is defeated.

It can also be argued that there is something obviously unsatisfactory about the succession of Fortinbras. This is something you feel when watching the end of the play. Perhaps it is because we are seeing 'power nakedly materialised' in the figure of Fortinbras. Stories about what makes kings sacred, and the monarchy an enduring and unifying paternal reassurance in an unstable world, are embarrassingly and revealingly stripped away in this moment (Barker 1993: 51).

The new historicists' ideas are opposed by the British school of Shakespeare critics known as the *cultural materialists*. They see in the plays subversive ideas that not only deny the 'naturalness' of absolute monarchy, but even speak up for the marginal and dispossessed – the poor, the outcast and women. They contest the idea that the historical and tragic drama of the time always represents the total dominance of male power, the court and the monarch. They see within the ideology a *series of conflicting stories*, not a *single* story that will always finally contain the others. For the cultural materialists there are *dissident* stories that undermine and call into question (or subvert) that story which supports the powerful and is most widely believed (i.e. is dominant). That story, however, according to the new historicists, will always ultimately endorse the rule of the king in the state and of the father in the family (a simple definition of the term *patriarchy*). We can look at these two theories about how power works by examining the depiction of women in the tragedies.

Tragedy and gender

Many feminist critics have written about the tragedies' portrayal of women and their relationships with men. Feminist critics are not all of a type. Here by 'feminist critics' I mean those who feel that literature, like our society, is, and has been, unjustly dominated by men. In their writings, these critics seek to show the nature of that male dominance as it appears in different forms in the texts being studied. *Gender* is, for them, part of that dominance, because it is seen as socially created; *sex*, on the other hand, is a biological fact (though there are obviously grey areas here too). Thus women naturally have breasts, are equipped to conceive, bear and nurture children, and so on. These are sexual characteristics. Most feminists, on the other hand, would say that being submissive, gentle and taking trouble over your appearance are qualities that society tends to make women want to have: they are not 'naturally' female, as are the sexual characteristics of female bodies. Gender relates to a set of ideas and assumptions that are attributed variously to men and women, but have no *necessary* connection to their bodies' sexual characteristics. In a society dominated by men, the qualities of the female gender will reflect that power imbalance, and place women at a disadvantage.

There is, of course, no doubt that women's position in society was considerably worse in Shakespeare's time than it is today, though it was not as bad as some people assume. Unmarried women and widows, for instance, had independent rights over property superior to those enjoyed by females in the late eighteenth century. The restrictive sexual prudishness of the mid-nineteenth century did not exist then. Yet women were generally regarded as inferior. Some influential authorities held them to be incomplete men, as earlier observed. The rational and logical element believed to distinguish the male was lacking in the woman. Women were governed by the moon, as their menstrual cycle revealed. Consequently they were inconstant and changeable. Women could never shake off the responsibility of mother Eve for the Fall of mankind in the Garden of Eden. Once their virginity was lost, they were likely to be sexually demanding and to lead men into sin. A gentlewoman was supposed to be a virgin at marriage so that her husband could be sure that the children she bore were his own, and he could then control her sexuality. Legitimate birth was, after all, the principal qualification for the transfer of property in this society (see Box 7, p. 69). Silence and obedience were politely regarded as the highest of female graces. All these ideas are evident, perhaps dominant, in Shakespeare's plays; but there are also female characters who clearly present quite different qualities.

The power of men over women can be seen not only in the way women are represented but in the assumptions that the plays make about the nature and place of women in society. The response from its audience that *King Lear* expects would seem to be based firmly on an idea of female subordination. Goneril and Regan's treatment of their father can be seen as wrong not just because it is cruel but, crucially, because it reverses the 'natural' and unchangeable law that daughters must always obey their fathers and husbands. In Act I, the now-retired Lear and his troop of badly-behaved knights are staying at the home of his daughter Goneril. When she requests that he slims down this riotous crew – for Lear the first concrete sign of resistance from his older daughters – he is angry with her not for her lack of respect, or because she went back on the terms under which her power was established; what rouses him to fury is that *his daughter* could *disobey* him. He immediately denies that she is really his daughter (I 4 218), and keeps repeating the idea; he pretends he can't recognise her (I 4 236), then says she cannot have been fathered by him (I 4 254). Female disobedience is to him unthinkable. Finally, in a horrible curse, he calls upon 'nature' herself to make Goneril incapable of bearing children:

Lear Hear, Nature, hear, dear goddess, hear!   275
       Suspend thy purpose, if thou didst intend
       To make this creature fruitful.
       Into her womb convey sterility,
       Dry up in her the organs of increase,*
       And from her derogate* body never spring   280
       A babe to honour her!

                                                    (I 4 275–81)

* [279] *organs of increase* her womb [280] *derogate* debased, or perhaps incomplete, disabled

Not only does Lear think that as a (retired) king he has the right to command a goddess: he thinks nature will agree to go against her own course (i.e. render a fertile woman infertile) as a punishment for a daughter disobeying her father. Female disobedience is more unnatural even than infertility! The speeches that condemn Goneril and Regan concentrate on their *unnaturalness*. Albany, Goneril's weak but honest husband, calls them 'tigers, not daughters' (IV 2 40); the heavens themselves must surely quickly punish such a subversion of the natural order, or else

'Humanity must perforce [i.e. of necessity] prey on itself/Like monsters of the deep' (IV 2 49–50). 'Proper deformity shows not in the fiend [i.e. the devil]/So horrid as in woman' (IV 2 60–1). In fact the devil, the bringer of all evil into the world, is overtly connected with female sexuality in Lear's shockingly vicious description of the female genitals (IV 6 118–29). This may be seen as prophetic. It is the lust they share for Edmund that leads to the destruction of them both – Regan is poisoned by Goneril, and Goneril, in despair when Edmund is mortally wounded, kills herself.

It might be objected that Cordelia shows disobedience to her father but is nevertheless presented as virtuous. At first glance, this looks true, but Cordelia is actually only standing up for the right of a husband to take some of the love that a daughter, prior to her marriage, owes solely to her father. And, indeed, even though disowned by her father, by the end of Act I Scene 1 Cordelia, as the betrothed of the King of France, has a new master. Unlike her sisters, she has never challenged patriarchy at all:

Cordelia Good my lord,   95
    You have begot* me, bred me, loved me: I
    Return those duties back as are right fit,
    Obey you, love you and most honour you.
    Why have my sisters husbands if they say
    They love you all? Happily, when I shall wed,   100
    The lord whose hand must take my plight* shall carry
    Half my love with him, half my care and duty.

                                 (I 1 95–102)

   * [96] *begot* fathered [101] *plight* wedding vow

When the two are finally reconciled, she even denies that she has a reason to resent the way he has treated her (IV 7 75). The whole dramatic development of the play seems slowly to build up our sympathy for Lear, and never seems to put us in a position to question the play's subordination of women. A feminist critic may therefore condemn the play altogether. Alternatively, the critic may continue to take pleasure in the play as drama while withholding approval of what the play may be saying (McLuskie 1985: 98).

Or, again, the critic may actually find readings of the plays that subvert the apparent sexist assumptions of early seventeenth-century plays. These readings might not detect a hidden feminism in Shakespeare – though some critics, like Juliet Dusinberre (1996a), claim to have done so (see p. 128). Rather, they uncover the social and economic roots of injustice and inequality, and expose the contradictions within them. Or they find clearly expressed in the plays a plea for treating everyone fairly, simply because we are all human.

Such a project can be conducted for *King Lear*, but I would like to discuss it with relevance to *Othello*. Emilia, Iago's wife, puts in context much of the play's male behaviour in a speech she makes at the end of Act IV. Desdemona is getting ready for bed, for the last time – though she does not know this, of course. When Othello comes to bed he will kill her because he has been persuaded by Iago that she has slept with Cassio. *Are* there women, she asks Emilia, who would be unfaithful to their husbands? She would not be so for the whole world. If you had the world, replies Emilia, it *would* be up to you whether or not it was wrong. And this is the play's point about male jealousy and possessiveness: it is the men who have the power and make the rules. But if men realised that women were the same as them and treated women as equals, not as possessions, the catastrophe which is about to occur would never arise. That whole code of behaviour which makes men feel that they must use violence to defend their collective honour against a treacherous and rebellious womankind would fall away, to everyone's advantage (Ryan 1989: 57). Feminist critics could then read Othello's violent jealousy as the product of a social system where women are dominated and possessed by men. More equal relationships between men and women, in which one party did not see the other as their property, would make such actions seem absurd.

Desdemona Beshrew me, if I would do such a wrong
    For the whole world.
Emilia Why, the wrong is but a wrong i'th'* world;   80
    and having the world for your labour, 'tis a wrong in
    your own world, and you might quickly make it right.
Desdemona I do not think there is any such woman.
Emilia Yes, a dozen; and as many to th' vantage* as
    would store the world they play'd for*   85
    But I do think it is their husbands' faults
    If wives do fall. Say that they slack their duties,*
    And pour our treasures into foreign laps;*
    Or else break out in peevish* jealousies,
    Throwing restraint upon us; or say they strike us,   90
    Or scant our former having in despite:*
    Why, we have galls;* and though we have some grace,
    Yet have we some revenge. Let husbands know
    Their wives have sense* like them; they see, and smell,
    And have their palates both for sweet and sour,   ` `95
    As husbands have. What is it that they do
    When they change us for others? Is it sport?*
    I think it is. And doth affection* breed it?
    I think it doth. Is't frailty that thus errs?
    It is so too. And have we not affections,   100
    Desires for sport, and frailty as men have?
    Then let them use us well; else let them know,
    The ills we do, their ills instruct us so.

                                 (IV 3 78–103)

   * [80] *i'th'* in the [84] *to th' advantage* in addition [85] *store the world they play'd for* populate the world they wanted to win [87] *slack their duties* neglect their wives in bed [88] *into foreign laps* into other women(!) [89] *peevish* childish [91] *scant our former having in despite* spitefully reduce how much money they allow us [92] *galls* the capacity to feel resentment [94] *sense* physical senses [97] *sport* fun [98] *affection* emotion

It worth noting that this speech does not appear in the Quarto version of the text, but only in the Folio (see Box 2, p. 25). No one knows why this is, but it may be connected to the controversial power and directness of Emilia's argument here.

Such feminist readings of the plays do not seek to prove that Shakespeare was a feminist, or indeed a sexist. Instead they try to reveal the ways in which ideology operates both to oppress women and to trap men into a way of behaving that entails violence. Sometimes this violence can even be directed against themselves, as we see in *Othello*.

We have here an indication of the approach of contemporary critics to the tragedies. They are not about heroic individuals with 'flawed' characters whose lives are lived out in a world where good and evil are engaged in a mighty struggle. Rather, critics look at how tragedies show human suffering to be the result of society's contradictory forces – forces that we can recognise on stage, and therefore, perhaps, seek to change in the world.

Summary

- Shakespeare lived at a time when the medieval world was giving way to the modern one. The principal characters in tragedies can be destroyed because they are trying to live in a world that no longer has any secure basis, or, more often, because the contradictions within the way they understand the world make their lives impossible.
- The tragedies show the operations of power in society by revealing how the stories and displays of those in authority convince those without power of their superiors' right to rule, baseless though these stories may well be.
- In particular, the tragedies reveal the ideological means by which men at this time ensured dominance over women.
- How might you apply the idea of a character destroyed by a changing or contradictory ideology to Antony and/or Cleopatra in *Antony and Cleopatra*? Or Brutus in *Julius Caesar*? Or Coriolanus in *Coriolanus*? What might you gain by applying this sort of feminist reading to the depiction of Tamora and Lavinia in *Titus Andronicus*?

Further reading

O'Toole (1990) is a lively and radical re-reading of the tragedies in their historical context, and is a very good place to start. I have made extensive use here of Holderness (1989b), a paper written for A Level students. More difficult, but certainly accessible, is Belsey (1985), which deals very interestingly with tragedy and gender. More difficult, but very important, is Dollimore (1984).

Chapter 9

Understanding the mixed-genre plays

Measure for Measure
and *Troilus and Cressida*

Not all of Shakespeare's plays fit neatly into the conventions of comedy, tragedy, history or romance. Those that don't have often puzzled critics because neither their narratives nor their moral and political outlooks seem to fit the preconceptions that these writers brought to Shakespeare. Consequently these texts became known as 'problem plays'.

It can be argued, in fact, that these plays reveal more about the worries and conflicts of the period in which they were written than many of the better-known and more frequently studied plays. To radical twentieth-century readers, these plays seem to cast doubt on and undermine many of the ideals and beliefs of 'traditional' English society, and this has given them new appeal. Indeed, it is thought that *Troilus and Cressida* could have been first performed not in Shakespeare's lifetime but in Germany in the 1890s. Certainly in England it lay unperformed in its original version between the first decade of the seventeenth century and the first decade of the twentieth. Today it is very popular: between 1993 and 1999 there were five professional productions in London alone.

This is not to say that these plays were 'ahead of their time'. That makes little sense. It is rather that the century which has just ended found that it could see itself more clearly in these works than in certain other plays.

The language of love

In the 1997 Riverside edition of Shakespeare's plays both *Measure For Measure* and *Troilus and Cressida* are categorised as *comedies*. Love and marriage are certainly principal concerns of both, as they are for the plays traditionally classed as comedies. In these two texts, however, the interest seems to be more in the *stories we tell about* love and marriage – and how those stories come into conflict with the facts of life as we find them.

One of the main ideas of new historicist criticism (see pp. 204f.) is sometimes expressed in the notion of *historicising the text and textualising history*. This means, first of all, that these critics believe we can read the text as a historical document about the times in which it is written ('historicising the text'). Equally, however, the only way we can know about the times in which a text was written is by reading other texts from that period – both literary and non-literary. But, crucially, these non-literary texts – whether letters, diaries, government documents or parish registers – are not regarded as any the less subject to the interpretation of the reader than are the plays or the poems (this is what they mean by 'textualising history'). All history (in the sense of what historians reconstruct of the past) is a kind of literary criticism and all literary criticism a kind of history. The two blur into each other. It certainly *could* be objected that this position ignores the specifically literary and dramatic types ('registers'; see pp. 21ff.) of language that make these texts what they are. But in the view of these critics reality itself is to an extent merged with textuality. We read the past from the present as a story which in the end reflects the stories (texts, narratives and ideas, both written and spoken) that *we tell about ourselves*. The French philosopher Michel Foucault (1926–84), whose ideas greatly influenced the new historicist critics, believed that when we write about both the past and the present we do so in order to circulate stories that convincingly give power to the tellers: *that* is what writing is.

So, in Shakespeare's time, as in ours, the texts produced partake of the fabric of life itself. They show the strategies used by the rulers, consciously and unconsciously, to maintain their power. New historicists consider that these plays show us, for example, how ideas that threaten the dominant and powerful are allowed expression only to be quickly suppressed. Thus only the true prince can bring harmony to Vienna in *Measure For Measure*, reconciling the sinner and the virtuous in the merciful institutions of the state, despite all the troubles of the city. In *Troilus and Cressida*, Cressida's independence of mind leads only to whoredom and despair; same-sex love leads to barbarism and cruelty.

The plays can, however, be read as radical texts, which is how the British cultural materialists regard them. They see the plays as historical documents which reveal the contradictions in the ideas and stories by which people lived, and consequently point forward to a more free and humane future.

Look at the stories told about love and lovers by the characters in these plays. These narratives provide the protagonists with their situations in the plays; and the actions of the protagonists are restricted to the positions offered by those narratives The stories are the structures of feeling and action in which love must happen.

But what if two lovers speak, in effect, *different languages* about love? What chance is there ever of a man and woman uniting harmoniously in a gender-divided, unfair society where the very words they speak about the *same* emotion make real communication impossible? If Troilus speaks of love in an idealised-heroic way, what chance does he have of real union with Cressida, who can talk of love only in a pragmatic, cautious, yet analytical way. The resolution can come only with the language of the powerful overwhelming and absorbing the language of the weak To modern audiences and readers, Troilus' position is morally the weaker, but politically his power over her is unquestioned.

Cressida's uncle Pandarus has problems communicating with a satirical servant when he has to bring a message to Prince Paris: 'Friend, we understand not one another', he says. He concludes that this is because 'I am too courtly and thou art too cunning' (III 1 27–8). This could be said to sum up the relationship between Troilus and Cressida. Troilus, as we saw above (I 1 98–104, see p. 28), has an absurdly inflated view of his lover, seeing her as a mixture of sensuous delight and, revealingly, financial prize. This is the courtly lover's idealisation of the warrior's mistress: an impossibly divine creature who acts as saintly patron of his deeds of battlefield violence.

The same confusion of battlefield and bedroom occurs later. As he awaits his first sexual encounter with her, he fears that he will not be able to discriminate the different sensual pleasures which he is about to experience:

Troilus I do fear besides
   That I shall lose distinction in my joys,
   As doth a battle when they charge on heaps*
   The enemy flying.

(III 2 26–9)

* [28] *As doth a battle when they charge on heaps* 'Just like when a battalion charges on a routed enemy, piling up their slaughtered enemies in heaps'

Like Othello, the courtly warrior cannot separate his love from his conduct and honour as a warrior (see pp. 192f.). Cressida, however, has a far more pragmatic view of sexual relationships between men and women.

When they first meet, both find it hard to speak. Cressida's feelings for Troilus aren't based on the idealisation of the courtly love tradition but come from the physical attraction she feels when she looks at him. However, she knows that once she starts to talk openly about her feelings the words she must use will transform her emotions into something she doesn't intend. She can talk to the *audience* about her feelings, but once she is involved with other characters in the play those emotions will be transformed by the language which the characters use to each other. This is a world ruled by men, and the language of love is their language. Cressida reveals herself to the audience as a woman who guards her own independence, but the only real power she has is to say no to men's advances. She cannot approach a lover (III 2 126–9); she must wait for his advances; and yet once she says yes to him he will have power over her. She knows this in the first act of the play. Here is the last part of her first soliloquy:

Cressida Yet I hold off. Women are angels, wooing:
    Things won are done, joy's soul lies not in the doing.
    That she beloved* knows naught that knows not this:
    Men prize the thing ungained more than it is.
    That she* was never yet that never knew   290
    Love got* so sweet as when desire did sue.
    Therefore this maxim out of* love I teach:
    Achievement is command; ungain'd, beseech;*
    Then though my heart's content firm love doth bear,
    Nothing of that shall from mine eyes appear.   295

                                (I 2 286–95)

    *[288] *she beloved* woman who is loved [290] *she* woman [291] *got* gained [292] *out of* derived from [293] *Achievement … beseech* 'When a man has gone to bed with you he will be in command – because you have nothing for him to beg for any more'

When the courtly and idealistic Troilus and the pragmatic and realistic Cressida finally speak it is only suffer a series of misunderstandings. He talks of the heroic deeds he would wish to perform to prove his love for her – eating rocks, taming tigers and so on (III 2 78). He concludes that his ability to perform these feats is limited by the facts of living in the physical world; Cressida, however, thinks he is engaging in a more down-to-earth piece of sexual banter:

> *Troilus* This is the monstruosity* in love, lady, that
>   the will is infinite and the execution confined, that the
>   desire is boundless and the act a slave to limit.
> *Cressida* They say all lovers swear more performance
>   than they are able, and yet reserve an ability that   85
>   they never perform; vowing more than the perfection
>   of ten,* and discharging less than the tenth part of one.
>
>   (III 2 81–7)

> * [81] *monstruosity* monstrosity, absurdity [84] *performance* skill as a lover [86–7] *vowing more than the perfection of ten* 'promising more than ten perfect lovers could perform'

He does not pick up on her tone, and she is forced to declare her love boldly and simply (III 2 114–15). Once she has done so, she is confused and regretful, and fears that he will now 'play the tyrant' with her (line 119). Silence is her best option. She ends her speech with the words 'Stop my mouth' (line 133), which Troilus immediately misinterprets as an invitation to kiss her, and does so. There is no real communication between them here. Cressida feels divided: she loves Troilus but fears the power he will have over her once they are lovers. The courtly discourse of love is written entirely in his terms, leaving Cressida locked in contradiction: she wants his love but doesn't want his love:

> *Troilus* What offends you, lady?
> *Cressida* Sir, mine own company.   145
> *Troilus* You cannot shun yourself.
> *Cressida* Let me go and try.
>   I have a kind of self resides with you;
>   But an unkind self, that itself would leave

To be another's fool. I would be gone. 150
Where is my wit? I know not what I speak.

(III 2 144–51)

But she must start to speak and, in the world of the play, once they start to talk she is inside his language. It seems that they are groping for some common ground on which to meet. Both of them attempt to fix their love by swearing oaths in their own names, trying to hold down the future by the magical power of words (lines 172–83). But they cannot control the future meaning of their words. Their words will control them. The name 'Cressida' for Shakespeare's audience referred to a proverbially unfaithful woman, so that even before she comes on stage, the word which is her name will already have certain connotations likely to affect their response to her. They could be no more un-prejudiced about her character than a Christian audience would be about a fictional character named Judas, for example. Almost everything about her is controlled by the language in which she has been socially constructed, even before the play was written.

Cressida *does* break her oath to Troilus, in circumstances which non-feminist critics have found hard to excuse. She is returned to her father Calchas, a Trojan defector in the Greek camp, as part of a prisoner exchange. As soon as the Greeks see her, they read her very appearance as a sexual provocation. Cressida's face and body mean something specific to them whether she likes it or not; that's the way they read and understand the world. To them, women who look like Cressida need sexual attention from men; and their honour as men and pride in their masculinity require that they give it. Diomedes, who leads to Troy the Greek embassy that is to effect the prisoner exchange, immediately remarks:

Diomedes The lustre in your eye, heaven in your cheek,
　　Pleads you fair usage, and to Diomed
　　You shall be mistress, and command him wholly.

(IV 4 118–20)

He really means that his desire for her will command his actions;

she will do as he says because she will have no choice if she is to have a man's protection in the predatory world of the Greek camp, as future scenes will reveal. Her appearance means that she will need a protector once among the Greeks. The truth behind his courtly language is very soon revealed when Troilus threatens him for making such an advance to her. 'When I am hence', boasts Diomedes, 'I'll answer to my lust' (IV 4 131–2).

When she reaches the Greek camp, Ulysses expresses the same idea: women who look like her are asking only for one thing:

> Ulysses Fie, fie upon her!
> There's language in her eye, her cheek, her lip,   55
> Nay, her foot speaks; her wanton* spirits look out
> At every joint and motive* of her body.
>
> (IV 5 54–7)

> * [56] *wanton* here, sexually inviting [57] *motive* movement

She has *said* nothing yet. It is *his* language, with its constructions and assumptions, that has created her identity, not, in fact, her own appearance or desires. Yet she must live in this world, and play this role – for it is the only one available to her. She succumbs to her guardian, and becomes Diomedes' lover. She knows, both as Troilus' sworn lover and as a woman who has a mind of her own, that she is living a contradiction; but by the end of the play she has forgotten her desire for independence and is living entirely in the world created by the language of these men. They believe that women have no control over their desires, and that their irrationality will always overwhelm their individuality or reason. Women in this language are base creatures, and she accepts her fate:

> Cressida Troilus, farewell! one eye yet looks on thee,
> But with my heart the other eye doth see.
> Ah poor our sex! this fault in us I find,
> The error of our eye* directs our mind.   110
> What error leads must err; O then conclude,

Minds swayed by eyes are full of turpitude.*
[*Exit*]

(V 2 107–12)

* [110] *The error of our eye* 'Our inability not to find other
men attractive' [112] *turpitude* baseness, being morally despi-
cable

The watching Thersites concludes she is now a whore. She accepts
the role that her appearance demands she play, according to the
world as it is constructed by male language. For his part, Troilus
cannot accept the shock her infidelity delivers to his courtly
ideology: the lover's mistress is by definition chaste and faithful –
otherwise he, a true knight, wouldn't have been attracted to her.
He cannot reconcile himself to this fact without his whole world
becoming fractured. If Cressida's engagement – not with the
audience but with her lover – transforms her into a creature of
men, Troilus' language, which creates love as a function of his
warrior identity, soon faces up to its incoherence. Love will go to
the man who has the power, no matter what his personal feelings
might be. When men worship women they are actually worshipping their own power to elevate a woman above the merely
human. In worshipping a woman they are worshipping themselves. We have seen that the contradiction in the way love is
constructed produces a contradiction in the object of that love, in
this case Cressida herself. The experience for Troilus is so shat-
tering that he loses faith in the principles of logic itself. Hidden
from her sight, he has just watched her give his love token to
Diomedes prior to her final exit:

Troilus This was not she. O madness of discourse,
    That cause sets up with and against itself!
    Bi-fold authority,* where reason can revolt*
    Without perdition,* and loss* assume all reason   145
    Without revolt.* This is, and is not Cressid!

(V 2 142–6)

* [144] *Bi-fold authority* divided basis of thought; *revolt* contradict itself [145] *perdition* loss [of sense]; *loss* loss of sense [146] *revolt* contradiction

He also loses faith in any notion that war can be chivalric, telling Hector that he will show no mercy in battle, even to fallen and unarmed Greeks (V 3 37–49). He falls back on that brutality which is actually the truth about knightly combat and courtly love, and fights with utter ferocity and cynicism (V 5 37–42). He becomes the 'warrior avenger' (Dollimore 1984: 49).

Thus the play's problematic nature actually reveals political and social contradictions inherent in society's view of itself in Shakespeare's time; in particular it reveals that the power *inscribed in* male love comes into conflict with the actual nature of human sexual desire, as well as showing its own contradictory nature. By 'inscribed in' I mean that male love can't exist in this society without containing and being totally shaped by the inequalities of power between men and women which existed then. This inequality of power is 'written into' all the stories of love that are told because it is built into the language in which those stories are told.

The same exploration of sexual conflict is found in *Measure For Measure*. The Duke of Vienna, worried that sexual licence has grown out of control, pretends to go away from the city, leaving in charge his strict deputy Angelo. The duke expects Angelo to enforce the fierce law that makes sex outside of marriage a capital offence – he himself has been too lenient to enforce it. Meanwhile, disguised as a friar, the duke watches what develops. Angelo decides to make an example of Claudio, whose fiancée Juliet is pregnant. Claudio's sister Isabella, herself about to enter a convent, goes to Angelo to plead for her brother's life.

Their debate is carried out initially at the level of abstract discussion (II 2 25–136). But it is not her reasoning that has the most impact on Angelo. Claudio's friend Lucio had told her that she was the right person to sue for his life, because when a young virgin kneels before authority and asks for mercy, all tradition says that she will be granted it (I 4 80–3). In a society where virginity stands for moral purity, a pleading virgin must be impartial; to deny her mercy would be to deny 'fairness' itself, in both senses of the word (look at how Lucio greets her at first meeting [I 4 24]) (Piesse 1996: 61). Yet a virgin's moral power rests on the unstated premiss of her desirability; she is female beauty unsullied by the potent threat of awakened female sexuality. She is, in theory, outside the sexual struggle. Men are attracted to the unthreatening moral purity of the virgin – but they want her, obviously, in order to take that purity from her. The whole contradictory construction is based on fear of female sexuality and the power it has over men. But in this play men speak a language about love that controls and neutralises that sexuality.

Men want their sexual desire to be dominant. Yet women have a crucial and obvious advantage in this struggle: males require females in order to reproduce themselves. Husbands need to control their wives' sexuality if they are to have sons whose paternity is beyond question. The fear of this real power that women have recurs in the imagery of so many of the exchanges in this play.

It is when Isabella moves the discussion away from the abstract and asks Angelo to consider his own feelings that he sees her as an individual, and therefore as a particular woman, rather than a symbol of virginity. Has he not wanted to do the very thing for which he now condemns her brother?

Isabella Go to your own bosom,
    Knock there, and ask your heart what it doth know
    That's like my brother's fault. If it confess
    A natural guiltiness, such as is his,
    Let it not sound a thought upon your tongue   140
    Against my brother's life.
Angelo (Aside) She speaks, and 'tis
    such sense* that my sense* breeds with it.

                            (II 2 136–42)

   * [142] *such sense* reason; *my sense* my sensuality

Angelo suddenly finds himself sexually attracted to her. Isabella's ability to plead, Angelo's language makes clear, is not actually a function of her power of reason, but of her sexual attractiveness. An obscene pun, which Angelo unconsciously makes once she has gone, reinforces this: 'Is this her fault, or mine?', he says, at the beginning of his soliloquy (II 2 162). 'Fault' was used as a term for the vagina. His 'fault', however, as a man, can only be in reasoning or behaviour. Once she has gone he finds that he 'loves' her (II 2 176), but what sort of love it can be remains open to question. It may be a subconscious recognition that, since he has power over this individual woman, he can get sex from her and father his child on her. This would be his definition of 'love'.

Sexual attraction is common to all societies and eras, but is always constructed by the political and economic power structures of those particular societies and eras. Given the stories this society tells about female desire and virginity, sexual relations must inevitably be distorted. Angelo has the power, and therefore control over the meaning of words. Because Isabella, the novice-nun, talks about sex in the same religious language that Angelo uses to justify the law, her own words make her a subject of male power, as well as the contradictions within that power: men want women to be pure, but at the same time want to take that purity from them.

Isabella is quite unaware of how her words will be interpreted once her language is thought of in sexual terms – as it inevitably will be in the world of the play. She continues to use the religious language, unaware that it carries within it that denial of normal sexuality which is at the root of Vienna's problems. That form of Christian morality which regards all non-procreative sex as wrong simply does not fit with the facts of human life. When Pompey the pimp is arrested, he puts the matter to the magistrate very succinctly: 'Does your worship mean to geld [castrate a male] and splay [sterilise a female] all the youth of the city?' (II 1 230–1) The law must accept the fact of human sexuality, not impose a religious rigour which serves the interests of the powerful – who are in this case, since it is women who 'tempt', men.

Isabella herself applauds the law and hates fornication (II 2 29–30). But her own language is full of suppressed sexuality, even when she uses religious ideas. When she returns to Angelo to plead once more for her brother's life, she says she would rather die than yield up her virginity to save his life. Yet the language she uses is startling. He asks what she would do if a judge said he would pardon her brother if she slept with him:

Angelo What would you do?
Isabella As much for my poor brother as myself;
That is, were I under the terms* of death,   100
Th' impression of keen whips I'ld wear as rubies,
And strip myself for death, as to a bed
That longing have been sick for, ere* I'ld yield
My body up to shame.

(II 4 98–104)

* [100] *terms* sentence [103] *ere* before

She is unaware of the impact of her words. She gives an image of herself as receiving blows from a whip with pride and pleasure; and of herself undressing for bed – a bed which she had desired so much that it had made her sick. The discourse of Christian asceticism contains a repressed sexuality which makes her all the more attractive to Angelo. He sees her as a woman, and tells her that she must stop teasing him and become what she must be, a sexual partner to a superior man who desires her. But he also despises her *because* he desires her. She is attractive because chaste; but that attraction tempts a man to sin.

In a crucial speech she admits that women are frail, as men sometimes are, in the context of their powers of reasoning (II 4 117–23). But she goes on to pick up Angelo's promptings about the specific frailty of women. She agrees that women are inferior, and thinks she is talking about their natural susceptibility to male reasoning and power. But Angelo is alert to the sexual possibilities in her speech and tells her she must take up the role allotted to her by the language she is speaking.

Angelo Nay, women are frail too.
Isabella Ay, as the glasses* where they view themselves,   125
    Which are as easy broke as they make forms.*
    Women? Help, heaven! Men their creation mar
    In profiting by them.* Nay, call us ten times frail,
    For we are soft as our complexions are,
    And credulous to false prints.*
Angelo I think it well;   130
    And from this testimony of your own sex
    (Since I suppose we are made to be no stronger
    Than faults may shake our frames), let me be bold.
    I do arrest* your words. Be that you are,
    That is, a woman; if you be more, you're none;*   135
    If you be one (as you are well expressed
    By all external warrants*), show it now,
    By putting on the destined livery.*

                                     (II 4 124–38)

* [125] *glasses* mirrors [126] *which are as easy broke as they make forms* which break as easily as they reflect images; but also (of women) 'who conceive a child as easily as their virginity is broken' [127–8] *Men their creation mar in profiting by them* 'Men spoil their creation in God's image by taking advantage of women' [130] *credulous to false prints* easily persuaded of untruths; but also 'willing to conceive an illegitimate child' [134] *arrest* stop; but also 'take into my custody and control' [135] *if you be more, you're none* if you are more chaste than a woman really is, you're not a woman at all [137] *external warrants* outward signs (Angelo is using legal language to describe her female attributes!) [138] *livery* a servant's uniform – so *destined* livery has the sense here of 'the badge of the role which, as a woman, you were always bound to assume sexually with a man'

Women's ability to conceive is actually the same thing, in this story, as their weakness and inferiority to men. Her own words contain this admission, so she should accept that she is destined to be his mistress. She finally understands what he is saying and appreciates the sexual subtext. She pleads for a return to a plain, non-sexual, discourse which cannot implicate her – but how can they return to what wasn't there is the first place? He defines what love is, not her:

> *Isabella* I have no tongue but one;* gentle my lord,
> Let me entreat you speak the former language.   140
> *Angelo* Plainly conceive,* I love you.
> *Isabella* My brother did love Juliet,
> And you tell me that he shall die for't.*
> *Angelo* He shall not, Isabel, if you give me love.

(II 4 139–44)

> * [139] *no tongue but one* 'one level only of meaning to my words' [141] *conceive* understand, but yet another parallel between men making women understand them, and men fathering children on them [143] *for't* for it

Meaning in the play is actually a function of power. Those with power have the final judgement on what words mean. This is made explicit soon afterwards. If Isabella goes out and proclaims Angelo's actions to the world, his good name and political position will mean that people will interpret her accusations as baseless slander (II 4 154–9).

The strange ending of *Measure For Measure* plays with the generic ending of comedy, multiple marriage. But it uses marriage as a punishment. Angelo must marry his ex-betrothed, Mariana, a death sentence – which he thought his rightful punishment (V 1 370–4) – being waived. This what Mariana wants, for it gives the jilted woman the social status she thought she'd never have. Whether either will be happy in the union is another matter. Lucio, Claudio's witty and insolent friend who slanders the Duke, regards his sentence of marriage to Kate Keepdown, the prostitute whom he impregnated, as equivalent to 'pressing to death,/ Whipping and hanging' (V 1 522–3). Claudio and Juliet are happy, but they were happy in their love and prospective parenthood before the state intervened. It is not really surprising that the text gives Isabella no response to the Duke's surprise proposal of marriage (V 1 534–7). Marriage in this scene is used to punish and control. Like Cressida, Isabella perhaps now realises that once you speak the language of the powerful you will implicated in their system.

Measure For Measure shows how the imposition of patriarchal law distorts sexual desire. This *may* reveal the resourcefulness of the powerful; or it may indicate a community's need to control the destabilising force of lust outside marriage. Alternatively, it may point forward to a utopian sexuality wherein desire and procreation find their own level free from legal constraint.

What I have argued in this section, it should be noted, is not that Shakespeare wrote *Measure For Measure* as an attack on marriage. Instead I have followed that contemporary critical approach which finds the source of the 'problems' of these plays not in the writer's design or dramatic skill – both plays work brilliantly on stage – but in the contradictions and absurdities that, from our perspective, are evident in the ideas about sexual love current in Jacobean London. In the comedies written in the 1590s love and marriage, while never simple, were not interrogated so darkly. There does seem to have been a shift in outlook with regard to these issues in the plays written after 1600.

Rulers and ruled

Macbeth has frequently been read as a struggle between good and evil, and as a warning against unjustifiable ambition; *Julius Caesar* has been seen as demonstrating that any violent opposition to established rule is bound to make matters worse. The mixed-genre plays are much less susceptible to simplistic readings of this kind. There is one famous speech in *Troilus and Cressida*, however, which is frequently quoted on its own as a demonstration of Shakespeare's own anti-egalitarian credentials. Indeed, it was quoted by Nigel Lawson, the British chancellor of the

Box 12: London

In 1600, nine-tenths of England's population lived in the countryside and its small market towns. Farmland, forest and moorland were punctuated by enclosed parks kept by noblemen for hunting deer and boar. Norwich, Bristol, York, Salisbury, Newcastle, Exeter and Coventry were the only towns with populations in excess of 5,000, and there was only one city by European standards: London. It was here that Shakespeare spent most of his working life, and aspects of the city are revealed in many of his plays.

Between 1550 and 1600 the population of the capital city trebled to around 150,000. In Europe, only Paris and Naples were larger. Maybe 15 per cent of Londoners were wealthy: the court, the aristocrats and important merchants. The vast majority of England's trade passed through London and here the merchants increased their wealth and power. Merchants had to be members of the livery companies that regulated the market against new competition. The senior officers of these companies governed the City of London and made its laws. Junior members – craftsmen, clerks, shop-keepers, apprentices – represented the typical 'citizenry' of London. They tended to be Puritan in their religious observance, and very proud of their status. Below them were the great mass of servants and, beneath, the genuinely poor who eked out a living one way or another.

London's 150,000 inhabitants were crammed into an area from the Tower in the east to Westminster in the west. The old city walls still stood, and the gates were locked at night, but increasingly new buildings were being erected outside the walls. London's great public buildings – the Tower and Whitehall Palace (sites of royal power), Westminster Abbey and old St Paul's Cathedral (symbols of the Church's importance), the Guildhall (the site of City government) and the Royal Exchange (the site of trade) – were spread across the city and surrounded by the parish churches, houses, shops, taverns, inns, schools, prisons and workshops of the rest of the population. The mansions of the rich, mostly along the Strand, were surrounded by the hovels of the poor in a warren of narrow, mostly unpaved, streets. The administration of the City of London did not extend fully north of the walls or south of the river. These areas were known as the 'liberties', and it was on the South Bank, beyond the control of the Puritan councillors, that The Swan, The Rose and The Globe theatres stood, along-side pits for bear-baiting and cock-fighting and a large number of brothels.

There was only one bridge, 'London Bridge', situated near the Tower in the east. Houses and shops lined its sides, and the heads of executed felons stood on pikes over its southern gateway. The Thames was the main artery of transport, with watermen rowing passengers among the ships and barges of merchants and traders.

London was a crowded, dirty and dangerous place, with a high mortality rate. Each 'ward' of the city had its 'scavengers' who were supposed to deal with sanitation, but most sewage just went down a gutter in the middle of the street, towards the Thames or one of the other London rivers. Plague was a constant bringer of sudden death, with bad outbreaks in 1593, 1597 and 1625, when 40,000 died. Clean water was not easily available, and it was probably typhoid from infected water that killed Shakespeare (Honan 1998: 407). Beer was safer than water to drink, and most people drank beer from an early age. Some historians have remarked that the violence of early modern city life may have been connected to the general low level of sobriety.

It was easy to get away with criminal activity in London, and many home-less and unemployed people, supporting themselves by begging, trickery and prostitution, drifted towards the capital. Many men went about armed, and fatal brawls were common. Shakespeare is very satirical about the inefficient police system of watchmen in *Measure For Measure* and *Much Ado About Nothing*. As well as the sight of violent street brawls, Londoners would have been used to public executions, the carcasses of slaughtered animals around them and, not so very rarely, corpses in the street.

London was nevertheless the most exciting and energetic place in the country. Money and power flowed through its streets alongside its stench and ever-present danger. Its merchant class, which was to defeat the forces of absolute monarchy later in the seventeenth century, were the most progressive and dynamic group in the country – even if they usually opposed the theatre.

Shakespeare's first play, *King Henry VI Part I*, seems to have been first performed in London in March 1592. His long poem *Venus and Adonis* was registered with the government censor and literature licensee, the Stationer's Office, in April 1593. We know that until 1585 he was in Warwickshire. What he was up to between 1585 and 1592, and how it was that he should suddenly have appeared in London as a writer have been subjects of considerable speculation. There are tales of deer-poaching, fighting against the Spanish in Holland and of visiting Italy, but there is no firm evidence for these stories. Evidence that he was a tutor to a Catholic family in Lancashire (Honan 1998: 65) is inconclusive. We know little, in fact, other than that he made his name in London. The world of its taverns, brothels and palaces is represented in many places, vividly so in *King Henry IV Part I* and less explicitly in *Measure For Measure*.

exchequer in 1983 as conclusive proof that 'Shakespeare was a Tory' (Wilson 1997: 65). In fact this play, taken as a whole, serves to undermine conventional notions of authority and hierarchy, just as *Measure For Measure* can be read as exposing the realities of arbitrary royal justice.

Ulysses is an important character both in the story of the Trojan War and in the play Shakespeare wrote about it. In mythology he is famed as 'the man of many wiles', as the first line of Homer's *Odyssey* puts it. In *Troilus and Cressida* he makes the most significant contribution to the Greeks' debate in Act I about why they have failed to capture Troy after nine long years of siege. Ulysses tells the assembled princes of Greece that their failure stems from lack of obedience and due deference to superiority in the army. After all, nature itself obeys order and precedence:

Ulysses The heavens themselves, the planets and this centre*
    Observe degree,* priority and place,   85
    Insisture,* course, proportion,* season, form,
    Office, and custom, in all line of order.
    And therefore is the glorious planet Sol*
    In noble eminence enthroned and sphered
    Amidst the other; whose med'cinable* eye   90
    Corrects the influence of evil planets,
    And posts* like the commandment of a king
    Sans check* to good and bad. But when the planets
    In evil mixture to disorder wander,
    What plagues, what portents, what mutiny,   95
    What raging of the sea, shaking of earth,

Commotion in the winds, frights, changes, horrors,
Divert and crack, rend* and deracinate*
The unity and married calm of states
Quite from their fixture! O, when degree is shaked,   100
Which is the ladder of all high designs*
The enterprise is sick! How could communities,
Degrees in schools,* and brotherhoods* in cities,
Peaceful commerce from dividable shores,
The primogeniture* and due of birth,   105
Prerogative* of age, crowns, sceptres, laurels,
But by degree stand in authentic* place?
Take but degree away, untune that string,
And hark what discord follows.

(I 3 84–109)

* [84] *this centre* the earth [85] *degree* rank, place in a hierarchy [86] *insisture* a planet's apparent stopping at certain
times on its orbit (Ulysses is doing his best to sound authoritative); *proportion* symmetry [88] *glorious planet Sol* the sun –
in the old Ptolemaic version of the universe the sun was the
planet that went round the earth, at the centre [90] *med'cin-
able* healing, correcting [92] *posts* sends fast messages [93]
sans check without hindrance [98] *rend* tear; *deracinate* root
up [101] *the ladder of all high designs* no great project can
succeed without a hierarchy, which acts like a ladder for
ascent [103] *degrees in schools* academic ranks and orders of
achievement; *brotherhoods in cities* trade guilds [105] *primogeniture* right of the first-born legitimate male to inherit [106]
Prerogative special rights [107] *authentic* authoritative

There is no ironic intention in the wording of this speech. It is a
highly rhetorical presentation of the medieval argument for the
importance of hierarchy in society, that would be read out by
order of the monarch to congregations in Elizabethan churches
(the 'Homily of Obedience'), and represented in the work of
political writers of the time like Richard Hooker. Nature itself is
built on a system of hierarchy and obedience. He draws on the

widely held belief that when there is a disturbance in the order of the heavens, a disturbance on earth soon follows. It is therefore only a matter of nature that we should obey our superiors in everything we do, or else chaos will follow.

It is also what Agamemnon, the commander in chief, would like to hear, for it is clearly an attack on the insubordinate stance of Achilles, their greatest warrior, who is currently refusing to fight. Yet Ulysses' sincerity is soon thrown into doubt by his account of Achilles' behaviour. According to Ulysses, as Achilles lazes in his tent, he is being entertained by his lover Patroclus' satirical impersonations of other Greek leaders. Ulysses goes out of his way to give precise details of Patroclus' performance – which he could not possibly have seen. In an earlier speech, his first in the play, Agamemnon had described the Greek predicament in language that is remarkable for its sonorous emptiness (see pp. 20f.). Ulysses now spends ten lines comparing Agamemnon's way of talking to the noise made by an actor stamping on the stage to sound impressive in order to hide the fact that he cannot act (I 3 153–6). His language is 'to-be-pitied and over-wrested [over-tightened, exaggerated] seeming [i.e. pretension]' (I 3 157); his words are so absurdly pompous that they would seem exaggerations if they were used by the monster Typhon, mythological father of hurricanes (I 3 159–61). As we've already seen the truth of this description, Ulysses is either being extraordinarily tactless or extremely cunning. Either way, in this public parade of his leader's failings Ulysses is himself showing exactly the lack of respect for his superior that his previous speech condemns.

The truth of the theory of natural superiority is further undermined when the Trojan emissary Aeneas arrives soon after and has to enquire which one of the Greek leaders *is* Agamemnon; it seems that he cannot tell by looking who is supposed to be the most senior. Presumably the position of the actors on stage should indicate seniority. If that is so, Agamemnon cannot look as if he is in charge despite his position. If not, then the stage picture shows the audience that the Greeks themselves do not realise that they are revealing a lack of belief in the 'specialty of rule' (I 3 78) – the obligation to obey the ruler – and natural hierarchy.

Aeneas brings a challenge from Hector, Troy's greatest warrior.

He claims that the woman he loves is 'wiser, fairer, truer' (I 3 275) than any of the Greeks' mistresses. He will, moreover, prove this boast in single combat. Ulysses knows that Hector's challenge is really directed at their best fighter, the recalcitrant Achilles (I 3 321–3). He decides that it would be a very bad idea for Achilles to fight Hector. If Hector wins, they lose their chief asset; if Achilles wins, his pride will make him even more difficult to control. He therefore arranges to hold a rigged ballot for the right to meet Hector, fixed so that the very strong but very stupid Ajax will fight him. If the rest of the Greeks then praise him as their champion it will humiliate Achilles and they will have their revenge on him: 'Ajax employed plucks down Achilles' plumes' (I 3 385). It is obvious that natural hierarchy is not what really matters to Ulysses. What matters is to gain political advantage within the jealousies of the Greek camp.

In fact, the whole plan fails disastrously. First Hector breaks off the fight with Ajax because they are actually related to one another (IV 5 120–3) – or, perhaps, because he is having the worst of it and realises he might lose (IV 5 114–16). Then Ajax, after all the praise heaped upon him by the Greek leaders, grows so proud that, like Achilles, he too refuses to fight when battle comes (V 4 14–15). Both join the fight only when someone close to them is killed (Patroclus, in Achilles' case), so that personal revenge rather than obedience and loyalty is the motivating force.

The events of the play show that Ulysses' cunning is not to be relied upon: he is a duplicitous plotter and schemer, and not even a very effective one. His 'policy' (political cunning), says the foul-mouthed servant Thersites, 'is proved not worth a blackberry' (V 4 12). *Troilus and Cressida* shows a world where both conservative political theory and Machiavellian politics are revealed to be as hollow and rotten as the warrior 'in sumptuous armour' (V 6 26, sd), who, when killed, is shown to be a 'Most putrefied core, so fair without' (V 8 1). Whatever might be the best justification or method of ruling a country, it is not to be found in this play.

Neither does the duke in *Measure For Measure* present a model of the ideal ruler. This was not the view among early twentieth-century Christian scholars. The influential critic

G. Wilson Knight wrote in his 1930 book *The Wheel of Fire* that the play is a Christian parable: 'The Duke's sense of human responsibility is delightful throughout: he is a kindly father, and all the rest are his children.' He is, wrote Wilson Knight, 'automatically comparable with Divinity' (quoted in Watts 1986: 119). This version sees the duke as a deity who leaves fallible mankind to sin and realise its own frailties, only to return and show mercy to all who have sinned *and* are contrite. True purity and virtue – in the form of Isabella – are rewarded. Yet what deity would play such self-indulgent games as the duke's? Audiences and readers often want to know why the duke lies to Isabella about Claudio's death, causing her a great deal of unnecessary grief. The only reason he gives, 'To make her heavenly comforts of despair/ When it is least expected' (IV 3 109–10), begs the question of *why* he should want to deliver such a dramatic surprise to her in the future when it would make her so happy now. We later suspect that casting himself in the role of divine restorer of what had seemed lost will help only *his* personal suit to her. Why should he also play with Angelo and Mariana's feelings as he does, first threatening death and then going back on his judgement? When it seems that Claudio is certain to be executed, why doesn't he just reveal himself and save Claudio's life, rather than participate in all the scheming and plotting? And what has actually changed in Vienna after the play's last judgement? Angelo's period of rule does not seem to have brought about a reform in public morals. The duke's own philosophy of justice is delivered as shallow doggerel (III 2 261–82), in jingling verse, quite out of spirit and tone with the rest of the play.

The critic A. D. Nuttall found a closer parallel to the duke's behaviour in a tactic which the infamous Italian tyrant Cesare Borgia used, according to Machiavelli's *The Prince* (see pp. 200f.). Borgia used a 'cruel and able' man, one Remirro de Orco, to mercilessly subdue a crime-wave in one of his dominions. Once order was restored, he had de Orco brutally executed. Thus Borgia both took the credit for solving a problem which his own misrule had created *and* was seen to redress the injustices which his deputy, not he himself, had committed in solving those problems (quoted in Watts 1986: 120–1).

It seems also that the duke may have been partly modelled on the actions of King James I. The patron of Shakespeare's company had toyed with the lives of three noblemen sentenced to death for their part in Sir Walter Raleigh's conspiracy against him in 1603. He wrote death warrants, to which he then sent a message of reprieve; then he cancelled the reprieve, dashing their hopes again. Only at the very point of their execution, with all their confessions made, did his own messenger, unexpected by all, arrive with their pardons. Their gratitude to him and the response of the watchers of this drama were compared by one contemporary to the events of the final scene of a play (Piesse 1996: 55). Maybe Shakespeare's duke was seen by King James as a sort of tribute to his own dramatic sense of regal mercy. But what did audiences then – and what do they now – make of this autocratic and self-indulgent judicial action? Is the play a tribute or a satire? Its contemporary ambivalence would seem to reflect the insecurities about rule by one person which are now very widely shared.

Idols and ideals

If the duke is a god-like figure brought down to earth by the play's denouement, the undermining of idols seems all the more pronounced in *Troilus and Cressida*. One of Shakespeare's sources was the playwright George Chapman's translation of *The Iliad*, the story of the Trojan war written by the ancient Greek epic poet Homer. Shakespeare's audience would have regarded the heroes of this text (who were familiar to them through a whole range of myths and stories) as examples of men who lived lives greater and more admirable than any that they knew: *The Iliad* told of the 'golden age' of heroes. But Agamemnon, as we have seen, is a bombastic bore, not as in Homer paramount leader of the greatest force assembled in mythical antiquity; Ulysses, again, is not the super-cunning schemer whose brilliance eventually took Troy and saw himself safe home to Ithaca despite everything hostile gods could throw at him; rather, he is an arrogant bungler. Achilles does not kill Hector in a fair fight, man to man, as he does in *The Iliad*, but sets his troops to slaughter him when the Trojan is unarmed and exhausted after the battle (V 8). In the context of the cynical world of the play, Hector himself seems a somewhat bizarre throw-back to chivalric ideals in his challenge to the Greeks. Having, to all intents and purposes, won the argument about giving Helen back (II 2), he then immediately concedes to his opponents, because, it seems, reason is less important to him than honour (II 2 188–93).

Why such a thorough debunking of the source material? Today many readers and audiences lack familiarity with the characters and stories which must originally have given the play its impact. Nor are we aware of the importance of the Troy myth in the way educated Londoners saw themselves as English men and women. Though Geoffrey of Monmouth's *Historia regum Britanniae* (*The History of the Kings of Britain* [1136]) was no longer believed to be authoritative, the idea that London and the English monarchy were founded by Brutus, the Trojan grandson of the hero Aeneas, himself the mythical founder of the Roman race, was at the time still well known. It conferred an ancient dignity and glory on the nation and, after the Reformation, gave the Protestant English state an antiquity to rival Rome's own (Hyland 1989: 12).

But Troy itself fell, it was believed, because of its own internal divisions. The play seems to have been written around the time of Elizabeth's death – the first reference we have of it is its appearance on the Stationers' Register for 7 February 1603. Fear and uncertainty about the succession – and the unrest and the civil war that might well follow it – were rife. A series of poor harvests in the 1590s had created much poverty and hunger. Unemployment and the crime rate remained high. In particular, the country was tired of the long wars with Spain and in Ireland. Everyone knew the Spanish war should end, but no one in the divided government could summon the political courage to seek a peace treaty. Elizabeth's last years had not inspired confidence in the monarchy, and all her potential successors were unknown quantities. Was England to have a glorious history, or a fall like

Troy's? The mood of the play perhaps reflects the mood of this particular historical moment.

The first seven books of George Chapman's translation of *The Iliad*, one of the play's main sources, were published in 1598. This work was dedicated to Robert Devereux, Earl of Essex (see pp. 185f.), whom he described in the Dedication as

> THE MOST HONOURED
> *now living Instance of the Achillean vertues*
> *eternized by divine Homere*
>
> (Chapman 1957, vol. 1: 503)

Further on, in the Preface, he begs Essex to

> let not the Pessant-common polities of the world, that count all things servile and simple that pamper not their private sensualities ... stirre your divine temper from perseverance in godlike pursute of Eternitie.
>
> (ibid.: 504)

If Shakespeare, in the wake of Essex's foolish and fatal rebellion in 1601, was aware that Essex had been called the 'English Achilles', we can see why he might present Achilles as he does in this play. Essex was regarded by many as a vain man, given in fact to 'private sensualities', though he saw himself as England's greatest warrior and perhaps fit to be monarch. Certainly he powerfully resented his periods of royal disgrace – for which he blamed his political opponents, not his own behaviour. Shakespeare's Achilles is an egotist and a sadist, as can be seen from the epicurean delight he takes in claiming the credit for his men's slaughter of Hector:

> *Achilles* My half-supped sword that frankly would have fed,
>   Pleased with this dainty bait, thus goes to bed.
>   *(He sheathes his sword)*
>
> (V 8 19–20)

Historicising the text in this way enables us to understand something of the political motives Shakespeare will have had for pulling the classical idols from their pedestals.

From our own perspective, these two plays' cynicism about patriarchal, chivalric and autocratic ideals might point towards a future where this cynicism can be turned into a new idealism. The new historicists, whose views I mentioned at the beginning of the chapter, generally deny that the meaning of a text can escape from the historical circumstances in which it was written. We are, however, reading these texts in the twenty-first century, and cannot stop ourselves finding in them our own concerns and hopes; after all, we can read them only from where we are today. But in doing so, are we actually finding more than is *actually* there? Are we reading too much into it? Some think not. Works of literature, the critic Jerome McGann has written, 'imagine more than they know'. He says of *Oresteia*, the great tragic trilogy of the Greek playwright Aeschylus, that it is

a far greater work, in those future contexts of reality it had not discussed and did not desire, than it is when we read it merely in the context of its own grandiose – and mistaken – self conceptions.

(McGann 1989: 97)

It cannot be claimed that these plays consciously desire a less violent and oppressive world; but it seems to me to be true that they have all the more quality for anticipating a better future in the way in which they depict life as Shakespeare knew it then.

Summary

- In both *Measure for Measure* and *Troilus and Cressida*, we can see how inequalities of power between men and women are built into the very fabric of the way men and women talk to one another. Because they can only express themselves by using this language, individual characters cannot love one another as equals. Inequality in their society is part of the basis of their language, so only in the submision of the weak (woman) to the strong (man) is any communication possible. A fulfilling love between equals is doomed.

- The two plays show a cynicism about both rulers in general, and about the mythical heroes in the past in particular. This may be a product of the political uncertainties and instabilities of the time in which they were written.
- To a modern audience, however, the plays questioning of the power of both males and kings might make them seem to point towards a future where power is more equally shared among people.
- How might these ideas about language, gender and power apply to Ophelia and Gertrude in *Hamlet*? Or in the special case of Cleopatra in *Antony and Cleopatra*? Think especially about the difference in the way men (Enobarbus, Octavius) talk about Cleopatra and the way her own language constructs her? Furthermore, does this idea suggest that there might be something *tragic* about the fates of Cressida and Isabella? Compare the ways in which martial heroism is undermined in *Troilus and Cressida* with the way juxtaposition is used to similar effect in *King Henry V* (see above pp. 167–70; 174–5.

Further reading

McLuskie's 1985 'The patriarchal bard: feminist criticism and Shakespeare: *King Lear* and *Measure For Measure*' gives a strong counterview to this chapter's optimistic reading of *Measure For Measure*. Piesse's 1996 essay 'Self-preservation in the Shakespearian system: gender, power and the New History' gives a demanding but very interesting perspective on gender and power, and I have drawn on some of Piesse's ideas in this chapter. Hyland (1989) is a brilliant introduction to many aspects of *Troilus and Cressida*'s complexity, and is particularly useful on the play's contexts. Watts' 1986 contribution to the same series is extremely useful, too, and covers a great deal of critical ground. Dollimore (1984) is challenging but, I think, very illuminating.

Chapter 10

Understanding romance

The Winter's Tale and
The Tempest

John Fletcher was the dramatist who became The King's Men's principal writer after Shakespeare retired in about 1613. In 1610 he published his play *The Faithful Shepherdess*. Though not a success in the theatre it heralded a new fashion, which Shakespeare himself began to follow at the end of his career. Fletcher's play, like its imitators, features shepherds and shepherdesses engaged in amorous misunderstandings – sometimes comically presented – which nearly lead to tragic conclusions. The happy resolution is effected with the help of magic herbs, a satyr and the god of the river. As the genre developed, the more serious roles were filled by noble characters, but the importance of magic and divine intervention in the plot remained.

Shakespeare's four plays in response to this new genre *tragicomedy* are generally known today as his 'romances': *Pericles* (1607–8), *Cymbeline*(1609–10),

The Winter's Tale (1610–11) and *The Tempest* (1611). The term 'romance' here has nothing to do with its modern sense of a boy-meets-girl story. It was first used in the thirteenth century to refer to Old French poems that told tales of daring deeds done by the knights of King Arthur and Charlemagne, or by the heroes of Greek and Roman mythology. It became the name for tales about heroes on quests in which magic and improbable coincidence would lead to a happy resolution, and where sundered families and lovers are eventually reunited, often after much suffering on the way. In Shakespeare's plays the protagonists, similarly, must travel, be shipwrecked, or be lost. The movement of the plot is from sorrow to joy, from division to unity.

To be fair, it should be stated that the term 'romance' is a label attached to these plays by later critics, notably the Victorian writer Dowden in 1877 (Orgel 1996b: 2). In the early seventeenth century these plays would have been regarded as 'tragicomedies' (though both *The Tempest* and *The Winter's Tale* are actually classified as comedies in the First Folio). As Orgel says (1996b: 3), critics talked about genres as a way of identifying the elements of a play, rather than as fixed pigeonholes in which to file a play. It remains, however, a useful observation that these plays share many of the conventions of romance.

The medieval versions often sought to illustrate a moral point. Shakespeare's romances can also be seen as making a statement of some sort. The plays seem to demonstrate an awareness of the improbability of their own stories. The combination of myth and fantasy characteristic of this genre gave a writer as sophisticated as Shakespeare, now late in his career, two tempting opportunities. It gave him a pretext to reflect upon the way art and the imagination operate in creating our understanding of the world. It also provided an appropriate context in which to show the world not only as it is but as it *could* be were its potential to be fulfilled.

In Shakespeare's romances it seems to be the role of children to make good the errors of their parents and bring harmony where once was discord. The loves of Perdita and Florizel in *The*

Winter's Tale, and of Miranda and Ferdinand in *The Tempest*, are the means by which the courts of Sicilia and Bohemia, Milan and Naples, are reconciled. For the future to be better than the past in these plays daughters must fall in love with other men's sons – with or without their fathers' permission. Women and their relationships with men are therefore central to these plays.

Romance and gender

In the tragedies there seem to be two types of woman: the chaste and virtuous (Ophelia, Desdemona) and the sensual and apparently untrustworthy (Gertrude, Emilia). These female stereotypes are even more obvious in the romances, where the mythical nature of the stories and the tradition of courtly love from which they sprung tend to produce female characters who, at least on the surface, are seen to fit what some early twentieth-century critics called two 'archetypes' of femininity: the submissive and chaste wife/daughter on the one hand ('the angel'), and the garrulous, sexually promiscuous, harridan on the other ('the whore'). By 'archetype' I mean more than a stereotype. 'Archetypes', said some critics and psychological theorists, are symbols or ideals that correspond to profound and eternal truths about the nature of human beings; they last from generation to generation, unchanging over time. The psychologist Carl Gustav Jung (1875–1961) thought they lived in the 'collective unconscious' of humanity. In Celtic mythology, for example, the three 'phases' of woman were the virgin, the wife and the crone, and certain characteristics went with these archetypal phases.

Of course, if something is said to come from the 'unconscious', then by definition you can't know it's there because you're not consciously aware of it. Consequently many critics and readers find these archetypes to be rather dubious notions with which to work. One of the philosophical bases of the contemporary criticism with which this book is concerned says that all symbolic representations are produced by particular historical, social and political circumstances at actual moments in time. Nothing is outside time and history. It makes more sense and is much more useful, it is contended, to ask in whose interest these views of the nature of women actually *are*. Early modern writers didn't have the concept *archetype*, but they did think women had a very distinctive *nature* which was different from that of men. But these plays reveal their own ideas about that nature in interesting ways. In fact, their views about gender were perhaps not as rigid as some twentieth century ideas.

In *The Winter's Tale*, Hermione, the wife of Leontes, the King of Sicilia, is suddenly and unjustly accused by her husband of being pregnant by his best friend Polixenes. Polixenes is the King of Bohemia and has been staying with them for the last nine months. The innocent Polixenes flees home, accompanied by Camillo, the nobleman ordered by the madly jealous Leontes to kill his guest. Hermione's reaction to her husband's accusation, and her general demeanour when put on trial for her life baffle many modern women. Though she shows great dignity and composure, she never once directly responds to her husband's mad behaviour with a counter-charge of gratuitous cruelty. When first accused she blames the configuration of the planets (II 1 105–7), not him; she immediately obeys his command and goes meekly to jail. On trial for her life she resolves that her best defence actually lies in not offering any testimony at all; she will rely on the gods to make her false accusers feel ashamed (III 2 22–32). One of the reasons she is not afraid of death at his hands is that she has lost the main joy in her life, his love (III 2 91–6). To many modern women her passive reaction is not exactly a source of inspiration. On stage, however, her patience and forbearance convince everyone other than the king himself of her innocence. Indeed, in the case of Hermione, chastity is closely connected with saying little, with suffering everything but doing nothing – as we will see.

There is, on the other hand, a woman – Paulina – who does speak out against the king's absurd accusations. But Paulina is quickly accused of sexual infidelity *because* she speaks out. She brings Hermione's new-born child into Leontes' chamber, in front of all his lords, in the hope that when he sees his new daughter he will be moved to realise his error. When he is not, she lets him know exactly what she thinks of him. Antigonus, Paulina's husband, is also present.

Leontes A nest of traitors!
Antigonus I am none, by this good light.*
Paulina Nor I, nor any
　　But one that's here – and that's himself; for he
　　The sacred honour of himself, his queen's　　　　　85
　　His hopeful son's,* his babe's, betrays to slander,
　　Whose sting is sharper than the sword's …

(II 3 83–7)

* [83] *this good light* Antigonus swears by the sun [86] *His hopeful son's* Leontes already has a son, by Hermione, called Mamillius

The king calls her a 'bawd' (II 3 69) and a 'callat [whore] of boundless tongue' (II 3 91–2). She is a 'gross hag' (II 3 78) whose tongue cannot be silenced. She is also accused of being a witch (II 3 68, 114). Her husband, Antigonus, is ridiculed by Leontes because he cannot control her (II 3 75–6, 108–9); she is like a horse, says Antigonus, who won't always obey the pull of the reins (II 3 51).

But why should female silence and patience in the face of injustice be regarded as chaste and virtuous, and the willingness to speak out against injustice be seen as a sign of sexual looseness, or even of witchcraft?

To call early modern English society *patriarchal* is to say that it was ruled by men and, in particular, by fathers (*pater* is the Latin word for 'father'). Patriarchy as an ideology (see pp. 195), then as now, is sustained by a number of philosophical and political beliefs as well as by myths, stories and associations of ideas. The philosophical view of men in power in this period is well represented in Sir Thomas Elyot's *The Book of the Governor*:

A man in his natural perfection* is fierce, hardy, strong in opinion, covetous of glory, desirous of knowledge, appetiting by generation to bring forth his semblable.* The good nature of woman is to be mild, timorous, tractable, benign, of sure remembrance,* and shamefast.*

(Quoted in Orgel 1996a: 107)

* *natural perfection* state of completeness; *appetiting by generation to bring forth his semblable* eager to produce children in his image; *of sure remembrance* never forgets her duties and her place; *shamefast* modest and afraid of shame

As regards fiction and myth, the moral of story after story emphasised the virtues of silence and patience in the face of suffering: patient Griselda, for example, in Chaucer's *Clerk's Tale*. Low-born Griselda endures her children being taken away by her noble husband – apparently to be killed – because of his shame at marrying as humble a woman as she is. She then must suffer her impending replacement by the new young bride of her husband, to whom she must act as a servant (he claims to have obtained permission from the Pope to annul their marriage). When the husband reveals that he did all this to test (over a dozen years!) Griselda's virtue, she accepts it all meekly: he is her husband, and she will do as he wishes.

Audiences would also be reminded of Lucretia (Lucrece), whose story is told as a model of virtue in Chaucer's *The Legend of Good Women*, the Italian writer Boccaccio's collection of stories *The Decameron* and in Shakespeare's own *The Rape of Lucrece*. Having been raped by Tarquin, Lucretia kills herself in front of her husband and her father so that she can bring no more shame on her family now her body has committed adultery, albeit against her will; Antonio's wife in Cyril Tourneur's *The Revenger's Tragedy* (published 1607) suffered the same fate and took the same action:

Antonio her honour forced,
　　[She] Deemed it a nobler dowry for her name*

to die with poison than to live with shame.

(Tourneur 1967: I 4 46–8)

* *Deemed it a nobler dowry for her name* thought it better to ensure a good reputation for the future by ...

Dying is the ultimate way of remaining silent, of course. Male power over women rested partly on their physical ability to restrain and hurt them. Military and legal power were entirely in the hands of men; before a state prison system of any size had come into being, the sentence of law was enforced physically on the bodies of those whom it found guilty, by whipping, pillorying, mutilating or hanging. Women literally couldn't fight back, even had they wanted to. They could talk, however; as Vittoria explains while on trial in John Webster's *The White Devil* (published 1612): 'O Woman's poor revenge/Which dwells but in the tongue' (Webster 1972 : III 2 285–6). *Talking* was the way in which women could assert their needs and wants, and for that reason had to be controlled under patriarchy. Female speech, it was thought, if unrestrained, could become a torrent of scolding and nagging which could wear men down. For this reason 'scolds' could be sentenced by magistrates to be physically bridled with an iron bit, the branks, to prevent them from talking. It was Eve's tongue, after all, that had persuaded Adam in Eden and led to the Fall of mankind.

Female attributes in general seemed to patriarchal attitudes to be *unrestrained*. Compactness, hardness and closedness were features of the male body which seemed particularly appropriate in a world where being an emotionless, fit and skilful warrior was one definition of virtue. Female bodies were soft and expansive, and given to the production both of extra fluids (milk, menstrual flow) and children. Their sexual appetite was supposed to be insatiable compared with that of men. One of the stories which used to be told of our culture was that it was usually the men who were after sex and the women who tried to avoid it. Popular culture in the early modern era portrayed it exactly the other way round. The never-ending desire which a woman acquired once she lost her virginity was always provoking men to sin. Were it not for gold and women, says the cynical Vindice in *The Revenger's Tragedy*, 'there would no damnation –/Hell would look like a lord's great kitchen without fire in't' (Tourneur 1967 : II 1 254–5). Again and again female speech is described as the woman's 'tongue'; its sensual, fluid quality and the fact that it is both a site and a giver of pleasure is so often implied. As Ferdinand tells his sister the duchess in Webster's *The Duchess of Malfi* (published 1623), women 'like that part, which .../Hath nev'r a bone in't ... I mean the tongue ...' (Webster 1972: I 2 257–60). Promiscuity and talking too much were connected.

Though men were certainly dominant in this society, female sexuality was a powerful threat to men. Hence chastity was the principal female virtue. It was argued that chastity and sexual fidelity were the female equivalents of male heroism in battle: both required physical courage in order to win glory against powerful natural instincts. Here the male view of woman's sexual nature is abundantly clear. By elevating female chastity to the peak of moral behaviour men's anxiety about the sexual threat to them is made very plain. An adulterous wife had the power to turn a man into a ridiculous beast, the cuckold, whose symbol was a man with horns growing from his brows. In the case of men of property she could also undermine the system of inheritance by the first-born *legitimate* son, which was the basis of the vast majority of property transfers. If men could not be sure of their wife's fidelity the stability of society itself would be threatened (see Box 7, p. 69). Both the mouth and the vagina are focal points of male insecurity about women, and are associated one with the other in the patriarchal discourse of the period. Unruliness in both must be checked: unruliness in one can lead to unruliness in both.

And yet the scold was accepted as a character in literature who was allowed to get away with more than one, at first glance, would imagine. A woman might also be a prophetess. Women's talkativeness *could* become privileged, like that of the fool who is allowed to be impertinent because in his ramblings there might be some profound truth. It is this kind of privilege that allows

Paulina to get away with the accusations she aims at the king. It might be thought perhaps that, because she was a woman, what she had to say would not be taken too seriously. But her pleadings seem to move Leontes to back off from the immediate destruction of the child. And there is a further paradox, here: in the end, it is Paulina and her 'witchcraft' with the 'statue' that bring harmony and reconciliation to Leontes' court (a *paradox* is statement which contradicts itself, and yet can still make sense despite appearances).

It is too easy, in fact, to see misogyny (hatred of women) as a single simple force running through all of society in Shakespeare's time. It clearly wasn't like that. England was after all ruled by a woman, Queen Elizabeth I, from 1558–1603, and ruled very successfully. How did that fit in with patriarchal ideology?

In the British feminist critic Lisa Jardine's *Still Harping on Daughters* (1983: 169–79) it is suggested that Elizabeth was proclaimed, indeed proclaimed herself, an exceptional woman whose rule served only to demonstrate by comparison the frailty and failings of other women. Thus her learning and knowledge placed her beyond her sex, and reminded everyone of how women were normally incapable of such achievement. More significantly, she created herself, not as a woman at all, but as an emblem or symbol of perfection in womanhood. She embodied qualities that were female ideals, but which no real woman could possess. Thus her chastity, the paramount female virtue, became the centre of the state cult around her. She became the idealised object of courtly-love literature and fantasies; she was closely associated with the classical goddess of chastity, Astraea. Furthermore, the public celebration of her person in progresses (official visits), tournaments and ceremonies was seen by many to have replaced the *worship* of the Virgin Mary – a powerful and ancient cult which had been suppressed only twenty years before she came to the throne – in Protestant England. Thus her political success was not the product of the actions of a *real* woman at all. This, at any rate, is how one argument has it.

Back to *The Winter's Tale*. Hermione, in her obedience and

chastity, can be seen as a sort of Griselda or Virgin Queen (or *maybe not*: she does insist in her trial on her dignity as a woman – see III 2 91–123, for example – and, I suppose, has the determination not to return to her husband until the loss of her daughter has been made good, even after sixteen years). But it is the actions and words of Paulina that are the agents of renewal and harmony. The play doesn't pretend that she is some kind of female beyond the ordinary in Act V. Leontes no longer regards her as a 'mankind witch' but now sees her as a trusted adviser, who he indeed allows to take liberties with him (V 1 1–84; V 3 1–3). At the moment when he thinks he has lost his wife he is happy to give her free rein to speak, in fact: 'Go on, go on:/Thou canst not speak too much' (III 2 214–15). Some might think it is magic that she employs in the final scene (V 3 89–91, 96–7, 105), but if it is, says Leontes, 'let it be an art/Lawful as eating' (V 3 110–11). She not only brings a statue to life, as it seems, she apparently even brings Hermione back to life. But she's no witch, as Hermione explains (V 3 125–8). If patriarchy is so strong, how can representations like this be performed in public, and, indeed, before the king, as the play was on 5 November 1612?

Strict 'sumptuary' laws forbade the wearing of certain rich fabrics and colours by those whose income and status didn't warrant them. But why was no law passed or legal action taken against the fashionable young women who cut their hair and went around in men's clothes in the first decade of the seventeenth century? They adopted male dress the better to show off their figures in unbuttoned doublets (jackets) and tight hose (tights). Why was it that trade guilds at this time had so many women in trades like carpenters and masons (48 per cent in Southampton in 1600 [Orgel 1996a: 73])? Why did men accept the authority women had over them in very many social and domestic situations as mothers, nurses, housekeepers, estate managers and the like?

An ideology, even a powerful and dominant one, is not a set of rules to be universally applied; nor is it a rigid mindset applying across all classes and peoples. One way of understanding it is as a myth of the 'norm', a set of ideas which indicate normal behaviour in a society; the perfect example may not actually exist, but it is a story that seems 'natural', and seems to tell the truth about that society to those who live in it. How do we then explain these cases, both in literature and in life, that so startlingly seem to contradict it? English society in Shakespeare's time *was* patriarchal, after all.

The new historicist (see pp. 204f.) explanation is to say that in order for a dominant idea to stay dominant it has to create threats to itself so that it can be seen to accommodate and absorb those threats: it has to reveal its nature in conflict in order to show its teeth, even if in this case patriarchal power isn't actually under serious threat. For the cultural materialists (see pp. 205), on the other hand, these cases are examples of contradictions within this ideology that expose the arbitrary (not 'natural' or God-given) and unnecessary power structure which is patriarchy. Furthermore, it points out the material forces (actual people and events, representational and otherwise) whose challenge will one day damage that power structure and overthrow it. Patriarchy may not be dead, but its grip on women in 2000 is certainly not that of 1600. In this play, then, Paulina – and perhaps even Hermione – can be seen as *utopian* figures. By this I mean that, as the intellectual and moral equals of men, they look forward self-consciously to a much fairer world than the one depicted in the play – or even known by the author and original audiences (a *utopia* is an ideal society).

I do not think the same kind of utopian undercurrent is evident in the depiction of Miranda in *The Tempest*. She doesn't look forward at all. In fact she is there to be looked at, as her name (the Latin means 'worthy to be wondered at') suggests. And more than just looked at: now she has reached the age (of about 15, it seems) at which she can produce children, she has become the object of several men's desires to produce offspring by her.

Prospero, her father, was once Duke of Milan. Twelve years earlier than the action depicted in the play he had been overthrown by his brother Antonio, with the help of Alonso, King of Naples. Prospero and the infant Miranda were set adrift in the Mediterranean with the barest of provisions, their clothes and Prospero's books of magic spells. Coming ashore on an island,

Prospero soon took control of both the environment and its inhabitants. These comprise Ariel, a spirit who had been imprisoned in a pine tree by the witch Sycorax because he would not obey her commands, and Caliban, a 'savage and deformed slave' (as it describes him in the *dramatis personae* – 'characters of the play' in the Folio). Caliban is Sycorax's son. Now a ship containing Antonio and Alonso is passing the island and Prospero uses his powers to 'wreck' the vessel. He does this without harming crew, passengers or ship. He disperses them around the island so that he can take his revenge upon the appropriate people by his own chosen means. The first of the shipwrecked to come to his attention is Ferdinand, son and heir of Alonso. He arranges for Miranda and Ferdinand to meet and fall in love. Thus they will produce an heir who will unite the city of Milan and the kingdom of Naples in future peace and harmony.

But there are others who have designs on Miranda as a sexual partner. Caliban had attempted to rape Miranda in the hope that he could people the island with his own kind (I 2 349–51). Stephano, Alonso's drunken butler, teams up with Caliban in a comic attempt to seize the island for himself and become king, with Miranda as his consort (III 2 106–7). Caliban's enslavement to Stephano through drink can be seen as an undercutting parody of the magic power by which Prospero enslaves him. It mocks Prospero's power through a comic replication of the main action, as happens the history plays (see pp. 73–5 and 167–70). But Prospero (acting through Ferdinand), Caliban and Stephano all see Miranda's body as a piece of property to be cultivated, from which each hopes both to produce a future for himself and to establish his own identity, at the same time cementing his authority over some territory in the future: Milan, or the island, and, by the same token, Miranda's body. Prospero will win. He has magic; he is the father.

Miranda, then, stands symbolically for the island itself. This maiden is the virgin territory that is to be conquered so that the conqueror may establish his identity and authority over part of the world.

Contemporary critics often write about *The Tempest* as a narrative of colonialism. Shakespeare's source material clearly draws on the recent adventures of an English fleet in Bermuda, and the play was written in a period when there was considerable investment and settlement taking place in the English colonies in the New World, particularly Virginia (in what is now the southern USA). Though geography, strictly speaking, would indicate a Mediterranean location (Alonso's ship is *en route* from Tunis to Naples), Caliban's name is clearly some sort of corruption of the word 'cannibal' or maybe 'Carib', the name of the original West Indian islanders wiped out by European disease and genocide, the murder of a whole people. A New World colonial setting is often assumed by critics. (Though, as the British critic Jerry Brotton has argued, to assume this is to ignore so much of the play's Mediterranean geography. The play is actually set in an area which was a point of conflict between Catholic Europeans and Muslim Turks. In this struggle the Protestant English pursued profitable, but embarrassing, commercial alliances with the Turks. The play, he argues, totally ignores this subordinate relationship to the 'infidel', and looks westwards to easier pickings, perhaps [Brotton 1998: 36–7]). There was also, of course, the continuing struggle to establish English rule in Ireland, over a people regarded by many English writers and colonisers as scarcely, if at all, human. 'Masterless men', like Stephano and his sidekick the Jester Trinculo, were also seen as a threat to order and good government, even in the heart of London. The play can be seen to explore, with various degrees of explicitness, the issues of colonisation and legitimacy of government current at the time. What gives one people the right to dominate another? What makes a government the just authority in a particular territory?

The association of the land to be colonised with the female body is an interesting one, and one which tells us much about male attitudes to women and women's sexuality. As Paul Brown points out (1985: 51), it is common in the discourse (by which is meant a 'distinctive' way of saying things) of colonialism to talk about 'opening up virgin territory', or 'making the land fruitful'. But there are also the temptations of the wilderness, which might lead the virtuous and saintly European astray. The colonisers will encounter the amoral and anarchic lives of the 'savages', whose careless enjoyment of nature's gifts and sexual licentiousness might lead the settler astray. Stories told about the uncivilised often made their lives seem like a tempting utopia, even if the Europeans knew it was actually a myth – see Gonzalo's account of his imaginary commonwealth, and Sebastian and Antonio's justifiable response to it (II 1 141–64). There is something tempting and mysterious about this unknown world, which drives the authorities to place it all the more fiercely under their control. This wild and anarchic utopia is figured as female in the symbolic function of Miranda, and the subversive delight of female sexuality as an ungovernable threat to male power runs through *The Tempest* in various forms. Prospero knows in his heart that his power is a dream ('an insubstantial pageant' [IV 1 155]) which might any moment dissolve into nothingness. Yet his nagging fear seems to be that he will lose control over his own daughter's sexuality (IV 1 14–23, 51–4).

Prospero admits, half-jokingly, that he has only his dead wife's word that Miranda actually is his daughter (I 2 56–7). Leontes in *The Winter's Tale* is actually driven to the edge of madness by his suspicions that he may not be the father of Hermione's child. Neither he nor Prospero can know for sure. Richard Wilson (1993: 158–83) argues that the late plays expose, among other things, historical moments at which men have sought to gain control over what, until then, had been a dark mystery presided over entirely by women: conception, pregnancy and childbirth. Doctors began to take precedence over midwives in supervising births. They began to adopt a new scientific medical practice based on the observation of women and the anatomy of corpses, animal and human, rather than the employment of folklore and quasi-magical operations based on the old medieval theories of resemblances (see pp 33f.). No one knew exactly how the man's seed becomes the child; no man could ever have proof, apart from his wife's word, that her child really was also his own. Men didn't attend the birth of children. The attempt by doctors and lawyers to regulate the practices of midwives was an attempt by men to bring light (the male gaze) to a darkness which they had obviously found alluring – but also constituted a threat to their power and sense of identity. (Interestingly, Shakespeare's son-in-law, John Hall, was one such doctor.)

Miranda wields power over men, first, because she is sexually attractive to men of all classes (both Stephano and Ferdinand) and cultures (Caliban), and, second, because she is the one with real magic in the play: the mysterious power to produce new versions of the man who is her lover. This is why she must be controlled by the man who seeks political dominance in the play, just as the new science had to replace the folk medicine of the past to establish its authority – even when such methods actually worked. The domination of women by men, a domination based on both desire and fear of the mysterious but essential 'other', is the model for domination by class, culture and race in the society of the time. It is, of course, an unstable state of affairs.

Strangely, Prospero's account of how he arrived safely on the island makes it seem as if he were courting a mistress who took pity on his distress (Brown 1985: 60). Miranda and he were left on their rotting boat

> To cry to the sea that roared to us, to sigh
> To the winds, whose pity, sighing back again,
> Did us but loving wrong.
>
> (I 2 149–51)

The winds became his lover in pity at the romance hero's troubles on his quest – a little like Desdemona in *Othello* (II 1 167–70). The goddess Fortune herself (luck, chance) and the very stars become lovers whom he must woo if his plan to take revenge on his brother and the Neapolitans is to come to fruition, as he tells Miranda:

Prospero Know thus far forth:
  By accident most strange, bountiful Fortune,
  Now my dear lady, hath mine enemies
  Brought to this shore; and by my prescience*   180
  I find my zenith* doth depend upon

A most auspicious* star, whose influence*
If now I court not, but omit,* my fortunes
Will ever after droop.

(I 2 177–84)

* [180] *prescience* foreknowledge [181] *zenith* high point, moment of greatest opportunity [181] *auspicious* a force for success; *influence* astrological power to affect life on earth [182] *omit* ignore

A man's whole future, it seems in Prospero's case, depends on his successful courtship of the female forces of chance and the stars that govern life. In the romances, the future is female. Male power has to come to terms with this fact. In *The Winter's Tale* Leontes learns this lesson over the course of sixteen years. It is the tender affection Ariel wants to feel for the vanquished and confused Neapolitans in *The Tempest* that makes Prospero decide to forgive rather than take vengeance (V 1 11–28). Tender feelings are usually unmanly in the culture of the period. But at this moment in the play they become 'human' (V 1 20), not womanly. Prospero recognises female qualities in himself; their exercise becomes the exercise of male 'noble reason' (V 1 26). Tender female feelings, even so, don't reign at the end of this play. But they have, for Prospero, replaced the male desire to dominate.

In the romances, then, despite the portrayal of women as either unruly creatures or merely beautiful and fruitful possessions, it can nevertheless be argued that there is in these plays a powerful undercurrent of 'female' qualities that will ultimately redeem the destructive 'male' desire to dominate.

Romance and utopia

Jonson [to Shakespeare] Your recent stuff's been pretty peculiar.
What was *The Winter's Tale* about? I ask to be polite.

(Bond 1987: 44)

What are these plays about, then? In the twentieth century one reading was fairly dominant, both among the conservative critics of the first part of the century and among the American new historicists of recent years. That view sees the romances as showing the God-given hierarchical social order being disturbed only so that it can be triumphantly reinstated, and thereby strengthened, at the end of Act V. Triumph, or even cosy reassurance, however, is not the feeling I ever get in the theatre at the close of these plays. At the end of *The Winter's Tale* there is a sense of wasted years – Hermione isn't as young as she was when Leontes last saw her (V 3 27–9), and there is also a feeling of unease about Paulina's sudden marriage (V 3 136–8). In *The Tempest*, Antonio is neither repentant nor contrite. It is true that Caliban, the would-be rapist and savage murderer (III 2 88–91), is now under control again, awed at Prospero's authority, and feeling suitably abashed for having acquired such unworthy new masters (V 1 261–2, 296–8). But there is something also in the crushing of Caliban and in the reinstatement of the old order that makes the reader or spectator feel a sense of loss. The recollection of the freedom and energy of the magic island, or of the joyously affirmative life of rural Bohemia in *The Winter's Tale* leaves one feeling that a better world has been glimpsed in these plays, even if palpably not achieved.

From where does our sympathy for Caliban come? Modern awareness of the wrongs done in the name of white imperialism, of course, prompts us to be more sympathetic to Caliban than many European audiences would have been in the past. Indeed, in Shakespeare's time the dominant attitude towards the original inhabitants of the Americas regarded them as semi-animals who had no language, or at best a defective one. Alternatively, the native languages were thought by some to be fundamentally the same as the European ones, describing the world according to the same concepts and the same social, political and religious ideas as the invading Spanish, Portuguese, French or English (Greenblatt 1990: 17–19). The former view seems to apply to Caliban; he has to be taught to talk, according to Prospero and Miranda (I 2 353–8). Yet he retains some sort of integrity and dignity. He has not become totally their creature, even though he is forced to think in their words. He is not an animal.

The invaders control the island by virtue of the violence threatened by Prospero's magic. Theirs is a language that contains the violence of their way of life, as Caliban immediately reminds them:

Caliban You taught me language, and my profit on't
 Is, I know how to curse. The red-plague rid* you
 For learning me your language!

(I 2 363–5)

 * *rid* kill

When Prospero and Miranda first came to the island, Caliban had no knowledge of their language, yet they treated him with affection and he treated them with love and care in return (I 2 332–9); the attempted rape seems to have happened after their concepts and ideas had been imparted to him more fully. Prospero and Miranda told him what his own words meant, and so had power over him; they gave him a language which replaced his 'brutish … gabble' (I 2 355–8). But they blame the rape attempt on his own savage nature (I 2 358–60), not on the view of the world which their acquisitive language has given him.

What Prospero has not quite managed to do, however, is destroy Caliban's capacity to think for himself. Stephano and Trinculo might sing that 'Thought is free' (III 2 123), but it is Caliban who knows the real tune, even if Prospero's spy Ariel knows it as well (III 2 124–5) (Patterson 1989: 161). Even under such surveillance, Caliban is not totally trapped by the system of hierarchy and oppression the invaders have brought to his island. Prospero is a usurper in Caliban's kingdom just as much as Antonio is in Milan, but it is still Caliban who appreciates the beauty of his home and can speak the the play's most tranquil lines, looking forward to future peace and happiness:

Caliban Be not afeared, the isle is full of noises,   135
 Sounds, and sweet airs, that give delight and hurt not.
 Sometimes a thousand twangling instruments

Will hum about my ears; and sometimes voices,
That if I then had waked after long sleep,
Will make me sleep again, and then in dreaming,   140
The clouds methought would open, and show riches
Ready to drop upon me, that when I waked
I cried to dream again.

(III 2 135–43)

The text seems to go out of its way to make us see how different is the ugly, violent and vengeful Caliban from the 'civilised' invaders, while still being totally human. Caliban has his own distinctive view of the world, his own sense of beauty and of what it is to be alive. We are aware of what Stephen Greenblatt means when he refers, in relation to another passage, to 'the independence and integrity of Caliban's construction of reality' (Greenblatt 1990: 31).

Caliban's ultimately independent view of the world, even if achieved in only a few places, stands out against the structurally oppressive language and ideas of the Italian invaders. Kiernan Ryan has pointed out (1989: 103–4) that Prospero's language is full of threat, aggression, violence and demands; even the love-promises of Miranda and Ferdinand are expressed in the language of master and slave (III 1 63–6, 84–6). As Ferdinand says, Prospero is 'composed of harshness' (III 1 9). Yet the voices of Caliban (and of Ariel – I 2 242–9) speak out for liberty, and we are given an even more startling anti-hierarchical perspective in the face of physical realities in the play's first scene. As the storm created by Ariel threatens the King of Naples' ship, the courtiers come up on deck only to be firmly put into their place by the boatswain:

Alonso Good boatswain, have care. Where's the master?
    Play the men.*
Boatswain I pray now, keep below.   10
Antonio Where is the master, bos'n?
Boatswain Do you not hear him? You mar our labour.*
    Keep your cabins – you do assist the storm.

Gonzalo Nay, good, be patient.   15
Boatswain When the sea is. Hence! What care these roarers
 for the name of king? To cabin! silence! Trouble us not.
Gonzalo Good, yet remember whom thou hast aboard.
Boatswain None that I love more than myself. You are a coun-
 cillor; if you can command these elements to silence, and
 work the peace of the present*, we will not hand a rope
 more. Use your authority.   21

                                                                (I 1 9–21)

 * [9–10] *Play the men* 'Act like men' [13] *You mar our labour*
 'You're getting in the way' [20] *work the peace of the present*
 'make everything quiet immediately'

The courtiers presume that their superiority is natural, and will
apply even over professional seafarers struggling to save the lives
of everyone in the teeth of a vicious storm. The scene shows such
superiority to be far from natural, and prepares for the other
challenges of the play that suggest the foundations of hierarchy
to be violence, not a God-given right to rule at all.

   Yet the play's ending sees the courtiers back in charge. Where
then does the egalitarian energy come from in these plays?
Kiernan Ryan suggests (1989: 83) that in both plays history is, so
to speak, speeded up, so that the guilt and wickedness of the
present is suddenly seen from the perspective of the future, and is
seen not to matter so much. Forgiveness becomes possible, and
we see human suffering from a different viewpoint, becoming less
entrenched in our passions and dogma. From the perspective of
people in their forties, for example, the jealousy someone felt over
a lover when they were 16 seems not very significant, and the
hurtful things they did then can be truly seen as the injustices that
they were. Most people thought it right and proper to imprison
homosexuals 100 years ago, but from a social perspective 100
years on that earlier stance can clearly be seen to be wrong – but
also forgivable. The world from this later perspective is a more
understanding and harmonious one, not so passionately vengeful
as it used to be. It is a better place in which to live. In *The Winter's*

Tale the figure of Time acts as a chorus between the two halves of the play. He moves the action on sixteen years, and reminds us exactly of this function:

Time … it is in my power
  To o'erthrow law, and in one self-born hour
  To plant and o'erwhelm custom.

(IV 1 7–9)

Thus the world in the first half of the play is one where passionate jealousy, in the hands of a man of power, destroys the lives of his wife, his son and two of his courtiers; his best friend is alienated and lost. A ship is wrecked and those on board drowned. A bear kills an old man carrying out an heroic act of kindness to a baby. This disasters are too much like the world as it is. After sixteen years, however, the original passions matter far less than the love which had existed previously The folly of inflexible and selfish human action is revealed. A new generation has grown to maturity which is not destined to repeat the errors of the past. In *The Tempest* Ariel's perspective on Prospero's vengeful outlook has the same effect. Standing outside the action, like Time, Ariel can remind Prospero what it actually means to be human.

Ryan's argument *is* fundamentally humanistic. By this I mean that it has the premiss that all people are basically the same and have the same basic needs, no matter to what period in history they belong. All of us should be treated with respect and dignity, and no one group can have a claim to special privileges simply by virtue of who they are. Injustice and suffering are produced by failure to recognise these facts. Time overwhelms the arbitrary divisions among people which we use to justify inequality (e.g. being a woman, being a Roman citizen, being homosexual, being the descendant of a Norman duke, being Jewish, etc.), showing all of them to be temporary. So seeing things from Time's perspective is always going to make us realise the folly of our excessive passions, unjust actions and special pleadings. Ariel, standing outside humanity and being able to see the similarities rather than the differences between us, has the same perspective. When romance relocates action to another part of the world, where things are viewed differently, we have the same shift in the point of view. Extramarital sex that produces unwanted offspring is the subject for a humorous aside among the shepherds of Bohemia (III 3 71–6). In the court of Sicilia it is a capital offence against the state.

Ryan's political project is fairly apparent. A non-humanistic sceptic, on the other hand, might argue that all time actually does is replace one set of arbitrary divisions between people with another set. Ryan is assuming that we can envisage a human society in which no one group of people is exercising power unjustly and to its own advantage over another group. There never has been such a society, it could be argued, since power and its exercise is everywhere in our lives; society simply cannot function without it – it is 'inscribed' in the very nature of social life. This would be a more *postmodern* view, one that is argued by critics influenced by the French philosopher Michel Foucault. Power is in constant circulation around the world, flowing now here, now there. No one really possesses it: it is simply active in every social exchange. We are all special pleaders in our own interests, all of the time. There can be no utopia according to this view.

The humanist argument does not suggest, however, that these plays show any sort of blueprint for the future. In fact the plays go out of their way to stress the provisional and outrageously fictional nature of the solutions they find to the problems of the narrative. When Antigonus was pursued off stage by a bear at The Globe or Blackfriars in 1611 (III 3 58, sd), it would either have been by a man in a bear-suit or a tame performing bear familiar to the audience from the Southwark entertainments. Both would no doubt have drawn laughter or cheers of a derisively affectionate nature. The mortal danger that the character of Antigonus is in would be immediately defused as a painful spectacle by the blatant fictionality of the moment. It is not scary or dangerous, this bear. Shakespeare is signalling that the play is shifting mood and genre in a big way.

Paulina never ceases to stress the preposterousness of the plot's conclusion, even though she has engineered it herself.

Shakespeare won't show us the obvious conclusion of the narrative from which we would expect to get our emotional satisfaction. We expect to see the tearful reunion of Leontes and Polixenes and the greeting by Leontes of his long-lost daughter, and her realisation of her true identity. But in fact this is relayed to us by two 'Gentlemen', one of whom has the cheek to tell us that we 'have lost a sight which was to be seen, which cannot be spoken of' (V 2 42–3). Instead of the expected dramatic denouement we get the scene where the 'statue' comes to life. It is an ending that some might attribute to 'wicked powers' (V 3 91), 'unlawful business' (V 3 96). Certainly it breaks many of the rules of decorum, just as the play breaks the unities (see pp. 71f.). More to the point, however, were this outcome to be recounted to you, it 'should be hooted at/Like an old tale' (V 3 115–16). A 'winter's tale', indeed, was an improbable story with which to pass a long dark evening.

By giving us a scene like this, however, the play highlights the *provisional* nature of its ending. This isn't the way the plot would end in the real world, and we know it. It's a symbolic fiction only. But by the same token it's not pretending that providence (see pp. 187f.) really exists. It's not even an ideal ending, as I have just argued. It is therefore not escapism. Its fictionality underscores the fact that it is an ending *made* by humans, not by God or the gods. It shows that just and humane resolutions are possible if we have the moral *imagination* and humanity to create them; but *we* have to make them.

The ending of *The Tempest* is even less ideal, as we have seen. But throughout the last part of the play Prospero seems to strive, at a level partly outside the drama of the play, to excuse himself from his own involvement in the injustice of the world in which he lives. Ryan (1989: 103) suggests that Gonzalo's speech about his ideal kingdom, and Sebastian and Antonio's response to it (II 1 144–67), foreground a paradox about power in the play: it draws attention to an interesting contradiction in the rulers' ideas. Prospero seeks to bring about liberty and justice through his use of absolute hierarchical power, but without any notion of his responsibilities to a wider community. By the last part of the play, however, he knows his power is arbitrary in its nature; it can be discarded at his will, and he chooses to discard it. In his speech after the end of the masque he reminds us of the insubstantial fictionality both of what we are watching and of his authority (IV 1 146–58), an estrangement device (see pp. 62f.) in itself. But most of all he calls on us, the audience, at the end of the play to release him from the island and his role there by our action of approval: applause (V 1 Epilogue). Just as we have committed injustices, he too seeks freedom from guilt; but it is a freedom he can only achieve outside his roles as duke and magician in the play:

Prospero As you from crimes would pardoned be,
   Let your indulgence set me free. *(Exit)*

(V 1 Epilogue 19–20)

The fictional exists in real historical time, just as the self-consciously fictional and the recognisably historical exist together in these plays. Our hopes for a more just world are there, realisable in the fiction; but the fiction is part of the real world, too. Plays happen in real time, in real places, and they affect the way we see reality. Romance gives us hope that our ideals can be brought to actuality, despite everything. Prospero says that we will, however, have to do it through our own actions.

Summary

- Women and their relationships with men are central to these plays especially, because in romance it is through the production of the next generation that the errors of the older generation will be redeemed.
- Though women are seen either as unruly and uncontrollable individuals, or as beautiful and fertile objects to be possessed, they nevertheless possess qualities that will make the world

> better, because they save men from the harshness and injustice of the masculine desire for power and control.
>
> - By their very obvious fictional contexts, and by showing how time can undermine all deeply held beliefs and structures except those that relate to our common humanity, these plays have a utopian vision, according to humanist critics, which looks forward to a more equal and fair world. Other critics would dispute this and say nothing has really changed at the conclusion to these plays.
>
> - Can the same arguments about the roles of women, time and the utopian vision also be applied to *Cymbeline* and *Pericles*? What comparisons can you draw between the portrayal of Perdita in *The Winter's Tale* and Miranda in *The Tempest*? What is their function in the renewal of the worlds of the latter two plays?

Further reading

Orgel's introductions to the Oxford editions of both *The Tempest* (1987) and *The Winter's Tale* (1996b) are very good places to start. There is brief and accessible information on genre, historical context, performance and criticism. Important new historicist work on *The Tempest* includes the title essay in Greenblatt (1990) and, at a slightly more demanding level, Brown (1985). I have drawn extensively on Jardine (1983) for the discussion here on 'shrewish' women. A very influential Marxist–humanist reading of the romances as utopian plays is Ryan (1989). Ryan has also edited a collection of relevant and useful essays (1995).

Conclusion

In England and Wales practically every secondary-school student must, by statute law, study Shakespeare. Indeed, all schoolchildren are tested on their knowledge of one particular play at the age of 14 and of a different text at 16. For many years government has seen Shakespeare's plays as part of the national heritage, as something essentially 'English' that will unite young people in a common culture. The plays will also, many have argued, provide a model of beautiful and memorable language. The plays are often praised for their 'universality', their ability to stand outside time and history and 'speak to' all people, past, present and future.

A similar function seems to be performed by these plays in other English-speaking countries, such as the United States, Australia and New Zealand, where their high cultural status makes them central to the study of English at high-school level. The plays are often described as part of a common cultural heritage which transcends the issues of national origin and politics. In other former British colonies such as South Africa, Zimbabwe, India and parts of the Caribbean Shakespeare's works seem to have a different educational status; but the notion of Shakespeare's *universality* and trans-cultural value is often employed as a reason for studying the plays.

I hope you can see from this book that at the higher levels of the education system the academic study of Shakespeare tends to march to a very different tune. Instead of the idea of Shakespeare as the creative genius who stands outside time, Shakespeare is seen as a writer whose plays are the product of the time in which they were written; the meaning of the plays is similarly seen to depend on the circumstances – the time and place – in which they are seen or their texts read. It so happens that current academic study of Shakespeare is concerned with an agenda that is seeking to promote neither a sense of national unity nor some timeless values whose purity is untouched by the fashionable opinions of today or tomorrow. Contemporary Shakespeare criticism looks instead at issues of power and social injustice; it is interested in gender, race and sexuality as concepts that are not only alive in the plays but important in the lives of those who read, teach, study or act Shakespeare. Shakespeare criticism has become *social* and *political*. It might be claimed that the presence of Shakespeare at secondary level is social and political, too, but that is another argument.

I hope this book has helped you to see how much more enthralling Shakespeare can be when it is part of this wider social and political picture. There are many things in this book which I hope you would want to contest, or think are misreadings, or miss the point. That is the way Shakespeare studies will move forward. Time moves on, and no doubt a new style of Shakespeare studies will emerge. Above all, I hope the book will add to the enjoyment you will derive from reading and watching the plays, and then producing those new arguments to take the subject through its next stage of study in this new century.

Chronology

Year	Events	Shakespeare – the theatre
1564	Gypsies expelled from England	William Shakespeare born
1576	Dutch rebellion against Spanish rule	James Burbage builds The Theatre, London's first purpose-built theatre, in Shoreditch
1581	Laws against Catholics passed	Worcester's Theatre Company play at Stratford-upon-Avon
1582	Plague in London	Shakespeare marries Ann Hathaway
1583	Rebellion in Ireland	Birth of Susanna, daughter to Ann and William
1585	War with Spain	Birth of twins, Hamnet and Judith, to Ann and William; Shakespeare leaves Stratford?
1587	Mary Queen of Scots beheaded by Elizabeth I	Philip Henslowe builds The Rose theatre on Bankside

1588	Spanish Armada defeated	Shakespeare now in the London theatre?
1589		First play:*King Henry VI Part I.*
1592	Successful English attacks on Spanish Treasure fleet; plague in London	*King Richard III*, *The Comedy of Errors*; Marlowe's *Dr Faustus*, *Edward II*
1593	Church attendance (Anglican) made compulsory; plague continues	Marlowe murdered
1594	Two plots on Queen Elizabeth's life; rebellion in Ireland	*The Taming of the Shrew*, *Titus Andronicus*; Lord Chamberlain's Company founded
1595	War abroad, unrest at home	*A Midsummer Night's Dream*, *Romeo and Juliet*, *King Richard II*; The Swan theatre built
1596	Essex destroys Spanish fleet; food shortages	Coat of arms granted to Shakespeare's father John; *The Merchant of Venice* and *King Henry IV Part I*; Hamnet dies
1598	Rebellion in Ireland	*King Henry IV Part II* and *Much Ado About Nothing*
1599	Essex fails to put down Irish rebellion	The Globe theatre built; *King Henry V*, *Julius Caesar* and *As You Like It*
1600	East India Company founded	*Hamlet*
1601	Essex's rebellion and execution	Death of John Shakespeare; *Troilus and Cressida*, *Twelfth Night*
1603	Death of Queen Elizabeth and Accession of James I	Shakespeare's last recorded stage performance, in Ben Jonson's *Sejanus*; Lord Chamberlain's Company becomes The King's Men

1604	Catholic priests banished	*Othello* and *Measure for Measure*; Marston's *The Malcontent*
1605	Gunpowder Plot	*King Lear*; Shakespeare makes land purchases in Stratford
1606	Expedition to colonise Virginia	*Macbeth* and *Antony and Cleopatra*; Jonson's *Volpone*; Tourneur's *The Revenger's Tragedy*
1607	Defeated Irish earls flee to the continent	Susanna Shakespeare marries John Hall; *Coriolanus*
1608	Conflict between king and parliament	The King's Men lease the indoor Blackfriars Theatre
1610	Parliament petitions the king with 'Grievances'	*The Winter's Tale*; Jonson's *The Alchemist*; Heywood's *The Fair Maid of the West*
1611	Parliament dismissed by King James; Scots Protestants settled on Catholic land in Ulster; translation of the Bible authorised by King James	*The Tempest*. Shakespeare now living mostly in Stratford?
1613		*The Two Noble Kinsmen* written by Shakespeare and John Fletcher; The Globe theatre burns down
1616		Susanna Shakespeare marries Thomas Quiney; William Shakespeare dies
1623		Publication of First Folio

References

Barker, F. (1993) *The Culture of Violence: Essays on Tragedy and History*, Manchester: Manchester University Press.

Bate, J. (1996) 'Introduction' to J. Bate and R. Jackson (eds) *Shakespeare: An Illustrated Stage History*, Oxford: Oxford University Press.

Belsey, C (1985) *The Subject of Tragedy: Identity and Difference in Renaissance Drama*, London: Routledge.

—— (1998) 'Love in Venice', in M. Coyle (ed.) *New Casebooks: The Merchant of Venice*, London: Macmillan.

Berry, C. (1987) *The Actor and His Text*, London: Harrap.

Blake, N.F. (1983) *Shakespeare's Language: An Introduction*, Basingstoke: Macmillan.

Blakemore Evans, G. (ed.) (1988) *Elizabethan–Jacobean Drama; A New Mermaid Background Book*, London: A. & C. Black.

—— (ed.) (1997) *The Riverside Shakespeare* (second edition), Boston, MA: Houghton Mifflin Company.

Bond, E. (1987) *Bingo: Scenes of Money and Death*, in *Bond Plays: Three*, London: Methuen [1974].

Brannigan, J. (1998) *New Historicism and Cultural Materialism*, Basingstoke: Macmillan.

Briggs, J. (1983) *This Stage-Play World*, Oxford: Oxford University Press.

Brook, G. L. (1976) *The Language of Shakespeare*, London: Andre Deutsch.

Brotton, J. (1998) ' "This Tunis, sir, was Carthage": contesting colonialism in *The Tempest*', in A. Loomba and M. Orkin (eds) *Post-Colonial Shakespeares*, London: Routledge.

Brown, P. (1985) ' "This thing of darkness I acknowledge mine": *The Tempest* and the discourse of colonialism', in J. Dollimore and A. Sinfield (eds) *Political Shakespeare*, Manchester: Manchester University Press.

Bulman, A. C. (1996) 'Shakespeare and performance theory', in A. C. Bulman (ed.) *Shakespeare, Theory and Performance*, London: Routledge.

Chapman, G. (1956) *The Iliad, The Odyssey and the Lesser Homerica*, ed. Allardyce Nicoll, London: Routledge and Kegan Paul [1598].

Coyle, M. (ed.) (1998) *New Casebook: A Midsummer Night's Dream*, London: Macmillan.

Davies, S. (1995) *William Shakespeare: The Taming of the Shrew*, Harmondsworth: Penguin Books.

Dawson, A. B. (1996) 'Performance and participation: Desdemona, Foucault and the actor's body', in A. C. Bulman (ed.) *Shakespeare, Theory and Performance*, London: Routledge.

Dessen, A. C. (1986) 'Shakespeare and the theatrical conventions of his time', in S. Wells (ed.) *The Cambridge Companion to Shakespeare Studies*, Cambridge: Cambridge University Press.

Dollimore, J. (1984) *Radical Tragedy: Religion, Ideology and Power in the Drama of Shakespeare and His Contemporaries*, Brighton: Harvester Wheatsheaf.

Dubrow, H. (1997) 'Twentieth-Century Shakespeare Criticism', in G. Blakemore-Evans (ed.) *The Riverside Shakespeare* (second edition), Boston, MA: Houghton Mifflin Company.

Dusinberre, J. (1996a) *Shakespeare and the Nature of Women* (second edition), London: Macmillan.

—— (1996b) 'Squeaking Cleopatras: gender and performance in *Antony and Cleopatra*', in A. C. Bulman (ed.) *Shakespeare, Theory and Performance*, London: Routledge.

Dutton, R. (ed.) (1998) *New Casebooks: The Merchant of Venice*, London: Macmillan.

Greenblatt, S. (1990) *Learning to Curse: Essays in Early Modern Culture*, London: Routledge.

Gurr, A. (1992) *The Shakespearean Stage 1574–1642*, Cambridge: Cambridge University Press.

Heinemann, M. (1985) 'How Brecht read Shakespeare', in J. Dollimore and A. Sinfield (eds) *Political Shakespeare*, Manchester: Manchester University Press.

Hibbard, G. R. (1987) *The Oxford Shakespeare: Hamlet*, Oxford: Oxford University Press.

Holderness, G. (1989a) *Hamlet*, Milton Keynes: Open University Press.

—— (1989b) 'Are Shakespeare's tragic heroes fatally flawed? Discuss', *Critical Survey* 1(1).

—— (1989c) *King Richard II*, Harmondsworth: Penguin Books.

—— (1992) *Shakespeare Recycled: The Making of Historical Drama*, Hemel Hempstead: Harvester.

Holland, P. (1993) 'Professional productions in the British Isles, January to December 1990', *Shakespeare Survey 45*, Cambridge: Cambridge University Press.

—— (1994) *The Oxford Shakespeare: A Midsummer Night's Dream*, Oxford: Oxford University Press.

Honan, P. (1998) *Shakespeare: A Life*, Oxford: Oxford University Press.

Howard, J. E. (1994) *The Stage and Social Struggle in Early Modern England*, London: Routledge.

Hyland, P. (1989) *William Shakespeare: Troilus and Cressida*, Harmondsworth: Penguin Books.

—— (1996) *An Introduction to Shakespeare: The Dramatist in his Context*, London: Macmillan.

Jardine, L. (1983) *Still Harping on Daughters: Women and Drama in the Age of Shakespeare*, Hemel Hempstead: Harvester Wheatsheaf.

—— (1996) *Reading Shakespeare Historically*, London: Routledge.

Jonson, B. (1962) *Volpone*, ed. D. Cook, London: Methuen [1606].

Kettle, A. (1964) 'From *Hamlet* to *Lear*', in A. Kettle (ed.) *Shakespeare in a Changing World*, London: Lawrence & Wishart.

Kiernan, P. (1996) *Shakespeare's Theory of Drama*, Cambridge: Cambridge University Press.

Krieger, E. (1979) ' "A Midsummer Night's Dream" ', in R. Dutton (ed.) *New Casebooks: A Midsummer Night's Dream* (1996), London: Macmillan.

Levi, P. (1988) *The Life and Times of William Shakespeare*, London: Macmillan.

Margolies, D. (1988) 'Teaching the handsaw to fly: Shakespeare as a hegemonic instrument', in G. Holderness (ed.) *The Shakespeare Myth*, Manchester: Manchester University Press.

McGann, J. (1989) 'The third world of criticism', in M. Levinson, M. Butler, J. McGann and P. Hamilton (eds) *Rethinking Historicism: Critical Readings in Romantic History*, Oxford: Basil Blackwell.

McLuskie, K. (1985) 'The patriarchal bard: feminist criticism and Shakespeare: *King Lear* and *Measure for Measure*', in J. Dollimore and A. Sinfield (eds) *Political Shakespeare*, Manchester: Manchester University Press.

Montrose, L. A. (1996) ' "Shaping fantasies": figurations of gender and power in Elizabethan culture', in R. Dutton (ed.) *New Casebooks: A Midsummer Night's Dream*, London: Macmillan [1983].

Moston, D. (ed) (1998) *Mr William Shakespeares Comedies, Histories and Tragedies: A Facsimile of the First Folio, 1623*, London: Routledge.

Newman, K. (1986) 'Renaissance family politics and Shakespeare's *The Taming of the Shrew*', in G. Waller (ed.) *Shakespeare's Comedies*, Harlow: Longman.

—— (1987) 'Portia's ring: unruly women and structures of exchange in *The Merchant of Venice*', in M. Coyle (ed.) (1998) *New Casebooks: The Merchant of Venice*, London: Macmillan.

Orgel, S. (1987) *The Oxford Shakespeare: The Tempest*, Oxford: Oxford University Press.

—— (1996a) *Impersonations: The Performance of Gender in Shakespeare's England,* Cambridge: Cambridge University Press.

—— (1996b) *The Oxford Shakespeare: The Winter's Tale*, Oxford: Oxford University Press.

O'Toole, F. (1990) *No More Heroes*, Dublin: Raven Arts Press.

Patterson, A. (1989) *Shakespeare and the Popular Voice*, Oxford: Basil Blackwell.

Piesse, A. (1996) 'Self-preservation in the Shakespearian system: gender, power and the New History' in Wood, N. (ed.) *Measure for Measure*, Buckingham: Open University Press.

Rackin, P. (1990) *Stages of History: Shakespeare's English Chronicles*, London: Routledge.

Reese, M. (1965) (ed) *King Henry IV Part One*, London: Edward Arnold.

Ryan, K. (1989) *Shakespeare*, Hemel Hempstead: Harvester Wheatsheaf (second edition 1995; third edition London: Macmillan, 2000).

—— (ed.) (1995) *Shakespeare: The Last Plays*, London: Longman.

Sinfield, A. (1986) '*Macbeth*: history, ideology and intellectuals', in A. Sinfield (ed.) *New Casebooks: Macbeth*, London, Macmillan 1992.

—— (1992) *Faultlines: Cultural Materialism and the Politics of Dissident Reading*, Oxford: Oxford University Press.

Tennenhouse, L. (1986) *Power on Display: The Politics of Shakespeare's Genres*, London: Routledge.

Thomson, P. (1983) *Shakespeare's Theatre*, London: Routledge.

Tourneur, C. (attrib.) (1967) *The Revenger's Tragedy*, ed. B. Gibbons, London: A & C Black [1607].

Trussler, S. (1989) *Shakespearean Concepts*, London: Methuen.

Turner, J. (1992) *Macbeth*, Buckingham: Open University Press.

Vaughan, V. M. (1994) '*Othello*': A Contextual History*, Cambridge: Cambridge University Press.

Vickers, B. (1971) 'Shakespeare's use of rhetoric', in K. Muir and S. Schoenbaum (eds) *A New Companion to Shakespeare Studies*, Cambridge: Cambridge University Press.

Waller, G. (ed.) (1991) *Shakespeare's Comedies*, London: Longman.

Watts, C. (1986) *Measure for Measure*, Harmondsworth: Penguin Books.

Webster, J. (1972) *Three Plays*, ed. D.Gunby, Harmondsworth: Penguin Books.

Weimann, R. (1978) *Shakespeare and the Popular Tradition in the Theater: Studies in the Social Dimension of Dramatic Form and Function* trans. and ed. R. Schwartz, Baltimore, MD, and London: Johns Hopkins University Press.

White, M. (1998) *Renaissance Drama in Action*, London: Routledge.

Williams, C. (1933) *A Short Life of Shakespeare with the Sources Abridged from Edmund Chambers's 'William Shakespeare: A Study of Facts and Problems'*, Oxford: Oxford University Press.

Williams, P. (1995) *The Later Tudors: England 1547–1603*, Oxford: Oxford University Press.

Wilson, R. (1993) *Will Power: Essays on Shakespearean Authority*, Hemel Hempstead: Harvester Wheatsheaf.

—— (1997) 'NATO's pharmacy: Shakespeare by prescription', in J. J. Joughin (ed.) *Shakespeare and National Culture*, Manchester: Manchester University Press.

Index

Bold entries for a particular play indicate substantial discussion. Bold entries for an idea, term or concept indicate a definition.